HE'S NOT COMING HOME

HE'S NOT COMING HOME

*A story of love,
loss and discovery
in Rabaul during
World War 2*

GILLIAN NIKAKIS

Lothian
BOOKS

Thomas C. Lothian Pty Ltd
132 Albert Road, South Melbourne, Victoria 3205
www.lothian.com.au

First published 2005

National Library of Australia
Cataloguing-in-Publication data:

    Nikakis, Gillian.
    He's not coming home.

    ISBN 0 7344 0814 5.

    1. Spensley family. 2. Missing in action - Family
    relationships. 3. World War, 1939-1945 - Papua New Guinea -
    Rabaul. 4. World War, 1939-1945 - Missing in action -
    Papua New Guinea. 5. War and family - Australia. I. Title.

    940.53161

Cover and text design by Mary Mason
Typeset by MM
Printed in Australia by Griffin Press

To my brother with love

CONTENTS

APPENDICES

ILLUSTRATIONS

*(unless otherwise specified, all photographs
are from the Spensley Collection)*

Between pages 144 and 145

LINE ILLUSTRATIONS

INTRODUCTION

I find the events in Rabaul during the ten-year period from 1935 to 1945 fascinating, tragic and quite extraordinary. Situated at the north-east of New Guinea on the island of New Britain, Rabaul was a tropical paradise, a place of powerful extremes. Although a place of great physical beauty, it was also a place where the constant daily rumblings and eventual eruption of the volcano was followed by the horrors of the Japanese occupation. Interwoven with the story of my mother and father, Tick and Bill Spensley, are some of the experiences of four other people whose paths crossed during this time and whose stories help to give a more complete picture of the Japanese invasion and occupation.

I do not presume to present myself as an expert on Rabaul as my time there was very short and no memory of it remains at a conscious level. Some of my material is anecdotal and this is confirmed with tapes of conversations, videos of interviews and transcripts, letters and personal manuscripts. I have spent many hours speaking to army people, nuns, nurses, old New Guinea residents and family members, and many hours at the Australian Archives, various libraries and the War Memorial in Canberra, checking my information; but I am not an army person and I am not a historian.

At the time of the Japanese invasion, there were fifteen hundred Australian soldiers including seventy men from the New Guinea Volunteer Rifles pitted against the might of the Japanese army, air force and navy. The Australians had completely inadequate equipment.

Requests by the Administration in Rabaul to evacuate civilians on a Norwegian ship in the harbour were refused. The Australian Government insisted on the ship being loaded with copra rather than evacuees.

There does not appear to have been a full inquiry into the events in Rabaul and one could be excused for questioning why this is so. A whole town disappeared! Over one thousand men marched out of the prison camp and were never seen again. These were the people the Australian Government decided were hostages to fortune and therefore expendable.

In October 1945 a telegram was sent to many of the families who had been waiting since 1942 for news of their missing relatives informing them that the Japanese ship, the *Montevideo Maru* carrying over one thousand prisoners to Japan, had been torpedoed by an American submarine off the coast of the Philippines. There were no survivors among the prisoners. It is the biggest maritime loss of life in Australian naval history and so quite surprising that so few Australians know anything about it.

I was amazed when I learnt of the long and sophisticated tunnels built by the Japanese in Rabaul to escape the Allied bombing attacks. They contained hospitals, operating theatres, X-ray departments, cafeterias and accommodation for 100 000 people. When reading about the invasion and the tunnels built by the Japanese it is impossible not to compare the efficiency and ingenuity of the Japanese with the lack of foresight and communication failure of the Australian Government and the Army. In their defence, world events were happening very fast and our allies had their own priorities. It was a dark period in this terrible war. Australia did not have the financial resources of countries like the United States of America and was dependent on support from its Allies who were pre-occupied in Europe and the Middle East. Australia, with significant forces located in the Middle East and Europe was not geared to defend its own shores. Japanese territorial ambitions were always known to be a threat but, politically, Australia, with other nations, gambled on Japan not entering World War 2. Japan's treacherous attack on Pearl Harbor on 7 December 1941 changed all that.

Eventually, heavy persistent bombing by the Allies cut off the Japanese supply lines and affected their morale, but it did not force them out of the tunnels. This happened only at the surrender by the Japanese Emperor Hirohito, following the bombing of Nagasaki and Hiroshima by the Allies.

As I decided to follow up information by conducting my own research, an unexpected picture began to emerge. I began to hear stories of cannibalism, vivisection, starvation, executions at sea, death marches, and of Japanese testing biological warfare on prisoners. I wondered if this information had implications concerning the fate of the prisoners reported to be on the *Montevideo Maru*. I knew there were some people who did not believe the prisoners were on the *Montevideo Maru* when it was sunk.

My mother, Tick, and many of the other widows have since died. Perhaps this has allowed some of the sons and daughters to proceed with their investigations free of guilt. We had no desire to cause our mothers further hurt.

The beautiful township of Rabaul is no longer the Jewel of the Pacific. It has been devastated by several more volcanic eruptions and much of it still lies under layers of pumice. For a period of approximately fifty years it was a thriving, exciting cosmopolitan township—until the day the people who helped create it disappeared.

ACKNOWLEDGEMENTS

The main characters in this book, apart from my parents Tick and Bill Spensley, are Colin Stirling, Sister Berenice Twohill, Lorna Whyte Johnston and John Murphy. I have used only parts of their experiences and want to acknowledge that many more books would be necessary to do each of them justice.

I wish to acknowledge the love and support shown to my family by Colin Stirling. He was always in the background prepared to help if necessary. He kindly and patiently shared his memories with us over the years. His paper, 'Reminiscences', has provided information concerning the last five months of Bill's life. Colin is the only person who could do this. Sadly, he died six weeks after reading the manuscript of this book.

Sister Berenice is an Australian nun with the order of Our Lady of the Sacred Heart. She spent three and a half years as a prisoner of the Japanese, first at the Sacred Heart Mission at Vunapope and later at Ramale Valley. Her observations of the behaviour of the Japanese during the occupation were extremely helpful to the Allies trying to piece together the events during this time. Sister Berenice and the other nuns showed great kindness and compassion to the nurses and patients who were also prisoners for some time at the Sacred Heart Mission.

Lorna Whyte Johnston, known as 'Whytie' to the other nurses, was the youngest of the Army nurses. I have referred to Lorna's account of the experiences of the Army nurses in Rabaul before they were shipped off to Japan on the *Naruto Maru*. They remained prisoners of war in Japan for three and a half years. There have been several excellent books written on their experiences so I have concentrated on their time spent in Rabaul.

John Murphy's story is quite exceptional. He was a brave man and I have drawn on his experiences to further describe the unpredictable behaviour of the Japanese. As John Murphy was the only Australian Army person found alive in Rabaul at the surrender, his observations were important.

Many people have contributed information and support. I cannot single anyone out as I am grateful to so many people. Those involved in the story: Jocelyn Best, Keith Colyer, Jean Cox (Big Jean), Jean Cunningham Cox (Little Jean), John Cox, Lex Frazer, Bill Harry, Commander Kemp Hewitt, Bill Larkin, Bob Lord, Canon John May, Marjorie Murphy, Oscar Rondahl; support and information: Dr Elizabeth Banks, Roma Bates, Jocelyn Best, Dr Peter Cahill, Cameron Eason, Barbara Eastgate, Margaret Henderson, Katherine Ingram, Pat Johnston, Jill Lewis, Ken McGowan, Diana Martell, Mary Mason, Geoff Melrose, Nina Mills, Kerry Murphy, Con Nikakis, Gael Penrose, Lisa Rennie, Albert Speer, Sally Spensley, Peter Stone, Alfred Uechtritz, Kaye Watson. I would also like to thank Peter Stone, Dr Jan Roberts, Yuki Tanaka and Joe Nason for allowing me to use excerpts from their fascinating books.

I have shared so much of this journey with my brother John, who has so often been by my side listening to stories and information. His interviews have been a joy to hear, as he brings out the most interesting information from his subjects. He has provided me with tapes, letters and photos and has always been there for me to discuss ideas. Although we have shared so much and he has been generous and unstinting in his support, this book is my personal experience.

THE FAMILY TREE

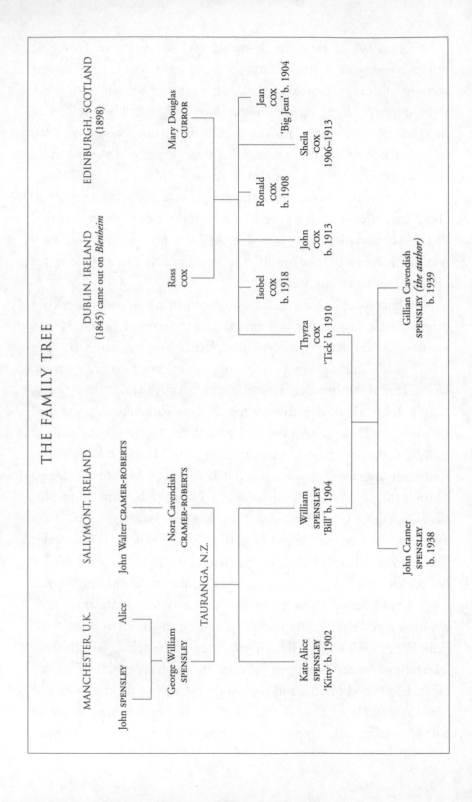

MANCHESTER, U.K.   SALLYMONT, IRELAND   DUBLIN, IRELAND   EDINBURGH, SCOTLAND
(1845) came out on *Blenheim*   (1898)

John SPENSLEY — Alice

George William
SPENSLEY — John Walter CRAMER-ROBERTS

Nora Cavendish
CRAMER-ROBERTS

TAURANGA, N.Z.

Ross
COX — Mary Douglas
CURROR

Kate Alice
SPENSLEY
'Kitty' b. 1902

William
SPENSLEY
'Bill' b. 1904

Thyrza
COX
'Tick' b. 1910

Isobel
COX
b. 1918

John
COX
b. 1913

Ronald
COX
b. 1908

Sheila
COX
1906–1913

Jean
COX
'Big Jean' b. 1904

John Cramer
SPENSLEY
b. 1938

Gillian Cavendish
SPENSLEY (*the author*)
b. 1939

CHAPTER 1

~

THE JOURNEY BEGINS

Truth is a shaft of light breaking through to

illuminate the mist-shrouded river.

A mere broken piece of bread may do the trick,

and the mists rise from off the eyes.

JOHN CARROLL, *The Western Dreaming*

I CLEARLY REMEMBER THE SCENE IN THE BATHROOM AS MY mother spoke the words, 'Your father will not be coming home'. My brother was sitting in the bath and I was standing beside it while she knelt and dried me with a towel. On the outside I was quite calm and did not shed a tear, but inside I remember the feeling. I wanted to yell 'Don't tell me! I don't want to know! I don't want it to be true!' I knew even at that age that my mother was very sad and that I must be good. As children often do when they lose a parent, I believed that somehow it was my fault. So I kept silent. It was 1945 and I had just turned six. In the bathroom that evening, our lives changed for ever.

Where do I start? The story really has only a vague beginning and no end. Throughout history, mothers have spoken those same words to their children and, sadly, will continue to do so.

As much of my family's history centres on New Guinea, this is where I will begin. Matupi, Vunapope, Kokopo, Kavieng, Toma: these names were full of mystery and romance for me as I grew up. I was born in New Britain, an island off the north-east coast of New Guinea, in the township of Rabaul, on 6 September 1939, three days after war was declared in Europe. In July 1941 when I was a baby of twenty-two months, I left Rabaul with my mother Tick and three-year-old brother John.

The last time Tick saw my father, Bill, he was standing on the wharf at Rabaul harbour, dressed in the favoured whites of Europeans in the tropics. Tick stood on the deck with me in her arms and John beside her. As the boat slowly moved away from the wharf, Bill waved and Tick waved back. She watched his figure disappearing into the distance as the ship sailed out of the glorious harbour. Both Tick and Bill thought their separation was to be only for a couple of months. They thought their life together as a family was just beginning. Neither had any idea of the enormity of what was about to happen. Four years later Tick finally received the news and spoke the words in the bathroom that night.

Tick did not want to believe that he would not return, so she had tried very hard to keep Bill's memory alive for John and me. She talked about our wonderful father, how much he loved us and how exciting it would be when he returned. So perhaps the loss was greater when the news of his death finally came. The four-year wait created unnatural circumstances and made it very difficult for Tick. John and I waited with high expectations for this wonderful man who would soon return. It was difficult for us to let go of this expectation.

It wasn't until I had my own children that I began to wonder what my father was really like. What sort of person was he? He was a New Zealander and had no family in Melbourne, so it was difficult to get a real sense of him. Tick would speak of him but only a romanticised picture would emerge. He was my son's grandfather. What sort of grandfather would he have been? Were my sons like him? Was John like him? The older I became the more I craved knowledge of him.

The person who had spent the last five months with him before his capture was Colin Stirling, a lieutenant in the Australian Army. Colin occasionally visited Melbourne from Launceston, Tasmania, where he lived. John and I subjected the poor man to intense questioning whenever he came to dinner. He answered every question: 'Yes, Bill had a great sense of humour. He was a great organiser. He was a brave man'. I remember becoming quite frustrated as I probed for the sort of snippets that would satisfy my feminine curiosity. I have often found that men think differently and what is important to them is not always as interesting to us women. I was looking for cameos about personal interactions and relationships. Nevertheless Colin did his best to give us what he thought we wanted to hear.

I don't think the full impact of my loss hit me until I was the same age as my father when he died. My children were also around the same age as John and I when we heard the news. It was at this stage that I began to unravel. With professional help I began to let go the grief that had stayed frozen inside for all those years. I felt like a five-year-old child as I sobbed my way through the session. The therapist did not interfere but encouraged me to just 'let it go'. Not only did I cry but I also raged at the unfairness of war, at the universe, at God and at my father for not coming home. I was stunned at the amount of grief I had been carrying around and felt the most enormous sense of relief.

In 1985 Tick and I flew to Rabaul. This was the first time she had been back since 1941 and my first trip to my birthplace. Sadly John was unable to join us so the trip was not quite complete. Our first stop was Port Moresby where it was uncomfortably hot. It was not a positive entrance to New Guinea as the airport was dirty and the airport workers appeared sullen and unfriendly. There was very little eye contact and we were quite relieved to leave. Rabaul gave a different impression entirely. It felt like coming home. I was struck by the colour. White, yellow, pinks, reds, purples and green, green, green. The New Guineans we met were relaxed and friendly and no one seemed to hurry anywhere. The romantic names began to take on real meaning rather than fantasy as Tick and I talked and explored her life in Rabaul.

People who lived in Rabaul before the Japanese invasion were known as 'B-4s' and they showed us around. We organised a trip to the War Cemetery at Bitapaka, some ten kilometres south of Kokopo. The silence except for the birds, the feeling of peace and the beauty of the surroundings seemed to cradle us both. We wept together for our own personal loss and the enormity of the wider tragedy, highlighted by the hundreds of white crosses and the plaques, nestling in the lush green beautifully kept lawns.

Tick began to talk about many things she had not mentioned before and I used a tape recorder and made copious notes. Taping was always an emotional event interspersed with roars of laughter and tears. But, in spite of her sadness, she was a joyous woman who did not dwell on her misfortunes. She had the most engaging talent for describing an amusing situation with just a few words, in a manner that was both whimsical and delightful.

During that visit to Rabaul I also discovered a different side of Tick that surprised me. We decided to visit the market and strolled around enjoying the smells and sounds and the fascinating panorama of colour that surrounded us. I took a photo of a New Guinean dressed in his glorious feathers, paint and 'arse grass' posing proudly between two parked cars. Laid out on banana leaves on the ground were the most wonderful displays of tropical fruits and vegetables. New Guinea women sat cross-legged on the ground minding their stalls, some with babies lying on banana leaves beside them. Tick began bartering with an old woman who stood beside her stall and display of painted coral shells and beads. I heard an imperious voice speaking in Pidgin, 'Olsem wonem. Nogat. Dia tumas!'

I realised with astonishment that it was my mother. I watched her moving from stall to stall, talking to the New Guineans, and it was as though she was another woman. She had become the colonial mistress, slipping into her old familiar character, so alien to the mother I knew.

During this trip I heard the first mention of Japanese cannibalism of prisoners. This occurred during a conversation over drinks with Arthur Brown who was in Rabaul at the time of the war trials. I must have dissociated from this comment, probably because I was with Tick and also because I did not want to believe it. I did not think of it again until I began researching material for this book.

We visited the New Guinea Club and I studied the aerial photos of Rabaul harbour on the wall. The harbour was full of Japanese shipping and the Americans had taken these photos during their bombing raids between 1942 and 1945. I was stunned. I began to understand the magnitude of what had happened in Rabaul. My interest grew, as did my desire to know more. But it was not until the commemoration trip to Rabaul in 1992 that I knew I wanted to write the story.

In the meantime, my work as a nurse had taken a different turn. I went back to study, updated my nursing degree, completed a psychiatric nursing certificate, updated my midwifery certificate and completed a unit of qualitative research. My work as a community health nurse had led me into the area of trauma and abuse. After twelve years at the Doveton/Hallam Community Health Centre, I moved into private practice. Although I was a general counsellor, a large percentage of my practice was with people who had been abused physically, mentally, sexually or all three. Working with people who have been abused, I was appalled and sickened by some of the stories I was hearing. I now believe that my work prepared me for some of the information I was to uncover while undertaking research for this book. I naively thought that writing a book about the fall of Rabaul would be some sort of relief from the traumas I was hearing about in my work. As the story unfolded, I realised that although professionally I was working with trauma at a personal level, I was now writing about it at a global level. For months I was in the jungles of New Guinea, living the horrors of the people I was writing about.

Tick died in 1989. The older I get, the more I realise what an amazing woman she was. I often wish I could have her back for half an hour so I could tell her how much I love and respect her. I would also like to apologise for the times I was just too busy to give her time. She never complained and very rarely showed anger to John or to me.

She experienced an earthquake, evacuation, and loss of her husband and her home. She was a widow at the age of thirty-two. She brought up two children, worked, sent us to private schools and provided us with a happy supportive home life. Her professional life was exciting and interesting. She was intelligent and well read and she stimulated both her children into pursuing interesting careers. She did all this without support. One of Tick's favourite sayings was 'possessions mean nothing, its people that count'. Having experienced single parenthood, I can appreciate the sacrifices she made for us.

After she died, I discovered letters written by my father and sent to her in the six months before the Japanese invasion. I also found Tick's letters to him. I had not known of their existence. It was a most moving experience at the age of sixty, to find letters written by my parents to each other discussing the development of my brother and me. A more realistic picture of my father began to emerge through these letters, but they were also a history of events leading up to the Japanese invasion.

When reading books about Rabaul I began to realise how survivors create history and myths. Facts and reality can become blurred and people who played major roles may be relegated to minor parts and in some cases erased from the story altogether. What is important to one person is not to another. In traumatic situations some details are crystal clear and others just disappear into the realms of the unconscious. That's just the way it is. I do not want my father to disappear without acknowledgement.

During the commemoration trip to Rabaul in 1992, a tremendous amount of sharing went on. There were surviving members of the 2/22 Battalion, army nurses who were POWs, Sister Berenice, a teaching nun and POW and eight people whose fathers were reported lost on the *Montevideo Maru*. We talked over dinner, over drinks, and in the bus. I was fascinated by the stories told to me by Sister Berenice, Lorna Whyte/Johnston and Colin Stirling. Listening to their experiences greatly broadened my understanding of the events that took place in 1941 and 1942.

So this story is about many things. It is about my search to discover what really happened to my father and to the other civilians and army people supposedly on the *Montevideo Maru*. It is a story about a tragedy that happened on a beautiful Pacific island and the threat posed to Australia. It is also about the ingenuity and cruelty of the Japanese in Rabaul during the occupation. It is about my parents and their lives together in this tropical paradise and through their letters, the experience of war and loss. It is also about confronting the myths and seeing things as they really are, both at a personal and global level. Through the eyes of Sister Berenice, Lorna Johnston, Colin Stirling, and my parents, I hope to share the trip I have been on over the last ten years. As my rose-coloured glasses were removed, I was also able to include some of the information I learned from John Murphy.

Tick is the person I have chosen to weave this story around. She is the centrepiece, the person who lived the experience. Her revelations are the mainstay of this book, and I begin with some of her early history. Her ambivalent relationship with her sister Jean is also relevant and cannot be omitted, as Jean had such an influence in our lives. It was through Jean that Tick found her way to New Guinea.

CHAPTER 2

TICK

The baby just born is a son or a daughter,

a person to be given a name and a place in the family.

The family itself is born when the gesticulating little bundle

is placed in a mother's arms for the first time.

LENNART NILSSON, *A Child is Born*

TICK'S REAL NAME WAS THYRZA BUT I RARELY HEARD HER addressed that way. The story of how she acquired the name of Tick has always fascinated me. Tick thrived on crisis and incident and looking back, this tendency started before she was even born.

It was 1910. The family lived in Brighton, a seaside suburb in Melbourne. Tick's father, Ross Cox, had arranged to go fishing with a friend. His wife Mary was pregnant with Tick, their fourth child. She decided to go for a walk and watch the men leave from the pier. Ross and his friend were concentrating on preparing the ketch for sailing and did not see Mary approach. The boom swung around and struck Mary across her head causing her to lose consciousness and fall to the ground. Unaware of the drama behind them, the men sailed out to sea happily anticipating a full day's fishing. Mary regained consciousness and staggered home by herself. But from that day she developed a white streak across her hair where the boom had hit and when my mother was born at full term, she weighed only three and a half pounds (about 1.7 kilos), although perfectly formed and with no other signs of prematurity. Her aunt, visiting from South Africa, took one look at the tiny new baby and exclaimed, 'She's no bigger than a South African tick'. In spite of the family names she had been given, 'Tick' is the name that stuck. Other variations developed, namely 'Ticky' and 'Ticko', and in later years she signed notes and cards with a tick and a zero '✓0'.

Including Tick, three of the six children of Ross and Mary Cox found their way to New Guinea and fell in love with this tropical island. Jean, Tick and their brother John are important participants in the Rabaul part of the story.

The first crisis in Tick's life occurred when she was three years old. Tick's older sister Sheila developed a cough which their mother thought was croup. Sheila's condition began to deteriorate: her glands and face started to swell, her voice became hoarse and she found it hard to talk. Mary called Dr Aitcheson, their family doctor, who informed the anxious parents that their daughter had diphtheria. Sheila began to have difficulty breathing. Tick watched anxiously as the adults moved in and out of Sheila's room, always closing the door behind them and speaking in whispers so the children could not hear.

On Mary's birthday, 9 October 1913, her daughter Sheila died. Sheila was seven years old and a beautiful, gentle child, adored by Mary. The family was devastated by her death. Mary sank into a depression and cut herself off from the family. She did little around the house and was unable to look after the other children. Jean, as the oldest child was forced into taking responsibility early and assisted her father Ross in running the house.

Tick attended the Esperance Primary School in Brighton. She hated school and when the teacher informed the children that the school was to break up, Tick searched excitedly through her father's workshop and found a hammer. She took it to school and was very disappointed to discover that the teacher's idea of the school breaking up was not the same as hers.

Tick always maintained that she was the runt of the litter. In one portrait taken of the three eldest children, Tick has been removed and a hydrangea put in her place. Ronald, Sheila and Jean are resplendent in lace, bows and sailor suit. Tick had dark, straight hair with not a trace of a curl. Her hair was cut in a pudding-basin style, which did nothing to enhance her little round face.

When Ross and Mary were married, Ross and his two brothers were running the Abbotshall vineyard in Wahgunyah, near Rutherglen. The vineyard was very successful, until phylloxera was discovered in the vines. This was followed by a drought and the brothers were forced to sell the vineyard.

Ross became manager of the Australasian Tobacco Company, where he worked for some time until he developed nicotine poisoning and a duodenal ulcer. The ulcer perforated while he was travelling on a train to Brighton. He haemorrhaged and was rushed to hospital. Tick watched her mother sitting at the kitchen table, her head on her arms, sobbing, while the family waited to hear whether Ross would survive. He did survive, but was forced to leave his position at the tobacco company, and the family's struggles began. Mary was pregnant at the time and her baby, Isobel, was born two weeks later.

Ross was still very sick and Dr Aitcheson advised the family to move away from the city. Ross and Mary bought a house with an apple orchard at Flowerdale, a country town in north-east Victoria, hoping that the country air would improve Ross's health.

Because of all their domestic upheavals, Tick was never long at any school and her education was very sketchy. Most of her education came from her parents guiding her reading. She read voraciously and widely and developed a passion for Shakespeare and

Dickens. Her parents were good teachers and encouraged their children to use their dictionaries constantly.

'Don't use a word if you don't know its meaning. Look it up!' Much of the teaching took place around the meal table at night or after the dishes were cleared away. The children and their parents sat at the table and read by the light of the kerosene lamp. Sometimes their mother would play the piano and the family would sing songs and ballads such as 'Sally in our Alley', 'Kathleen Mavourneen', or 'Bonnie Bonnie Banks of Loch Lomond'. Ross, whose family had come from Ireland, had inherited the Irish love of music. He particularly liked Gilbert and Sullivan and fancied himself as a fine singer. His rendition of 'Tit Willow' had the family rolling around the room with laughter. If Ross couldn't sleep, he would cajole one of the children into playing cribbage till late into the night. The smell of the roots of apple trees burning continuously in the fireplace added depth to the warmth of these memories.

During the day Tick and her young brother John sat at their father's huge desk working on their correspondence lessons. Living at Flowerdale on a property was a wonderful experience for the younger children. Apart from their correspondence lessons, they spent as much time as they could out of doors, riding horses, mushrooming, picking wildflowers and helping their mother in the orchard. Tick and John spent much of their time creating games involving their horses. Their favourite fantasy was competing in horse shows, jumping and parading. They both loved their horses. Their games were never violent although there was some competition. There was no television and they saw no violent films and the idea of a war game never entered their heads.

There came a time when Ross was unable to keep up the payments on the orchard and it had to be sold. It was difficult for him to get a job but he managed to find a position share farming. The children rose at 2 a.m. to help milk the cows before going to school. They would then walk six miles (11 kilometres) to the local school. Tick's milking record was twenty-eight cows and she was extremely proud of this achievement even sixty years later.

During the family's time at Flowerdale and later when share farming, Ross and Mary taught the children to love and care for their animals. There was no dinner for anyone before the animals were fed and this rule was strictly kept. No child was allowed to use a saddle until he or she could ride bareback.

Jessie the cow took a fancy to Ron, Tick's older brother. She would give a low moo as she followed him everywhere. One day, to the delight of the other children, she followed him into the kitchen and gazed at him longingly. The other children could not understand why she chose Ron, but assumed love had given her rose coloured glasses. Ron was modestly proud at being singled out from the herd.

Mary, Tick's mother, became quite bitter over the years. She came from a comfortable middle-class family in Edinburgh where her father owned his own bank. She was unable to cope with the family tragedies and their poor financial situation.

Before coming to Australia from Scotland and marrying Ross, Mary had travelled to Norway with her singing teacher to study music with Edvard Grieg. She was considered to have a great future ahead of her as a singer or concert pianist. When she decided to stay in Australia and marry Ross, her career as a concert pianist disappeared for ever. There was one occasion where Mary's talent was witnessed by an audience, however. One night, much to the family's delight, Ross decided they would all go to the local picture theatre. Scrubbed and excited, they set off. When interval came a distressed manager approached the family and spoke directly to Mary. He had heard of her talent and his usual piano player had been taken ill and could not play. Would she assist him by playing during the interval? Reluctantly, but pushed by her excited children, she climbed up on the stage, sat at the piano and began to play. There was silence in the theatre, as the audience became aware of the beauty of the performance they were witnessing. When she had finished, the audience gave her a standing ovation. The children were very proud of their mother and, although she refused ever to play again in public, they spoke of her performance years later as proudly as if it were yesterday.

Mary worked as an untrained nursing volunteer, but when the family became poor, she seemed to lose heart. By now Jean was running the house and Mary became increasingly jealous of her. Jean was close to her father and his favourite. Mary had difficulty controlling her temper and lashed out at Jean physically and verbally. Jean in turn used the same behaviour with her siblings. Ross tended to side with his daughter Jean and this infuriated Mary. Eventually the relationship degenerated to such an extent that Mary confronted Ross: 'You must choose between your wife and your daughter!' Jean was found a position as a nanny with friends of the family until she was old enough to begin her nursing training.

When Jean left home, family life was much more peaceful for everyone and the next years were happy ones for Tick. Jean began her nursing training at the Royal Melbourne Hospital and Ronald, the oldest son, commenced a law degree. Because of the family's poor financial circumstances and, happy to have an excuse to leave school, Tick found herself a job as a nanny. She was fourteen.

The idea of Tick leaving school so early was too much for her godmother, Aunt Thyrza. She insisted on sending Tick to St Michael's Girls School for her final years of schooling. Following this, Aunt Thyrza decided to enlist the assistance of her friend Myra Bull, who was the matron at Lauriston Girls' School. Lauriston was a small private non-denominational school for young ladies. Tick was found a position as student housemistress and was paid 10 shillings (about 1 dollar) a week. She lived in the turret of the beautiful old ivy-covered Victorian building which was the Boarding House. She was able to study French and Maths while she was at the school. At seventeen, she was not much older than the senior girls and recalled her time at Lauriston as lots of fun.

Aunt Thyrza specialised in literature and was determined that her god-daughter should receive a good education. Elocution and pronunciation were extremely important to her and she organised elocution tutoring for Tick with the Misses Taylor.

At eighteen, Tick was old enough to follow her sister Jean into nursing.

CHAPTER 3

JEAN DISCOVERS
NEW GUINEA

The native believes that the mind, emotions and

desires are seated in the belly, more intensely in the liver.

When he is endeavouring to recollect something

he will say — 'Askim gut liva bilong yu.'

(Ask well liver of you.) Examine your conscience.

JOHN MURPHY

JEAN WAS AN EXCELLENT NURSE, AND RECEIVED THE HOSPITAL prize for midwifery. She was a skilled theatre nurse and when the newly opened Alfred Hospital requested help from the Royal Melbourne Hospital to set up their operating theatres, Matron Jane Bell sent Jean to help them do this. After several years as a Staff Nurse, Jean found an advertisement in the newspaper under the heading of 'The League of Nations' asking nurses to go to New Guinea to work. She applied and was accepted and although Matron Bell was not happy to lose one of her best staff nurses, she sent Jean off with glowing references.

Jean's appointment was the beginning of the family's involvement with New Guinea. Her letters home stimulated the family's interest and gave them some relief from the dreariness of the Depression. I was fascinated by Jean's letters when I first read them in 2001. I remember flinching as I read the language she used which would now be condemned as racist but is a reflection of the times and the paternalistic attitude shown to the New Guineans. On arriving in Rabaul Dr Sinclair, the senior medical officer, requested that Jean go to the hospital in Salamaua which was badly in need of some efficient restructuring.

The Salamaua Hospital in the early 1930s did not have a good reputation, and many of the miners admitted with Blackwater Fever failed to recover. Ion Idriess relates in *Gold-Dust and Ashes* that one miner, weak with Blackwater Fever, was being carried from the aerodrome to the hospital on a stretcher. The procession passed the pub and the sick miner waved weakly to the crowd and in a croaky voice asked them what the odds were on his recovery. 'Thirty-three to one against!' they shouted back. He took the odds to three fivers, and collected! A patrol officer and a Catholic missionary were not so fortunate. Both died in Salamaua hospital from arrow wounds received after being attacked by Highlanders.

The Salamaua Hospital provided the health care for the population of Wau, the Bulolo goldfields and Edie Creek. The planes only flew to Wau and Bulolo and they could often not get through because of the low clouds. All cargo, stores and visitors went by donkey to Edie Creek which had a population of about one hundred.

On 23 July 1930 Jean wrote the following letter to her family in Melbourne:

I found the hospital in a most filthy state, scarcely any linen and what was there was very badly laundered and full of holes. The boys couldn't understand me nor I them. Thanks to Dr. Sinclair in Rabaul I learnt

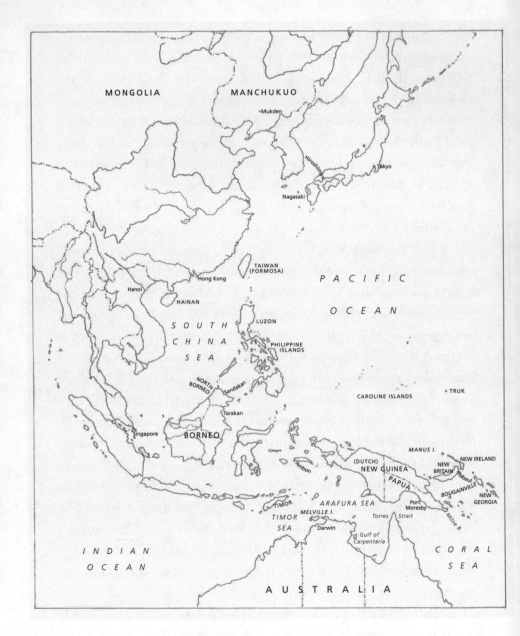

THE PACIFIC OCEAN AND SURROUNDING WAR ZONES

one or two words and the way the natives use certain phrases. It was very difficult tho' I can tell you.

About 10.30 am the boss boy came to me and said 'Time you go catchem cup of tea along Missus along House No 1.' I thought so too and went. By about the third day I managed to establish a sort of system and make each boy responsible for certain things. The next morning I arrived and found the work almost finished and fairly well too, so the price of boys rose to a great height. I grieve to say it didn't stay risen for very long. For one reason the ones I'd trained so well were all changed onto 'watch along night' so my troubles began again. I think I'll gradually get them licked into shape but I do think that a preliminary school for hospital boys could be instituted in this territory with impunity.

There is only one really good boy who mostly stays good. I have only once so far caught him smoking on duty. The others are more or less incompetent young devils who would sooner catch butterflies or pull pulls (ferns) than work.

I've been having great fun teaching the laundry boy how to make starch. That effort was particularly satisfactory and he now makes excellent starch and is so proud of it that he will persist in starching all the wrong things. He cannot see that my caps need any but my pyjamas and handkerchiefs are always like boards. He irons very badly and when I tried to explain how to damp iron my dresses he said: 'Fashion belong you missus me think you talk talk too much!' However I intend to persist in sending them all back till they are right. Men's trousers seem to be the only things they do really well. I can scarcely see myself decked in those all the time just for the sake of looking well laundered.

One day a whole tribe of New Guineans arrived at the hospital. When Jean appeared, the children yelled and ran in all directions. They had never seen a white woman before, let alone one wearing a starched white cap and uniform.

Pidgin English is glorious. If a thing is beyond recall and a boy wishes to tell you so—he says 'm'c' buggar up—finish missus'. My full title in this village is 'Missus belong House sick'. So far I haven't had anyone very sick just a few malarias whom I've managed to cure in a day or two. It's wonderful how quickly they improve with regular doses of quinine.

Referring to people by their illness was a custom still in operation when I began my nursing training in 1957. I suspect it is probably still the case. This made it difficult when meeting a patient we had nursed, outside the hospital. We could remember their diagnosis but not their name. It was not appropriate to say 'Good morning Mr Anal Fissure', or 'How are you Mrs Gall Bladder?' Nursing and medical terminology can be very dehumanising.

In September 1930 Jean wrote again to her family:

I've had jolly good luck with the boys so far and it's horrible to be rouse rouse all the time. There is one thing I'm sure of there is not one kanaka born who could be trusted, not even my Marawombe whom I occasionally find smoking on duty but not often I'll admit. He really is a treasure. You'd yell if you could hear him sometimes telling the others off. Politeness towards one another is quite beyond their understanding altogether and he keeps the juniors well in order.

11/12/30. I have not had one day off since I've been here and have been very busy lately too. Women patients in one after the other and as I have no indentured female natives I have to do everything for them myself which becomes somewhat tiring if too much of it.

Jean's attempts to run the hospital along the lines of the Royal Melbourne Hospital were constantly frustrated by the relaxed lifestyle of the New Guineans. They did not share her zeal, nor her belief in the importance of starch, sterility, shining floors and shiny monometal.

Marawombe took great pains to plant some watermelons in the middle of the path one day last week. I didn't dare suggest he should put them elsewhere for he takes it always as reproof and is so easily hurt. He also planted two rows of beans. They came up in two days so today instead of sweeping and dusting I found the old devil out making a rough fence for them to creep on. I never met such people for making excuses. Whatever outrage they commit they have the most plausible excuse on the tip of their tongue. What I admire though is the fact that if the Government men discipline them by kicking or hitting they stand quite still till they finish and never utter one word. Of course if they did answer back they'd go before the magistrate quick time and it would mean two weeks gaol and sand drill.

In *Race Relations and Colonial Rule In Papua New Guinea* Edward Wolfers states that a magistrate was the sole personification of the Government. He was a policeman, explorer, road builder, health inspector, social worker and prison warder. He acted as prosecutor, defence counsel, judge and jury. From 1890 magistrates could summon anyone they suspected of committing a 'forbidden act'. In 1913 disobedience became punishable by a fine of 10 shillings or one month gaol. The magistrate had wide powers to enforce the law.[1] (In May 1919 flogging was completely outlawed although the prevalent opinion among expatriates, even the officials, was that its abolition was a mistake.)[2]

Many of Jean's letters were written to her father. In several of her earlier letters she tried to persuade him to come to New Guinea but soon realised that unemployment was as much a problem in New Guinea as it was in Melbourne. In February 1931 she wrote:

The unemployment really is terrible. I do wish things would brighten up. It's just the same up here. Everyone seems to save up the whole time to have enough money to go South as it's imperative that one must leave the territory once in two years. There is more work here than anywhere and things should improve with Placer opening these new works as they are but quite the wrong type of men seem to be coming up. They do not understand the necessity of upholding the prestige of the white race. The native won't have any respect if it is not enforced, and these newcomers don't realise that the boys are here to work and that they are here to see they do it and that is all. (a resident of 9 months speaking.)

Wolfers gives a vivid description of Papua's expatriate settlers:

The world of Papua's expatriate settlers before the War was a dusty, lower middleclass, Australian version of the British Raj. It lacked the grace and magnificence of the Empire at its zenith. Its security derived less from a sense of pride in its technological superiority and splendour than from a mean and pedantic insistence on the importance of racial differences.[3]

Much of the legislation passed in the 1920s and earlier was punitive and paternalistic. After 1911 the law forbade 'all noise shouting beating of drums and dancing …in…(gazetted) towns and villages (after) 9 o'clock each night unless given permission by a Magistrate'.[4]

From 1920 all Papuans, both male and female, were forbidden to wear clothes on the upper part of the body, on pain of being fined between 10 shillings and one pound, or imprisonment for between one and two months and having their clothes destroyed. This legislation came about because it was felt that the New Guineans did not know how to look after their European clothes and lowered the standard of the colony; they were, therefore, to be discouraged from wearing such dress.

Wolfers wrote that in 1919 'a patient legislative lecture was preached to the clothed and erring':

Clothes are good to wear if they are kept clean, and if they are taken off when they are wet and dried before they are put on again. Otherwise they are bad, for they cause sickness and death. Some natives know how to keep their clothes clean and do not wear them when they are wet, but many others are foolish, and wear them when they are very dirty, and keep them on, and even sleep in them, when they are wet. To protect these foolish men and women it is necessary to make a law about the wearing of clothes.[5]

One of the most controversial pieces of legislation was the White Womens Protection Ordinance introduced in the 1930s. Governor Murray was seen to have bowed to pressure. Many felt that the Act was a reflection of the Europeans' insecurities and distrust of the Papuans rather than a genuine social need. In the 1930s if a white woman consented to a sexual relationship with a New Guinean who was not her husband she was committing an offence. A New Guinean who attempted to have carnal knowledge of a consenting white woman could be gaoled.[6] If a New Guinean was convicted of rape or attempted rape of a white woman he could receive the death penalty; in 1934 a Papuan was hanged for the rape of a white girl. Offences against white women could incur whippings and long gaol sentences; and many felt that it was important for the New Guineans to learn that the white woman was 'sacred'.[7]

While Jean was enjoying Salamaua, Tick was enjoying her nursing and her social life, often burning the candle at both ends. Jean received reports in New Guinea from her colleagues describing Tick's party going. This led to a stream of letters from Jean chastising her for her 'flibberty gibbet' behaviour. Comments such as 'you'll never be the nurse your sister is' accompanied Tick throughout her training. In spite of the dire warnings that she would fail if she didn't pull herself together, Tick graduated as a trained nurse and as a midwife. Reflecting on this years later, Tick thought she would have been wiser to have trained at a hospital other than where her sister was so well known.

Jean returned from New Guinea and she and Tick took over the running of a little private hospital in Canterbury called 'The

Bryson'. It is still there today. Jean was a most capable nurse and ran the hospital efficiently. Tick provided the warmth and caring. She loved looking after the mothers and babies whereas Jean lacked the patience. At this stage in their lives, the two sisters complemented each other. Tick was dependent on Jean and reasonably happy to let herself be organised.

Life was lots of fun. Tick had managed to purchase a Morris Cowley car with a soft top for £35. The local milkman taught her how to drive and she could be seen roaring along highways at 25 miles (about 40 km) an hour, scarf flying and feeling like Australia's answer to Isadora Duncan! The sisters developed a tradition of 'High Tea' on Sundays. They would produce a table laden with food and invite their friends to join them. One frequent guest was their handsome young brother John Cox. Tick had recently joined a theatre group known as the Cairns Memorial Players and many interesting people from this group were guests at these teas, as well as many outstanding personalities from radio and the arts. The company was always stimulating and entertaining.

But Jean was yearning to go back to New Guinea, and raised the matter again on Christmas Eve 1934. Tick turned to her and said, 'Well, why don't you go?' Four days later Jean left Australia. Tick organised the 'hand over' of the hospital to the new managers and followed her.

In the meantime Jean had discovered on returning to New Guinea that, if she wished to take on more responsible positions in her nursing career, she required further qualifications. She enrolled at Guy's Hospital in London to study Tropical Medicine and Ward Management. The sisters decided to work for a short time in the islands and then continue on to London by cargo ship.

CHAPTER 4

~

RABAUL
1935

George (if I may call you that)

Now my heart goes pit-a-pat,

For this moment, while you spoke

What no doubt is passion woke;

Though till now I never knew,

I believe I dote on you;

Love unguessed

Filled my breast

I will marry you—Yes Sir, Yes!

A. P. HERBERT, *A Book of Ballads*

NEW GUINEA LIES IN THE TROPICS BETWEEN THE EQUATOR and 10 degrees south. The climate is hot and steamy with tropical rains, and the temperature ranges from above 30 degrees Celsius during the day and rarely falls below 25 degrees at night.[1] Tick enjoyed the trip to Rabaul. She was twenty-five years old, full of fun, and a wonderful adventure was about to begin. On board the ship, she met some interesting people and received two marriage proposals. It was during this trip that Tick began a lasting friendship with Elsie Edgell, a tall dark elegant young woman who later became my godmother. Elsie and her husband Tony ran a plantation on Manus Island. Elsie had a relaxed unflappable manner and Tick listened enthralled to her description of life on a plantation.

As a young woman who had never before been out of Australia, Tick found her arrival in Rabaul unforgettable. A splendid sight greeted her from the wharf. Government officials dressed in white waited to welcome the ship and Europeans gathered to greet friends back from leave. The arrival of the large ships was an exciting event for visitors and the people of Rabaul. A wonderful heady smell of copra mixed with frangipani wafted up to the passengers on the ship. Every now and then a wisp of sulphur broke through and reminded them that Rabaul is surrounded by a ring of active volcanoes. Rabaul itself is situated on the rim of an extinct volcano that nestles around Blanche Bay, one of the most beautiful harbours in the world. Rabaul was known as 'The Jewel of the Pacific' and its natural harbour became a centre for trade between the South Pacific islands. Blanche Bay contains two inner harbours, Simpson and Matupi, and is capable of holding up to 300 000 tonnes of shipping, a fact that becomes of great significance later in the story.

New Britain is about 500 kilometres long and about 80 kilometres wide. Rabaul lies at its north-eastern corner in the area called the Gazelle Peninsula. The Baining mountain range is a formidable barrier to the south. The island's highest mountain, Uluwan, is known as 'The Father' and lies south of Rabaul. Tovanumbater, 'The North Daughter', is north of Rabaul. Kombiu, 'The Mother', is the largest of the volcanoes. Matupi is the smallest but is active to the north of Matupi Island.[2]

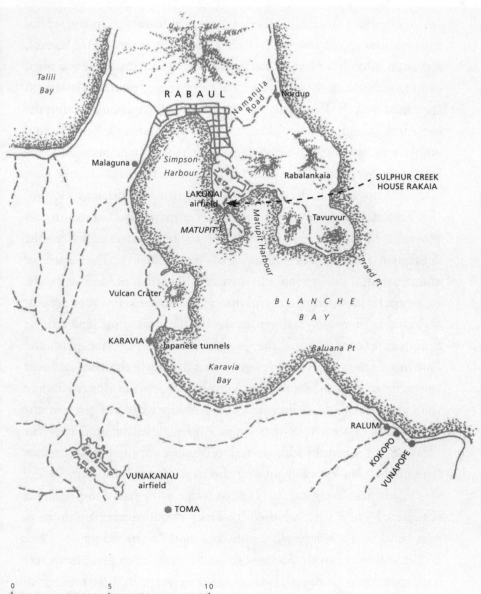

RABAUL

The New Guineans believe that the volcanoes possess powerful supernatural spirits known as 'kaia'.[3] Certainly, from 1937, Rabaul, although initially a place of much beauty, rapidly turned into a place of horror. Perhaps the volcanoes were expressing their displeasure as they observed the Germans, Australians and Japanese occupying the beautiful island of New Britain and imposing their rules and regulations upon a native population who were managing quite well before they arrived.

In 1884 Germany had proclaimed the archipelago of islands that includes New Britain as a part of German New Guinea. It was governed by Albert Hahl from 1901 to 1914 when it fell to the Australian forces at the outbreak of World War 1. The centre of administration under Hahl was initially at Kokopo or Herbertshoehe to give it its German name. Kokopo as a harbour was not as deep or sheltered as Simpson Harbour and so Hahl acquired the land around Simpson Harbour from the people of Matupi, Malaguna and Nordup. The mosquito-infested swamps were drained and the township of Rabaul was built.[4] Concern about volcanic activity and the close proximity of Rabaul to its volcanoes did not prevent the building of the town at that time. And yet the decision over the location of the central administration became a recurring issue in the lives of the people of Rabaul over the next fifty years.

Jean had arranged for Tick to lodge with Mrs Jones and her daughter Nancy. I was amused by Tick's description of her hostess. Mrs Jones was a fine English woman straight from the pages of one of Jane Austen's novels. She was acutely aware of her place in society and appearances were paramount, and maintaining the prestige of the Empire was of great importance. Her daughter Nancy, rather like Lydia in *Pride and Prejudice*, escaped from the fold on one occasion and returned home looking very contented. She was the pride of Mrs Jones' life, and she would hear no ill of her. She was a little concerned at Nancy's sudden weight gain and cautioned her to watch her food intake. One night she rang the doctor to say Nancy had a bad tummy ache from the spices she had eaten at dinner. The tummy ache turned out to be a fine bouncing baby boy.

Tick was enchanted by Rabaul's wide streets. The beautiful colourful casuarina, mango and rain trees provided soothing shade from the tropical sun. The gardens were beautifully kept and the green lawns provided a backdrop for glorious colourful frangipani, crocus and croton. These plants divided the properties as there were no fences. Tick had never seen such a profusion of tropical plants and colour. She had never before experienced the smell of the tropics and her senses were reeling. German built bungalows with red and green roofs were set in these gardens and stood up to 20 feet (6 metres) from the ground. Balcony lounges lacquered green, and pot plants brimming with luxurious maidenhair fern decorated the wide verandas which surrounded each house. Not only were the gardens full of colour, but so were the streets.

Gentlemen in their whites, some with elegantly dressed European women on their arm, strolled in the streets. Chinese women in brightly coloured silk with parasols shielding them from the tropical sun added to the picture. Tick noticed that many of the native people of Rabaul were a light coffee colour and some had blond hair. Mrs Jones explained that they used peroxide to lighten their hair and boot polish to darken it. They were Tolai New Guineans who lived predominantly on the Gazelle Peninsula and were regarded as the wealthiest, most advanced group of native people in Papua New Guinea. In the past they had eaten their enemies, but now most of them were Christian and monogamous.

Tick was amazed that Rabaul was so well planned and maintained. Mrs. Jones explained that the Germans were excellent planners: 'They know how to discipline the natives and let them know who's boss', said Mrs Jones. People who came thinking they would make friends with the natives would soon find the boys being insolent and the government men would have to discipline them again. Mrs Jones blamed the missionaries for many of these problems, and her words made Tick flinch. Her landlady sounded just like Jean when she spoke and Jean's way of talking about the New Guineans always left Tick feeling uncomfortable.

Tick knew that in 1921 Australia had been granted a mandate to administer the previous German New Guinea on behalf of the League of Nations. Rabaul remained the capital of the Mandated Territory of New Guinea. She had also learnt from her sister Jean that the Germans ruled the natives with an iron rod and that their methods were admired by many of the Europeans.

In Hank Nelson's *Taim Bilong Masta* one of the plantation owners describes how to control the native worker as 'the use of a bit of force, a swift clout or a boot to the area where it did most good'. When hitting, it was advised to do so with an open hand, as a closed fist could damage their skin which was paper thin. Newcomers were told to avoid hitting the natives on the body as this could be fatal. Many natives had enlarged spleens from chronic malaria. This approach continued into the 1960s.[5]

Many of the 'B-4' population, such as Geoff Melrose's father, did not like or approve of the paternalistic attitude and racist language.

The word boong was first used by New Guinea natives to describe the white man. This was because of the sound of the rifle shots made by the guns of the first white men they encountered. How the word came to describe the natives, out of the mouths of white men, is one of life's little mysteries. After WW 2 I used the word once or twice, only to be reprimanded by my dad that this was an unsavoury word. Native was OK as it was a reflection of 'this is my own, my native land'. Kanaka was permissible as it was freely used by the locals themselves. Bush Kanaka was just as permissible, as it also was in local use, but should be avoided by white fellas because it could be derogatory in the same way as cow cocky was a put down term in Australia. Coon and nigger were not to be used and this was supposedly Government policy pre-war. I never heard the word nigger up there but coon was used by some planters and miners—but never a second time in front of my father. Usually a calm man, he turned into an erupting volcano at that word. (*Una Voce,* March 2001)[6]

There were three Government doctors in Rabaul—Champion Hosking, Bob Cooper and Tom Brennan—and they were extremely good to Tick and Jean. Tom Brennan was the Director of Health and when he heard that the cargo ship to Europe was held up for a month, he invited Tick to work at the Rabaul Hospital. Tick signed the papers for him to send to Canberra registering her to nurse in Rabaul. Champion Hosking and Bob Cooper introduced the girls around and this soon led to the end of Tick's nursing career in the Islands.

Tick was a dark, pretty woman with beautiful cheekbones and a lovely smile, which lit up her face. She was slim and stood about 5 feet 4 inches (1.6 metres) tall. She was lots of fun and had an irrepressible sense of the ridiculous. There was no shortage of admirers. She wore dark-rimmed glasses and scoffed at the saying that 'Men don't make passes at girls who wear glasses'. Her most notable characteristics were her sweetness and her openness. She wore her heart on her sleeve. This sweetness did not prevent her having fun and making the odd bitchy comment, although these were rare. She was genuinely interested in whomever she was talking with, and people warmed to her.

Shortly after her arrival, a big party was held at the Kokopo Hotel to celebrate a large gold find by one of the well-known Leahy brothers. Tick and her date for the evening were enjoying a drink at the Rabaul Club as they waited for their lift to arrive. A handsome New Zealander walked through the swinging doors putting on his coat, and her heart skipped a beat. 'Here's our lift for the evening', said her date as he moved forward to shake hands with the newcomer.

'Tick, I want you to meet Bill Spensley.' They looked at each other and smiled.

'Look at that smile! That's the woman I'm going to marry.' These were the words uttered by my father to a friend when they arrived at the party.

Bill approached Tick as soon as he saw her alone, her partner having been waylaid by another guest.

'Would you like a drink? I'll ask the waiter to get you a pernod.' Bill had achieved considerable success in the past by convincing his quarry that pernod was a 'must'.

'No thank you', replied Tick. 'I'm strictly a gin and lemonade girl.'

Bill looked aghast. 'Good heavens, you can't do that to gin. Let me introduce you to pernod.'

'How does it mix with lemonade?'

'It doesn't.'

'Then I'll stick to my gin and lemonade.'

Defeated in the area of alcohol, Bill moved on to another subject.

'How do you like Rabaul?'

Tick's face lit up. 'I love it. It's so full of colour.'

Tick explained why she came to Rabaul. She told him about Jean's experience in Salamaua, and her desire to return to New Guinea. She also told him that she and Jean were waiting for a ship to take them to England.

'The Director of Health, Tom Brennan, has invited me to work at the Rabaul Hospital while we are waiting for the ship. The doctors have been very kind, particularly Tom, Champion Hosking and Bob Cooper.'

As they were all friends of his, Bill felt that it was a good time to emphasise this point.

'Come and meet Claire Cooper, Bob's wife. She was also a nurse, in Melbourne, I think.'

Bill took Tick's arm and steered her towards a group of people standing by the window. Tick greeted Bob Cooper warmly and he responded in kind. Tick's eyes moved to the tall elegant woman standing beside him, who exclaimed with surprise, 'Ticky Cox. Good heavens!' She turned to her husband and said, 'Tick and I trained at the Royal Melbourne Hospital together'. A clipped male English voice cut across their greeting.

'Introduce us to the young lady, Bill.' The demand came from a tall distinguished looking gentleman, wearing a monocle. Beside him stood a pleasant looking woman who smiled at Tick as she greeted her.

'Tick, I want you to meet Fred Mantle and his wife Phil. Fred is the District Officer in Rabaul and I warn you—don't play poker with him.' Bill explained to Tick later that Fred, an Englishman, was educated in Germany and spoke perfect German. He had worked with British Intelligence during World War 1 and was a unique and colourful character.

In the same group was the Harbour Master, Commander Webb, and his wife Taffy. He was always known affectionately as 'Webby'. He was very partial to his pink gin and his ribald sense of humour could shock on first acquaintance. It soon became clear that he was harmless, lots of fun and enjoyed shocking people. Tick enjoyed the repartee in the group and particularly enjoyed the knowledge that Bill did not seem to be able to take his eyes off her.

From this night on, Bill and Tick were inseparable. They spent the next months enjoying each other's company and discovering more and more about each other.

We were told that Bill's parents had died when he was three, and he and his sister were brought up by his maternal aunt in Auckland, New Zealand. He was certainly brought up by his aunt but recent investigations have shown that Bill's mother died when he was eighteen. She possibly spent many years in a sanitarium. His father died in Sydney in the company of a woman called Mary Fahey when Bill was fifteen. In days gone by, guarding the family reputation led to many lies being told and it is often difficult to sort out fact from fiction. I do not know if Tick knew the truth but I am sure it would not have made the slightest difference. She was happily, deliriously, in love.

Bill was sent to Dilworth, a school for impoverished young gentlemen. The school has always had an excellent reputation and has produced many outstanding citizens. James Dilworth was an Ulsterman, born at Donaghmore near County Tyrone. Possibly because he was childless, he decided to devote his substantial fortune to founding and running an independent boarding school for boys. These boys were either orphaned or had lost one parent, or seemed in every way worthy of a sound education beyond that provided by the state. Dilworth carried on the old world tradition of the endowed school. It had a strong emphasis on community and each member of staff knew every boy and the boys knew all the teachers. The school encouraged the active involvement of the Old Boys Association and this gave the school a sense of family. The old boys acted as support advisers and role models to other students and Bill was an active member before leaving for New Guinea.[7]

My father Bill was nine years older than Tick. After leaving school, he joined the South British Insurance Co. in Auckland where he worked for a short time until he was offered a job with Colyer Watson. This was a New Zealand-based small company specialising in skins and hides. Bill was sent to Christchurch to open another branch of the firm and lived there for several years. In about 1933 Mr Colyer decided to open an office in Rabaul. He had an agent there whose name was F.O.G. Greenwood who, with Laws, had an importing firm acting as agents for Colyer Watson.

Tick's sister Jean was in great demand in the colony for her excellent nursing skills, particularly her midwifery expertise, and she assisted in the delivery of talk-back radio personality, John Laws.

Mr Colyer believed that there was a big future in exporting copra, trochus and other products and decided to send Bill to Rabaul to set up an import and export firm. This was completely separate from the skins and hide business in New Zealand and Australia. Bill started at a desk in FOG's office and in no time at all had his own office, plus staff. Within two years he was managing a turnover of over £1 million ($2 million). Colyer Watson were the managing agents for the Norddeutscher Lloyd Shipping Company, a German company based in Bremen. Two ships called in to pick up the copra and trochus and brought in tinned meats and juice, cars and all kinds of other goods. The ships were the *Friderun*, which serviced the northern mainland ports like Manus, Wewak and Madang and the *Bremerhaven* which went to Kavieng and the Solomons. The latter was an old tramp steamer, reeking of copra and full of cockroaches.

Although a man of few words, Bill was dynamic, with a strong personality and a wonderful sense of humour. He had a handsome face with strong features. Tick fell instantly and deeply in love. Two months after their first meeting Bill proposed. Neither of them appeared to have any doubts. Bill was not the least intimidated by Jean who, in spite of losing some of her control over her sister, had a great respect for Bill. Tick's description of Bill was always so positive and clearly coloured by her feelings. She told us he loved all sports, particularly tennis, swimming, golf and rugby and was good at them all. He played rugby for his school and also for Auckland. He was popular with both sexes and in business he had a reputation for being tough but fair. He did not suffer fools gladly and had a tendency to make his feelings known. He did not offer excuses and encouraged Tick to follow his example: 'You don't need to explain. Just refuse'. Tick did not find this approach easy as she liked everyone to be happy.

As Bill was due to go to New Zealand in about a month after the proposal, they decided to marry quickly so Tick could accompany him and meet his family. Bill wrote to Tick's father requesting his daughter's hand in marriage and the arrangements were made. The approval arrived on the day of the wedding.

The wedding on 14 October 1935 was to be kept secret, but the wife of the Anglican archdeacon told the Sunday school group about it and the news spread quickly. Lady McNicoll offered Government House for the reception, but Tick and Bill decided to accept the offer of the home of Harold Page, who was the Government Secretary. Harold Page was a decorated World War 1 soldier and a brother of Sir Earle Page who was, for a time, Australian Prime Minister. Dr Champion Hosking gave the bride away, and Mike Donnelly, manager of the Bank of New South Wales, was the best man. Tick's wardrobe was limited. She had a leghorn straw hat which was all that was suitable. She borrowed a dress and had a frangipani muff made. She gratefully accepted the help of Jean and friends who decorated the church beautifully. The little Rabaul Anglican church was full to overflowing and the reception organised by Jean was a grand celebration. Sadly, the church was destroyed during the Occupation and today another church stands in its place. Tick and Bill spent their honeymoon aboard the *Friderun* sailing around the islands.

CHAPTER 5

LIFE IN RABAUL
1935–1937

The leaf of the black currant is coarse as canvas,

In the house there is laughter and the sound of ringing glass;

They are slicing, pickling, peppering,

Putting cloves into jars ...

BORIS PASTERNAK, 'Indian Summer'

RABAUL SOCIETY WAS VERY ORGANISED. It was described by Johnson and Threlfall in their book *Volcano Town*.

Rabaul in early 1937 was in its heyday as an inviolate enclave of the British Empire ... No Asians or New Guineans attended the public school. Rabaul was a racially stratified society in which the colonial 'mastas' were the 700 Caucasians, mainly Australian and German. Next in line, came the 1,000 Asians, mainly Chinese and a few Malays and last about 8,000 New Guineans, including many indentured laborers from as far away as the Sepik area and Manus Island...[1]

The Chinese community liked Bill and trusted him. T. C. Wee, a wealthy sawmiller and merchant, couldn't sign his name, so he asked Bill to write out cheques for large sums owing for goods that had been imported for him and, to authorise payment, he would then put his thumb print under the name which Bill had written.[2]

Tick loved Chinese New Year and she and Bill would call on all the old Chinese families where there would be great celebrations going on. They watched the fireworks and afterwards were served tea and little cakes accompanied by much ceremony and bowing. Tick found the Chinese in Rabaul to be fine people, and for this she was admonished by several of the European community. Fraternising with the Chinese community was discouraged, a fact which did not deter Tick and Bill.

Although the Australian Administration gave the Asians the same legal status as Europeans, the physical separation of the races was maintained. Chinatown was situated in the north-eastern corner, socially isolated from the European residential areas. There were three separate hospitals, one for each colour, helping to maintain the segregation of whites, blacks and yellows.

Tick's brother John, having decided to join his sisters in Rabaul, was soon employed running the picture theatre and, briefly, the local newspaper. He was a trained projectionist and had a lot of experience with radios. In fact, he was a man who could turn his hand to many things, looking for adventure and willing to learn anything and everything. John lived with Bill and Tick when he first came to Rabaul and John and Bill became firm friends. They prided themselves on being able to belch 'God Save The King' as a duet. When the native boys began to copy them, Tick had her hands full trying to put a stop to the duet which had now become a quartet. She threatened the New Guineans with a mouth wash and indeed carried this out, but I do not believe my father or uncle were subjected to the same punishment.

The girls were delighted to have their young brother in Rabaul and introduced him to their friends. John was a handsome young man with dark hair and brown eyes. He was over six feet (about 2 metres) tall with a lean, strong body. In shorts, his legs attracted admiring glances from the female community. Following in his sisters' footsteps, John began to enjoy his social life in Rabaul, and Bill's success in expanding Colyer Watson interests were about to have a big impact on John Cox's life.

Jean Cunningham was twenty-one when she arrived in Rabaul. Her father Dave had run a plantation in the Solomons and was persuaded by Colyer Watson to come to Rabaul to assist Bill. By 1936 the Colyer Watson firm had grown dramatically. Dave Cunningham arrived in Rabaul just before Christmas on board the *Neptuna*, accompanied by his wife and three beautiful daughters. They were greeted by Bill and Tick who had come straight from a fancy dress party at the New Guinea Club, Bill looking splendid as a Roman senator.

Jean Cunningham was the eldest of three daughters and the most striking. She was slim with thick lustrous dark hair and beautiful features. Her skin was lightly tanned, giving her an appearance of healthy youth. When she laughed it was the laugh of a joyful child and I remember clearly how infectious her giggle was. Her first twelve months in Rabaul, however, were traumatic. Mrs Cunningham became ill very soon after she and her family had arrived in Rabaul and was diagnosed with bowel cancer. As their father's work meant that he spent much of his time sailing around the islands, the girls were left with the task of caring for their mother. This was to become a very frightening experience particularly during the coming volcanic eruption.

Life in Rabaul for most Europeans was self indulgent and privileged. With labour so cheap, the women in Rabaul spent a leisurely existence shopping in the morning or playing mah-jong. Husbands often came home for lunch and, after a two-hour siesta, returned to work for the afternoon. The women often played a round of golf or some tennis before the rain came at 4 p.m. The husbands and wives would meet at one of the clubs for cocktails when the husbands finished work. Much of the social life centred on the New Guinea Club and the Rabaul Club. Membership of each depended upon status, the Rabaul Club having a more restricted membership.

Tick was a demonstrative person and she was able to bring this side out in Bill. They were very much in love, and whenever they walked into either club, the band began to play 'their' song, 'Cheek to Cheek'. After drinks at the club, people would meet at each other's houses to talk or listen to music. The local cinema played the same show all week and Friday night was the New Guineans' night at the movies.

The unremitting humidity could make personal hygiene a problem. When attending a party, men would be accompanied by a 'boy' whose duty was to take care of the four or five starched shirts and jackets brought so that the men could change during the evening.

When the ships came in with fresh meat and stores, a round of parties ensued. Twelve courses were often served. The expectation was that if one was invited to dine on another's fresh meat, the compliment would be returned. Eggs were sealed with Vaseline and stored in wet sand in a trunk under the house.

When they married, Tick and Bill moved to a house on Namanula Hill. Namanula Avenue stretched up from the township, past Government House and reached a 'lookout' which provided a view over Rabaul Harbour.

They had a long-haired fox terrier named Bobby Dog. He suffered from eczema, which seemed to localise itself around his tail and, during one particularly bad outbreak, his tail began to bleed. Feeling very sorry for him, Tick dressed his wound. She used a fingerstall and a blue ribbon to hold the dressing in place. Bobby Dog was well known in Rabaul and wandered around as if he owned it. After dressing his tail, Tick and Bill went off to the cinema where a local concert was being held. An aspiring singer began her performance only to find the audience roaring with laughter.

Looking around, she spied Bobby Dog walking across the stage looking for Tick with his blue-ribboned tail wagging enthusiastically.

Because of this unseemly performance, Tick decided it was time for Bobby Dog to have a female companion and settle down. She sent down South for a fox terrier bitch. When the dog arrived in Rabaul it was obviously a male. The bitch had gone to Madang where an excited couple waited for their male fox terrier. The swap was duly made and Bobby Dog began to take his new responsibilities seriously. Before long Patsy, Bobby Dog's new wife, was pregnant. She was always a bad-tempered little dog but this did not appear to worry Bobby Dog, and Patsy produced a fine litter of fox terrier puppies.

Bill had a share in a horse with a friend, Clarrie Archer, who was on the Custodian Expropriation Board.[3] The horse was called Romany Lad and had eight starts and eight wins, so attendance at the racecourse was another social event. Romany Lad won the Rabaul Cup in 1937 and there was much celebration following this momentous event! The racecourse was also the golf course and the aerodrome. Both Tick and Bill liked to gamble—roulette was a favourite—and Bill played poker quite often with Tom Brennan and some of the other men.

Bill and Tick spent a lot of time with Oscar and Phil Rondahl and later they invited Oscar to be their son John's godfather. Oscar was the son of Captain Rondahl, a Swedish officer who came to Rabaul around 1870. He made a lot of money trading around the islands and in Shanghai. In 1918, at the age of twenty-one, Oscar inherited £60 000 when his father died. He continued trading as his father had done before him. Oscar married Phyllis Cooper who was a member of the Coopers Brewery family from Adelaide.[4]

Oscar was Queen Emma's half-nephew, so he was related to one of the most colourful and best known personages in the South Pacific. I have always found Queen Emma's story to be quite fascinating and for anyone wishing to learn about New Britain, R.W.

Robson's account of her life will take one on an adventure full of drama, comedy, and colourful romance.

Emma's father was the American consul and her mother a Samoan princess. Queen Emma was beautiful, intelligent and a match for any man in the islands. She was also accomplished, cultured and politically aware. By 1878 Queen Emma was rich and very influential. She had two marriages and many lovers, defied convention and founded a commercial empire in nineteenth-century New Guinea. Her beautiful nieces surrounded Emma, and the wonderful parties and hospitality fascinated visitors. Her family was large and Emma liked to make sure her nieces married well. Many married visiting Germans who were mesmerised by the beautiful half-caste nieces and found the financial encouragement from Emma irresistible. Her youngest sister Phoebe married a brilliant young surveyor of Anglo-German ancestry, Richard H. R. Parkinson. He was also a skilled planter and botanist and became known as the 'German Professor'. Emma had observed the lucrative results achieved by the Germans planting coconuts in Samoa and she persuaded Parkinson to join her in planting coconuts in New Britain. He was reluctant at first as the New Britain natives were hostile cannibals and were not to be trusted. Their savagery was in part understandable. From about 1875 until the Germans took control in the late 1880's, countless shiploads of natives from New Britain, the Solomon Islands and Melanesia were carried off into forced labour on the plantations of Samoa, Queensland and Fiji. Sometimes there was a semblance of law, where the chief traded goods for labourers to be used on plantations for a stipulated period.

Emma and Parkinson recruited men from Buka, north-west of Bougainville, to act as bodyguards. The Buka natives were black, very strong and brave; they were also trustworthy. Parkinson and his bodyguard of Bukas accomplished more than any other single factor at that time in taming the country and laying the foundations of a great planting industry in New Britain.

Emma and the Parkinsons selected an area called Ralum to settle and build the home of Emma's dreams. The house was built on a high fertile terrace looking eastwards to the Duke of York Islands. It was called Gunantambu and is surely one of the most glorious sites for a home in the South Pacific.

Before Emma's house was built at Gunantambu, there stood a house built by a gentleman called Wilfred Powell, who built his house from native materials and surrounded it with a double fence of bamboo. When it was finished he invited his native neighbours for the opening feast, but was embarrassed when one petty chief brought along a human body as his contribution to the party.[5]

Oscar Rondahl was refused membership of the Rabaul Club and extensive investigation has left me unclear as to whether this was because of the Samoan connection or his Swedish ancestry. The Swedes were seen as German sympathisers. Whatever the reason, it made no difference to Tick and Bill's friendship with Oscar and Phil, but they were upset that he was not granted membership.

Oscar bought land at Kabakaul, a beautiful natural harbour, which was not as deep as Simpson Harbour. The plantation had its own private entrance and wharf at which Oscar moored his two schooners, the *Induna Star* and the *Kabakaul*. Imports such as copra and cattle were unloaded at the wharf at Kabakaul. The cattle were swung ashore in slings. Oscar built a magnificent mansion for his wife Phil. The walls were hand-plastered and he brought in skilled artisans from China to ensure that the marble floors and plastering was of the highest quality. Much of the material was imported from Italy. There is a story that the work was so boring and the bay so isolated that one of the Chinese artisans committed suicide.

Oscar's mother Grace (Queen Emma's half sister) was known as 'Ma' Schmidt. She married again after Captain Rondahl died. She ran a plantation in the Kokopo area and Tick and Bill were frequent visitors for lunch and dinner. It was a privileged, comfortable and happy time for Tick and Bill. They were young and energetic, and delighted in each other's company.

CHAPTER 6

VOLCANIC ERUPTION

1937

Enormous amounts of electrical energy are generated

in turbulent eruption clouds by the friction caused by

volcanic particles rubbing together within the cloud.

This energy builds up to a critical amount and is then

discharged as spectacular volcanic lightning that shoots to the

ground midst crashing thunder. The lightning and thunder

effect during the 1937 Vulcan eruption were especially

impressive, and contributed to much of the fear

experienced by those in the fallout zone...

R.W. JOHNSON AND N.A. THRELFALL, *Volcano Town*

THE EUROPEAN COMMUNITY OF RABAUL ENJOYED THEIR privileged existence accompanied by daily earth tremors and rumblings from the surrounding volcanoes. This was part of daily life. There was no vulcanologist in Rabaul to warn of impending disasters.

On Friday 28 May 1937 there were several earthquakes lasting about 30 seconds each. Several houses collapsed. A ship named the *Montoro* was discharging cargo when the crew noticed the ship beginning to tremble. The trembling became more violent until plates and cutlery on the table started to dance.[1] By mid-afternoon the tremors had stopped. Fluctuations were noticed in the level of the water in the harbour. Waters receded gently to about 100 metres out from the shore and then returned. On Vulcan Island, a small island in the middle of the harbour, the water receded and then it came back to approximately 150 metres past the high water-mark then receded to its normal level. Fish were left stranded.

The inhabitants treated the rumblings as a bit of a joke, even when they noticed the road moving! 'As long as father is smoking his pipe, the mother will be all right' was a common saying at the time, referring to the nicknames of the volcanoes.

Tick and Bill were resting after lunch on that Friday when a particularly violent guria (earth tremor) occurred. They heard later that an elderly German lady, Mrs Furter, was in bed with a fever when a wardrobe fell on her, breaking her leg. Bill became a little concerned as his firm Colyer Watson ran the freezer and the electricity supply. He was worried that the flywheel might shake loose and if it rolled through the township, it could cause great damage.

Early on Saturday morning Tick and her friend Claire Cooper drove down to the market together to buy some fish. They repeated the 'father smoking his pipe' saying to each other with a laugh as they observed the movement of the road. When they entered the stores, they saw that the shopkeepers were having difficulty keeping cans on the shelves.

When Tick arrived home from the market, she and Bill packed the car and set off for Toma, where they had been lent a house for the weekend. Toma is in the mountains and about an hour out of Rabaul. They often spent weekends there as it was more open to the sea breezes. They noticed that Lapin and the other houseboys were more agitated than usual. Tick laughed it off saying, 'If the top blows off, we'll all go bang'. She regretted the flippancy of her words in the days to come.

As they drove out of Rabaul, they noticed a big red spit of land which had not been there the day before. They arrived at the house at Toma and were sitting in the garden enjoying the breeze and a cup of tea when suddenly they heard two enormous explosions, that sounded like thunder.

At 4.10 p.m. on Saturday 29 May 1937 the eruption began. The water in the middle of the harbour began to bubble. It was like a giant cauldron full of boiling water. The sea began to break into waves and water began to spout towards the sky. Rocks were thrown high into the air with hot water, dust and pumice. Survivors described how a sailboat trapped in the disturbed water disappeared in the eruption cloud.[2]

Tick and Bill looked towards the harbour and saw giant stones as big as houses spitting into the sky. A huge cloud like a giant cauliflower began to spread across the harbour. There was some relief when they realised that the stones were spitting upwards and not sideways. They raced to the car and headed for the harbour. White smoke began to blot out all view of the harbour like a theatre curtain coming down. Bill and his friend Oscar Rondahl gathered a crew together and took the *Induna Star* out from Kabakaul to transport survivors to Kokopo.

The Cunningham family had then been in Rabaul for six months. Mrs Cunningham's condition had worsened and she was desperately ill. Dave Cunningham was at sea on the *Island Trader*, buying copra for Colyer Watson. The three girls were nursing their mother when the eruption happened, and they were unable to contact the doctors whose services were in demand. There was no public transport and the girls had no access to private transport. Their mother was bedridden and the girls were so concerned about her condition that they decided to stay put. In the meantime, the dense clouds of pumice thrown out of the volcano obliterated the sun and the only light was from the ferocious lightning. This created a weird and terrifying atmosphere.

Hospital staff, including Dr Cooper and Dr Watch, worked throughout the night. They treated dust-infected eyes and administered sedatives to shocked people. Eventually, the demands were too many and the decision was made to transport people from Nordup to Kokopo and Vunapope using all available craft.[3]

Fortunately, a couple of patrol officers had been detached to investigate all residences and bring any people they found to the hospital at Namanula. Next morning Mrs Cunningham and the girls joined the flotilla of craft and were ferried to the Sacred Heart Mission hospital at Vunapope. Mrs Cunningham died two days later.

Many people said that the most terrifying experience was the electrical storm that accompanied the eruption. Continuous blinding lightning, rolling thunder and darkness filled the sky. The volcano continued to spit giant rocks.

On the first night Tick took many people back to Toma. As the men continued their rescue mission far into the night, Tick and the others tried to catch some sleep, but the noise was horrendous and Tick found sleep impossible as her teeth were chattering uncontrollably. On the following day they rang around the plantations to find how many people could be billeted to each place and then set about organising the billets.

After a few hours rest, the rescue missions began again. The *Golden Bear* managed to escape the harbour, but lost its wireless operator who was swept overboard by a tidal wave. The *Golden Bear* managed to transport many survivors from Nordup to Kokopo assisted by a flotilla of smaller craft.

Tick helped to organise the billeting of survivors to the plantations. The Sacred Heart Mission at Vunapope provided sanctuary for many and, four years later, was to repeat this performance when the Japanese invaded Rabaul. Patients evacuated from the Namanula Hospital were housed at the mission hospital. One of Tick's friends, Betty Best, was very pregnant and delivered her daughter, Jocelyn, at the mission the day after the eruption. The cradle used was a beer crate placed on a table, the legs of which were placed in cans of water to prevent scorpions getting to the baby.

The Mission provided food for distribution to outlying stations. Approximately 1000 people required accommodation and food. The people of Rabaul were very grateful to the Sacred Heart Mission for their kindness and hospitality and readiness to assist in a crisis.

Bill and Tick, with Oscar and Phil Rondahl, spent the second night at the home of Oscar's mother, Ma Schmidt. They needed to be with friends as the world was erupting around them. Ma Schmidt's plantation was full of survivors, so they were all able to help.

The second eruption occurred at 3 p.m. on Sunday. Tick was standing on the wharf at Kabakaul waiting to welcome a boat full of women and children who were being transported from Matupi Island. The boat was about 500 yards from shore when Matupi erupted. Tick heard the most heart-rending poignant moan coming from the ship across the water as the women mourned their husbands left behind at Matupi Island. Five hundred people died as a result of the eruption.

There were many stories from survivors. One involved a Mr Chinnery and his wife Sarah and friends, who had decided to take a boat out to inspect the new spit of land that had arisen in the harbour. As they did, the land began slowly to come up under them and they had to leave the boat and run for their lives. An engineer was lost during the earthquake. He was due to leave Rabaul on the *Montoro* and had climbed Matupi to take photos of the steaming volcano before departing. Apparently fumes overcame him, for he was never seen again.

Tick and Bill's house on Namanula Hill provided shelter for many people. Prisoners were let out of gaol and some spent the night under the house, leaving messages of thanks scrawled in the ash. People made for the ridge and the north coast as mud and fallen trees made many of the other roads impassable. Some emerged covered in pumice, only their red eyes adding relief to the grey ash all over them.

Tick's brother John was busy at the other end of Rabaul. He tried to get through to see if the harbour was navigable, but there was a great sheet of pumice across it. John tried unsuccessfully to keep the phones going and spent the night at the police station helping with the evacuations and distribution of food. Tick was very worried about him, so Bill and Oscar sailed around to the north coast and eventually found him, but he refused to leave. Brother and sister continued their work on opposite ends of Rabaul. John Cox received a letter of commendation from the Australian Government for his work during this time. I recall Tick describing with distaste, people sitting on verandas having tea and scones, watching the eruption, while others pulled together to help the survivors.

The sulphur fumes were sickening, but worse was the damage from the pumice. Fowls died as pumice got into their crops and set hard. Palm trees looked like inverted umbrellas. Trees were stripped of leaves and uprooted in the main street. Pumice created a layer like glass across the streets making driving dangerous, if not impossible, and ash covered everything including cars and houses, inside and out. After ten days the noise settled down to a rumble and people with businesses were permitted to return to Rabaul when the Administration considered it was safe. Many cars could not be moved as they were covered up to their windows with pumice.

CHAPTER 7

THE AFTERMATH

Social life in Rabaul was soon resumed after the

re-occupation of the town and, like the frangipani

flowers that had so impressed Gordon Thomas and others,

it bloomed again in its former style.

The Frangipani Ball was inaugurated to celebrate

the rebirth of the town,...

R. W. JOHNSON AND N. A. THRELFALL, *Volcano Town*

*R*ABAUL WAS DEVASTATED, BUT IT WAS TIME TO START cleaning up. Bill and Oscar continued to assist in the billeting of people until the Administration gave permission to re-enter Rabaul, when Bill began transferring office equipment to Kokopo. Tick remained at Rainan, Ma Schmidt's plantation. She nursed Phyl Rondahl who had developed tonsillitis and was miserable.

People were instructed to wear masks, as the dust was everywhere, but there were not enough masks to go around and they had to use pieces of gauze dampened with glycerine and rose water.

Everything was covered in fine ash. There was very little pure water and teeth had to be cleaned in lemonade. All the water tanks and roofs were covered in pumice and everyone prayed that the rain would not come before they had time to clean the tanks as these provided the water catchments. Unfortunately, it did rain and the pumice set like cement causing more headaches for the house-holders. There were flash floods with water up to 1.8 metres deep covering elevated verandas.

When Tick and Bill returned to their house on Namanula Hill, they found their parrot had wreaked havoc inside the house. The bird had gnawed cupboards, toothpaste tubes and mustard tubes and had disappeared.

Gradually the quakes subsided and life began to return to normal, but from the time of the eruption Tick always had an emer-gency kit packed with essentials. The beautiful casuarina trees on the main road were cut right back to ensure future exit over the mountain in the event of another eruption. Since 1937 there has been a vulcanologist in residence in Rabaul. Dr Hosking was worried about the health risks following the eruption. The drainage system was a mess and he feared an outbreak of malaria. In his report to Sir Ramsay McNicoll, the Administrator, he suggested that Sir Ralph Cilento, Professor of Tropical Medicine at the University of Queens-land be invited to review the situation and write a report.[1] Sir Raphael Cilento shared Dr Hosking's fears of an outbreak of malaria and the need to take strenuous preventive measures. He supported McNicoll's decision to move the people at Kokopo back to Rabaul immediately. From a psychological point of view, he felt it was important to restore order as soon as possible so that people would begin to feel secure again. He did believe that the European population should live at 1500–2000 feet above sea-level away from 'native and Chinese areas'. His report was only a review of the medical situation but none the less racist—indicative of attitudes of the times.[2]

In contrast, Dr Charles Edgar Stehn, an experienced vulcanol-ogist, and Dr Walter George Woolnough, a geological adviser to the

Australian Government, in their first report stated they could not confidently say that further eruptions would not occur. '...we are, therefore, forced to the conclusion that reasonably early evacuation of Rabaul as the main administrative centre of the Territory must be seriously considered'. There was also '...the possibility that the whole of the capital invested in town and harbour may be jeopardised or wiped out of existence in a few hours by another serious eruption taking place under conditions not so extraordinarily favourable as those of the recent phenomena'. They were referring to the fact that the eruption happened in daylight, in the weekend when families were at home, when transport was in convenient positions, and there was easy access to escape points.[3] Stehn later changed his mind and suggested that Rabaul could remain as the Territory capital if a vulcanological observatory were established and if the warning signs were heeded.

The arguments continued. Moving the capital would be a very expensive process not to be entered into lightly. In 1910 the German Governor Hahl had made the decision to move the capital to Rabaul for economic reasons. Simpson Harbour was deep and sheltered and very attractive to shipping, and it was far less exposed than Kokopo. Governor Hahl clearly felt that the hazards from the volcano were apparently outweighed by the economic and political advantage. Tick and Bill, having experienced the terrifying power of the volcano, now believed that building a township in an active volcanic caldera was not a very sensible thing to do.

The following extracts from the local press speak for themselves.

Publicists and paragraphists in the Australian Press may write contentious articles regarding the advisability of rehabilitating Rabaul, proffering all sorts of arguments to bolster up their views; nature, however, wastes no time with words but acts to prove her points and, despite pessimistic pressmen, shows the world that Rabaul is much alive and the budding trees, the blooming flowers and the blades of new grass all show that Rabaul has flung her 'winter garment of repentance' in the fire of Spring…And the frangipanis bloom again. Rabaul, like a beautiful lady undergoing a facial 'mud pack' will emerge more beautiful than ever, after Time and Work and Patience. We must not be afraid to tackle the job, nor must we allow the flapper press in Australia to deprive us either of our faith or patience. It is illogical to pay attention to statements that another outbreak will occur in fifty-nine years because the last one took place in 1878. You can't work out averages from only two dates.

During critical periods there is always a division of opinion. Had the Administrator at the outset decided that Rabaul should be abandoned then there would have been a far greater cry of protest from the public and vested interests than has arisen over his present decision, at the prospect of abandoning hundreds of thousands of pounds worth of public and private property.

What town or city, which has been devastated by earthquake or eruption, has not risen again to a greater beauty and prosperity? Were 'Frisco, Tokyo, Napier and Quetta—abandoned? So why Rabaul?

The frangipanis and the hibiscus are blooming, and the lady will emerge more beautiful than ever from her facial mud pack. All we ask is that we be left alone to do the job of work before us, nor made the butt of political issues in Australia, which seems to be the aim of the Sydney 'Bulletin' in its issue of June 9. We can tolerate published inaccuracies in the sensation-loving newspapers of Australia but we certainly expect 'The Bulletin' to give us a 'fair go', and at least marshal its facts correctly.[4]

From the radio news this week we learn that Dr. Ch. E. Stehn, a vulcanologist of repute is to pay Rabaul a visit of inspection in order to report on its safety qualities.

Dr. Stehn is an official of the Dutch East Indies and has spent many years in making a personal study of that volcanic marvel Krakatan, which erupted in 1883. The Netherlands government established an observation post a few miles from the submarine crater and it was here that Dr. Stehn was in charge of the vulcanological service, which has amassed a fund of data relating to the habits of volcanoes, especially Krakatan which has been known to erupt as often as 6,800 times in the twenty-four hours.

In the Dutch East Indies they capitalise their volcanoes, and special tourist trips are made daily by boat and 'plane to enable travellers to inspect these interesting landmarks which manifest the 'breathing of the earth', as eruptions have been referred to by certain scientists.

Vulcanology has been termed 'the science of the living earth', and though it is one of the youngest sciences, and not yet properly organised, still a fund of information has already been obtained by such men as Dr. Stehn and Frank Perret, Director of the Volcano Museum in St. Pierre, which enables them to diagnose conditions at an active crater and, in many instances, predict its doings. We await with interest Dr. Stehn's report on our own situation here.

The fears of some have been allayed now that the analysis of the mud and dust of Rabaul shows it to be devoid of arsenical properties and unlikely to affect the drinking water.

Sir Raphael Cilento, the one time R.M.O. in this Territory and now reporting on health conditions for the Federal government, is making a very thorough survey of the situation but is naturally uncommunicative before presenting his report. Conditions are, however, greatly improved in comparison to what he expected to find and his recommendations no doubt will deal chiefly with preventive measures against a mosquito menace as was known in Rabaul in earlier years.

While scientific experts frame their reports and various expressions of opinion are voiced reflecting the result of individual psychological repercussions, the pick and shovel work goes ahead with amazing strides; more especially since the arrival of mechanical conveyors which do five times as much work as the boy with a spade. There is a big job of work yet to be done; and that can only be accomplished by good team work in the interests of the whole and the effacement of personal predilections.[5]

In a letter written by Tick to her family in Melbourne she gives a different point of view.

KOKOPO 7/6/37

We are still going strong and quite enjoying our excitements and altho' the volcanoes are still coughing and spitting they have died down quite a lot and the place looks a good deal healthier.

John has been in Rabaul all the time and doing very splendid work, helping get the women and children away and then stopping to send stores and get the radio station working.

Bill went over in a schooner many times to help get away the women and when the second crater went up he went over to find John and bring him back. John wouldn't come, so Bill has been doing some heavy work billeting people and goodness only knows what.

The Administrator says that he intends to rehabilitate Rabaul and is working to that end. Needless to say all the people are dead against it and I think there'll be one hell of a row before it's over. The business firms and banks refuse to go and have set up their offices here pro tem and they are all using all their influence in Canberra to have the Capital moved. Hope they succeed. Isn't it marvellous how quickly one can turn against something one has previously loved. That's how everyone is feeling just at present.

Bill is very busy setting up his offices here in Kokopo now and I don't see very much of him. Yesterday he went over to Rabaul to get things and he told me that he has never seen such a scene of desolation. The trees are just bare trunks and the roads are about 18" [45 cm] thick with pumice and dirt and littered with enormous branches. It seems unbelievable that our lovely town could look like that, but I hope to see it myself in a day or two.

CHAPTER 8

THE LULL BEFORE
THE STORM
1937–1939

Once upon a time

In a fairy-tale kingdom,

Spurring over

The burrs of the steppe,

A horseman rode to battle,

Through the dusk a dark forest

Rose to meet him

In the distance

BORIS PASTERNAK, 'A Fairy Tale'

IN 1937, WHEN TICK BECAME PREGNANT WITH MY BROTHER John, Bill decided that they needed a bigger house and they moved into House Rakaia, at Sulphur Creek. House Rakaia had been built by the Norddeutscher Lloyd shipping line for their senior staff and German business guests. It was then purchased by Burns Philp for the regional manager's residence. It was a magnificent two-storey timber hilltop bungalow and guest house set in acres of manicured lawns and tropical trees and gardens, with views over Blanche Bay. Sulphur Creek is a straight and narrow inlet from the harbour and runs about 450 metres into the centre of the craters.

The house was on the edge of Sulphur Creek, in quite a high and airy position. On one side it looked over towards the town of Rabaul and on the other side the land sloped quite steeply down into the remnants of a volcano. It was known as 'the house with a hundred windows'. Stone steps led up to the house from the drive, which was edged with vibrant orange crocuses and tulip trees. Wide sweeping lawns led to the guest house situated on a lower level to the main house. The managing director of Burns Philp, Phil Coote, lived there with his family until his wife Rhoda found the smell of sulphur too upsetting and they decided to move. Norddeutscher Lloyd shipping line took over the lease, and as Colyer Watson was their agent in the islands, Bill and his family were offered the house. Vulcan Island was called Rakaia and the name means 'explosion of the spirit' because of the violence of volcanic eruptions.[1]

Much of Tick's time was spent supervising the staff. She had six full-time staff and could call on more whenever needed. There was a houseboy, a wash boy, a cook boy, carboy and a gardener. In Rabaul the car boys often wore lap laps with initials or logos stencilled on them. They looked very impressive when they rode on the car's running board. Tick's main helper was called Tigary Lapin and John and I had two New Guineans as playmates.

In 1938 Tick and Bill decided to visit Melbourne. Tick wanted to have her baby in a familiar environment, close to her family. It was also an opportunity for Bill to meet his in-laws.

While Tick was in hospital, her Melbourne friends, Iris Hunt and Marjorie Ward, looked after Bill. These two women were part of Tick's single life before her marriage to Bill. Iris was a beautiful, voluptuous, extroverted woman, married to Ralph Hunt, the

Colyer Watson (New Guinea) Ltd.

COPRA   MERCHANDISE   SHIPPING

MANGO AVE.   RABAUL, T.N.G.

PHONE 26.   Telegrams: COLYERAM   Codes BENTLEYS, ACME   BOX 65.

Agents For:

CHINA NAVIGATION COMPANY LIMITED.
NATIONAL MUTUAL LIFE ASSOCIATION OF AUSTRALASIA, LTD.
UNION ASSURANCE SOCIETY LIMITED

Distributors of: CHRYSLER AND PLYMOUTH CARS.
FARGO MOTOR AND DIESEL TRUCKS.
ZENITH RADIOS AND WINCHARGERS.

Managing Agents: RABAUL ELECTRICITY LIMITED.
RABAUL FREEZER LIMITED.

Rabaul Times, 10 JANUARY 1941

American Consul. Marjorie was a petite, attractive young woman with enormous energy. The meeting with Bill was about to change Marjorie Ward's life. In a letter to me in 1995, she wrote:

Tick designated us to 'look after Bill', which was no hardship I can assure you. He was a beaut bloke and grand company. He would visit Tick at the hospital and then join us at the Capitol Theatre where we had booked 3 seats. This was in the days of Ray Milland and Dorothy Lamour. When Bill heard I was a stenographer and typist he said he was having trouble finding one in Rabaul and offered me a job, which at that time I turned down. However two years later I needed a change and thought of going to Brisbane when Iris reminded me of Bill's offer so I ended up in Rabaul, and a jolly good boss Bill was too! After I met John Murphy we used to babysit John and you and when Bill had to fly to Sydney on business I stayed with Tick. We had planned to work for another year before marrying. However the Powers that Be decided John had to take his leave when due, so Bill gave me away on the 6 January, 1941 at the Catholic Church in Rabaul and Tick gave us a lovely reception at Haus Rakaia, their abode.

A young Australian nun played the organ at John and Marjorie Murphy's wedding and was embarrassed when she realised the bride was half-way up the aisle before she had commenced playing. The nun's name was Sister Berenice and she and John Murphy play a large part in the following chapters. It was only recently that I learnt of this connection.

After John was successfully delivered, and old enough to travel, Bill and Tick happily returned to Rabaul. Shortly after this, much to Tick's embarrassment, she became pregnant with me. After several half-hearted attempts to abort me, by jumping off chairs and drinking gin, she gave up the idea. Tick felt that to be pregnant so soon after the birth of her first child was a little unseemly! I did not agree and refused to let go of my place in the world.

It was at this time that the romance between John Cox and Jean Cunningham began to develop. The Cunningham girls were very attractive young women and were receiving a lot of attention from the single men in Rabaul, who far outnumbered the women. A romantic experience was an invitation to view the fireflies in the cocoa trees in the beautiful botanical gardens. It was wonderful to see hundreds of twinkling lights glowing against the black velvety darkness.

After their mother died, the two eldest Cunningham girls were employed by the Administration. Female employees were housed in nice little houses next to each other. This group of houses was known as the 'Virgins' Retreat' and was opposite the New Guinea Club. Jean was twenty-one, and Gwenyth was eighteen. Their younger sister Dawn was 'sent south' to school. As their father was frequently away, the two older girls had to grow up quickly. They had been through two traumatic experiences–the volcano eruption and the death of their mother.

Shortly after the girls had settled into their new accommodation their houseboys from their old home presented themselves on the doorstep. They were from the Duke of York Islands, aged twenty and seventeen, and were eager to begin work again. One morning the younger boy came to the girls in great distress and as Jean could not understand his story, she sent him to the District Officer with a request for an explanation. The lad came back with a note saying, 'Your boy is the victim of sodomy'. Jean was a naïve twenty-one-year-old unable to appreciate the ramifications of this piece of news or, in fact, exactly what it meant. Jean's knowledge of sodomy was limited to her childhood and the strange tales told her by an ignorant young woman masquerading as a teacher—a Sunday School teacher, no less. She had explained such goings on: 'The way those ancient Jews filled in their time was positively disgusting. Co-habiting with animals and sodding about and of course they named a couple of cities after them—Sodom and Gomorrah. What they did in Gomorrah I hate to think'. Gwenyth was no help as she was even more naïve, so they decided the best thing would be to send the young boy home: 'Why we didn't send the cause of all the trouble home, I don't know. I don't think we even thought of that'. I assume the cause of the problem was his twenty-year-old countryman.[2]

Tick thought her brother John was interested in Gwenyth and was quite surprised when he announced that Jean was 'the one'. In the years to come, we referred to Jean Cunningham as 'Little Jean' and Tick's older sister, Jean Cox, as 'Big Jean'.

The export and import company, Colyer Watson, continued to grow and Bill found it necessary to increase his staff. He employed a man called Jack Evans who, in the following year, met, fell in love with and married Gwenyth Cunningham. It was becoming a family affair. Little did all those people enjoying their idyllic lifestyle know that the increasingly ugly developments in Europe would soon have their counterpart in South East Asia.

CHAPTER 9

∼

WAR IN EUROPE

Too often, people think that solving the

world's problems is based on conquering the earth,

rather than touching the earth, touching ground...

CHOGYAM TRUNGPA

*I*T WAS A DISTURBING AND THREATENING TIME IN EUROPE AS hitler intimidated, negotiated, broke promises, annexed Austria and began to show his colours as the bully of Europe. Big Jean had left Rabaul for London in 1937 and after completing a course in ward management, laundry and kitchen servicing, infectious and tropical diseases at Guy's Hospital, she did some home nursing.

I am nursing a Parson and the son of a Duke no less. They are very nice to me but I know I shall be oozing piety soon. I'm terrified I'll swear. Since starting this letter I've washed my parson, poulticed him, cleaned his teeth and run up and down stairs about 75 times. These English houses are the very devil...

In a burst of patriotic fervour, Jean joined the Queen Alexandra's Imperial Military Nursing Corps. She was appointed Charge Sister at St John's Hospital, Lewisham, where she spent 1939 anxiously awaiting news of Hitler's intentions.

27/8/39...No doubt you will all be in the same state of mind that I am in tonight—wondering to be or not to be? I listened to the 6 pm news bulletin which was quite uninformative and without a vestige of reassurance. It's all this waiting and suspense that makes things so much worse. Matron has a day off today but I have had to report to her every three or four hours. She calls herself the War Office. There was a great flutter on Thursday. That was the day that Von Ribbentrop went to Moscow and things looked specially grave. All sorts of orders came from everywhere. The Principal Matron of the Sector sent a few, the Colonel in Chief sent a sheaf, the local authorities sent a few more and so it went on. If it really does come to a show down there will be a fine old muddle.

Next day things looked a bit blacker, as you know, so I fitted all the nurses with gas masks, and looked out the service masks (the ones which are to be used by persons working amongst casualties) and even put the anti-dim stuff on so that they would be quite ready—incidentally this little job filled in a bit of time. Then came the 'Stand By' telegram from the Home Office, a horrid looking scarlet envelope all covered with black writing. This meant to send home all patients who could go, and not to admit any for ordinary operations. Matron came to me with a long face, and showed me the telegram and we both read it. We then sought feverishly for the very, very lengthy instructions for the evacuating of patients, which came the crisis before last, and which we had glanced through but not really digested. We each took a page and retired to read it.

All is now in readiness and an overwhelming calm prevails. The nurses are very sensible and taking things calmly. In actual fact they are all to be evacuated to Maidstone, down in Kent and out of harm's way. There they work in ordinary hospitals because all the sick are

being sent out of London. I think I told you before that we are a
casualty clearing station here. Forgive me if I go on and on about this
damned war business. There seems to be nothing else to speak about.
Ordinary mundane matters all seem so trivial. I must go now and tell
all the nurses that they must write and tell their families of the
arrangements for their evacuation. There will be such a helluva
dashing about tomorrow.

On 3 September 1939 Germany invaded Poland, and Great Britain
declared war on Germany. Three days later I was born, ten days early.

In October 1939 Tick's brother John returned to Melbourne
and enlisted in the 7th Division Signals. Little Jean followed and
they were married before he left for the Middle East on the *Queen
Mary*.

Europe seemed so far away and, although concerned about
'Big Jean' and her brother John, Tick was preoccupied with her new
baby (me), her thirteen-month-old son and the fear of another
volcanic eruption.

More changes were about to occur, however, and once again,
Tick and Bill were caught up in the turmoil of the times. Colyer
Watson was interested in expanding its interests and spreading its
operations to Hong Kong. In November 1939 Bill travelled to Hong
Kong for discussions with the Jardine family and took his family
with him. I was two months old and the trip proved fairly eventful
for me. Dr Bob Cooper gave me a cholera injection on the sole of
my foot and this caused a rather nasty allergic reaction. While
lunching at the Jardines' home, the nanny let go of my pram, it took
off across the rolling lawns and I was tipped out on my head. During
the return trip to Rabaul our ship was blacked out as we were chased
by a Japanese ship. We then encountered a horrific storm, so Tick
and Bill were pleased finally to arrive home.

In 1939 the Australian Army issued authority for the
formation of the New Guinea Volunteer Rifles by the white
residents. The NGVR, as it became known, was a militia unit of

volunteers. By the terms of the mandate under which Australia administered New Britain and New Ireland, Australia was prohibited from training native troops except for internal police purposes, and always scrupulously obeyed this prohibition. New Guinea was not supposed to be fortified or have a defence force.[1] The Tolais in Rabaul were very different from the natives of Papua who were trained and were a formidable fighting force. The Tolais had served under several masters and were treated condescendingly by the Europeans in Rabaul. They were considered impossible to discipline and useless from a military point of view. It was deemed important for them to 'know their place and keep it'. No wonder many of them saw the Japanese as liberators.

Indigenous New Guineans were not sought by the NGVR. The Government had responsibility to protect New Guinea, but they would only be used as soldiers as a last resort. The German Administration under Governor Hahl before 1914 severely punished any breaking of the law and imposed harsh penalties but was not overly concerned with the long-term welfare of the New Guineans. The Germans were primarily directed towards economic gain. They were much less interventionist than the Australian Administration and were content to let the New Guineans run their own village life. In contrast, the Australian Administration was paternalistic and racist and its legislation aimed at maintaining the superiority of the white race. No Asians or New Guineans were permitted to join the public service. After 1929, New Guineans were not permitted to carry a weapon when in town, except to sell it, to remove it after buying it or to carry it to or from work.[2] Also after 1929,

New Guineans were forbidden the use of any garden seat, arbour, summerhouse, or other convenience provided for the public in the Rabaul Botanic Reserve, and of any seat or other convenience that was provided for public use in the public streets, roads, parks and gardens of Rabaul, Kavieng, Morobe, Madang, Namatanai, Aitape, Lorengau, Kokopo, and Kieta townships.[3]

JOHN, TICK AND ISOBEL COX
(IN FRONT), FLOWERDALE, 1924

JOHN COX, AGED SIXTEEN

AFTER CRICKET PRACTICE: BILL SPENSLEY (RIGHT), NEW ZEALAND, 1932

BILL, NEW ZEALAND, 1935

TICK COX, *en route* TO RABAUL, 1935

BILL'S WEDDING PHOTOGRAPH, 1935

TICK'S WEDDING PHOTOGRAPH, 1935

BILL WITH BOBBY DOG, RABAUL, 1936

BILL SPENSLEY AND MAJOR AYRES AT THE
RABAUL CUP, 1937, WON BY ROMANY LAD,
CO-OWNED BY BILL SPENSLEY AND
CLARRIE ARCHER

VULCAN EMERGING OUT OF THE SEA

A CAR BURIED AND ABANDONED AFTER THE ERUPTION, 1937

ROAD WASHED AWAY AT WALAUR AFTER THE ERUPTION

ELECTRICAL STORM FOLLOWING THE ERUPTION

EVACUATION FOLLOWING THE ERUPTION: THE *Golden Bear* TRANSPORTED CIVILIANS
FROM NORDUP TO KOKOPO, 1937

HOUSE RAKAIA

BILL AT HOUSE RAKAIA, 1938

TICK AT HOUSE RAKAIA, 1938

TICK WITH JOHN, MELBOURNE, 1938

BILL WITH JOHN, MELBOURNE, 1938

COLIN STIRLING AND CAPTAIN TRAVERS, 1939

The Rabaul group of the NGVR consisted of about 150 members who formed a machine-gun section and one rifle company. My father Bill was one of its first members, having served eight years in the Militia in New Zealand. The NGVR became a small but efficient group, training in their spare time. In early 1941, during the Menzies government, the war cabinet authorised a force of 1399 Australian troops, known as Lark Force, to defend New Britain and, for the first time, men in khaki were seen around Rabaul. The average age of the men was eighteen years and six months. Their equipment included two six-inch coastal guns and two three-inch anti-aircraft guns. The Royal Australian Navy was represented by a small base staff of ten and meagre supplies of ammunition, and the Royal Australian Air Force had ten Wirraways and four Hudson bombers.[4]

Six army nurses under the command of Major Palmer accompanied the troops. Among them was an attractive, bright young nurse, Lorna Whyte. Lorna held the popular belief of the time that Japan was a poor nation full of myopic little men who could not fire a rifle. They were not considered a threat by the majority of the population, who were soon to learn to their peril how completely misinformed they were.

Kay Parker was the Sister in Charge. She was an excellent nurse, down to earth, sensible, and yet always very professional. She had a big heart and was loved and respected by the other army nurses, and she wasn't scared of showing some feelings if the situation arose. She would often give the patients a hug and say, 'You'll be all right, boy'. She cut through a lot of unnecessary red tape if she thought it wasn't appropriate.

Lorna and the other nurses found the heat unbearable. Their uniforms had long sleeves and the material did not breathe. Their stockings clung to their legs and were completely unsuitable for a tropical climate. The nurses decided to remove their stockings and cut the sleeves off their uniforms. A World War 1 nurse who lived on a plantation out of Rabaul saw the nurses in the township one day.

She immediately wrote to the Matron in Chief of the Australian Army Nursing Service, in Australia, complaining about the dress of the army nurses. A hostile letter arrived from Matron chastising the nurses and threatening to bring them back to Australia, if they did not obey the dress code. Kaye wrote a letter of explanation back to Australia but before she could post it, the Japanese invasion began.

When the nurses arrived home after spending three and a half years in Japan as prisoners of war, Matron was waiting at the wharf in tears: 'I have had a dreadful war. How could I write that awful letter to you. I'm so sorry'. When the nurses first arrived in Rabaul there was no army hospital and a hospital of tents was erected in a coconut grove. Although it was a picturesque setting on the seashore, Lorna found night duty could be quite frightening as huge bats flew from tent to tent and coconuts could be heard dropping on the tents. Shortly after the nurses arrived, the volcano Matupi erupted again and it was decided to move Government House to Lae because of the pumice being thrown up by the volcano. Rabaul Government House became the hospital of the 2/10 Field Ambulance attached to Lark Force and the nurses and patients enjoyed the beautiful surroundings until 20 January 1942.

Most of the nursing at this stage was for tropical ulcers, malaria and dysentery. There were also occasional limb fractures. The ulcers were treated with mercurochrome packs, and left for several days—a very effective remedy. There was no penicillin and nursing care and sulphur drugs were the main forms of treatment. Lorna learnt a lot about nursing in a tropical environment.

Among the members of 2/22 Battalion/Lark Force was a young lieutenant by the name of Colin Stirling, who had been working as an accountant with Price Waterhouse in Melbourne when he joined the Militia. He rose through the ranks and arrived in Rabaul in charge of a platoon. Colin was competent and charming, with a lovely sense of humour. He loved a drink and a good party and, consequently, was a popular guest at Rabaul social functions.

Soon after his arrival, Colin and his platoon were given the task of defending the Sulphur Creek area. The camp was close by the house where Tick and Bill lived and Colin became a frequent visitor to lunches, dinners and parties held at the house. A friendship began and lasted until Colin's death in 2001. Colin was always an important person in our lives and the reason for this will become clearer as the story continues.

In those early days before the beginning of hostilities, life was pleasant for the troops in Rabaul and the people of Rabaul made them welcome. In May 1941 the volcano Matupi erupted again and continued to rumble afterwards, intermittently spitting out filth and ash that found its way into everything. Tick and Bill were worried about John and me, as the sulphur was quite sickening when a south-easterly wind was blowing. The vegetation was slowly dying.

Bill and Tick discussed the problems caused by the volcano. It seemed that many of their friends had 'gone south'—including Clare Cooper and Ruth Brennan. Bill felt that Tick and the children should go too. Tick was reluctant, but Bill managed to convince her that she could go to Melbourne ahead of him and he would join his family as soon as possible.

In July 1941 Tick reluctantly packed our bags said goodbye to Lapin, Gelu, Toowong and all her friends. She hugged Bill, unaware that this was the last time she would do so. They had enjoyed six wonderful years together and both believed their life as a family was just beginning.

CHAPTER 10

~

MEN'S TOWN
JULY–OCTOBER 1941

There are many ways of living,

and reading is one of them...

When you are reading you are living,

and when you are dreaming you

are living also...

JORGE LUIS BORGES

ICK, JOHN AND I TOOK THE SHIP TO SYDNEY AND THEN FLEW
from Sydney to Melbourne. Tick found a very different situation
at home from the one she had left behind in 1935. The war had had
quite an effect on the family. Tick's brother John had enlisted and left
for the Middle East on the *Queen Mary*; her sister Isobel had also
enlisted and married a regular army man; both had been sent to
different areas. Tick's older brother Ronald gave up his law degree
studies and joined the Police Force. He had also married, and was
living away from home. The three of us moved in with Ross, my
maternal grandfather, who was living alone in the family home in
Malvern. Tick's mother Mary was living with a friend in Hamilton,

a country town in the Western District of Victoria, and although words like 'separation' and 'divorce' were not mentioned, Mary did not seem to have any intention of coming home.

Tick and Bill's letters became a daily diary. They mailed them to each other weekly, neither of them missing a week until all the mail to Rabaul stopped with the invasion. At first Bill's letters were full of happenings and updates on friends, but over the months they became a record of the lead-up to the invasion from a civilian's point of view. Bill refers to many different people and, judging by the calibre of the people mentioned in Bill's letters (see Appendix I), it seems likely that war-planning meetings took place at House Rakaia, the house at Toma and the Club.

As events in Europe were escalating and the general situation was becoming very serious, men in Rabaul were showing increasing concern for the safety of their wives and children, and the evacuation to Australia began.

The mail ship which visited Rabaul weekly was the carrier of letters passing between loved ones and friends. The letters exchanged by Bill and Tick were probably illustrative of such communications. They can be described as documents containing expressions of disquiet, fears and love under cover of an attempt to project an image of normality. For that reason, some fairly comprehensive extracts are included in this chapter.

15 July 1941… Things are getting serious. If anyone enlists up here now they are posted to the camp here. Parades are happening more often. I have been having some trouble with Gelu. [Gelu was housekeeper, cook and nanny.] The other night I was getting into bed when I heard a car arrive and go off again. My suspicions were aroused and I found the boy friend Sam, in Gelus room (the lady was in bed) with his shoes off and shirt off. He reckoned it was very hot and his corns hurt him. I cuffed him smartly several times and sent him off. I was very annoyed with Gel and asked her what she meant by it. She said Sam was drunk and wanted to marry her. I told her she was not to see Sam again and if I had any more trouble I'd send her right back to Manus. Emma has gone back to her place but I can't get rid of Toowong (wash boy) he wants to stay and wash. Gelu is cooking well and looks after me all OK. Went off to work this morning feeling pretty good except for a bit of a head which I put down to an overdose of sulphur dioxide from Matupi. However at 10am I got Tom [Dr Brennan] to take a slide and found the old fever again active. Came home and bed at 11am with a temperature of 103 degrees. Tom gave me a quinine injection in the buttock which fixed things. At 2pm temperature was 99.8 and at 4 PM—normal. It is now 7 PM and I feel as good as gold. I have managed to secure a bloke named Bob Bensley for the office. Previously our agent in Salamaua. He arrives in a day or two thank goodness. Oscar and Phyl were in to lunch and Oscar stayed the night. Colin McInnes and Ted Best came up to dinner also. Had some NGVR stuff in the afternoon and got all hot and bothered.

There appears to have been some friction between the colonial old guard and the newer, younger club members. As an enthusiastic, opinionated young man, Bill was determined not to be intimidated and in his position as secretary of the club made a stand against one of them.

My blitz with Savage is still on in spite of requests from Tom and others to give in. Tonight at 6 PM the Queen Carnival closes and I will attend in person as Pat [Savage] seems to have got the rest of Rabaul bluffed. 'I sticks by me guns.' He has lodged an appeal with the head Red Cross council so everything is flourishing. I will myself chalk up the votes tonight and take a full and proper control of things.

The Sou' East has dropped and the business now goes straight up and comes down hours later as fine dust. We still get it. The vegetation is slowly dying. Gee I am glad you and the kids got away. And then the Japs are not behaving themselves. All in all there is cause for relief.

25 July 1941. It seems like 6 months since you went away. I am glad you decided on flying through. If half the rumours we hear up here are true then you did the right thing. Hardie has been through Rabaul and returns again later. This makes more work. McDonald [The Minister for Territories] is here also Halligan of the Prime Ministers Dept. Big doings. Had him round at the club for a few spots Wednesday night. He doesn't drink but this did not stop us. He is not a bad lad. Had a conference with him yesterday. Just him an me an Halligan. Matupi is behaving itself. It would while the Minister is here.

We are crowning the Queen on Saturday night and I might have to put in an appearance. The Army Officers are turning on a dance at The Rabaul Club on the 9th August. I don't know what they are going to dance with.

I am expecting Norm Whiteley in with Hardie. There has been quite a wave of car stealing recently and many soldiers have appeared in court and had to cough up anything up to 30 pounds or 2 months.

Well darling now you tell me something about yourself and the kids. As I say no word from you yet is just hell. You've no idea how big and lonely that bed can get. However I'm getting along with the radio and an odd book or so and I also am taking work home. This Copra Pool is causing a lot of extra work.

Give my love to John and Jill. I hope Jill has developed good habits. Tell me all about them on the boat and whether you had a hell of a time or not. How did they take to the Balus [aeroplane].

31 July 1941. Well John is three and we are an old married couple. I don't feel so old though when you are about and while we may have been married a long time I have certainly never been bored. What about you Darling. I hope Jill treated her brother decently on his birthday. It won't be long now before she has one herself.

I went to the Queen Carnival dance last Saturday and stayed an hour. Lost 1 or 2 shillings on the Housey Housey and went home. The

Sou'East is still as strong as ever. Just on two months of it now. I have never known it so prolonged and so strong. All local schooners are tied up. Darling I'll call at the club now for a quick un and finish this later. Cheers in the meantime.

1 August 1941. I forgot to tell you Pip Appel called in the other day and mysteriously asked me out for a spot. I put him off but saw him later at the Club and the occasion was the birth of a son. It happened a couple of weeks ago but he only heard by airmail. The radio has not yet arrived. However we wet his head and all is well. His brother officers suggest he should have the initials of D.P. Appel as news of his arrival came up in the same mail as news that the lads are getting Deferred Pay. Well dear there is no other news. I only long for you. Miss you terribly also the kids.

7 August 1941. Going out to the Cootes for dinner tonight. As you can imagine I have been as busy as hell in the office. Matupi aint dead yet. Gave forth a couple of beautiful cauliflower bursts yesterday with the result the place is absolutely filthy again.

14 August 1941. The Officers Ball was a great success. I had 2 dances and lots to drink. Went home at 1.30am. It continued till 4.30 and plenty of sore heads next day. On Sunday night Tom, Saunders, Rich and I went out to Tovakundum for dinner and poker. Lost 30/- [30 shillings, about $1.50] but had a very pleasant time. I went up to Government House for cocktails on Friday. Tame and uneventful. Turned down an invitation to dinner there last Monday. Tonight am having a cocktail party at home for Carter, to return hospitality. It's a damn nuisance but Gwen is doing the decent thing by me.

Friday… Well the do was on last night with a vengeance. 30 odd people and Gwen did very well indeed with the supper. Everyone was very thirsty and no one would go home. Lorna Hosking and

Champ both let their heads go a bit. Still no rain and I'm running out of water.

20//8/41 Drill, drill and more drill.

 Went to Nonga where Frankie Saunders and Rich are dug in to avoid the muck. Orton and Ann Townsend, the Cromies, Noel O'Dwyer and some girl friend from the hospital, Clarrie Archer and self. Enjoyed the swim and run on the beach plus a beer or two. Chauncey and Tom Brennan came to dinner and went home early.

 Saturday was a bit hectic. A couple of Yankee warships arrived and believe me the run on the beer at the Club was hard to cope with. I took Carter down to the plane at 12.30, saw Phyl off and rushed back to Club to help Tom entertain some 30 officers. I enclose a card exchanged with one lad who took whisky by the half tumbler with a chaser. However got an hours sleep and then appeared at the Club annual meeting and cocktail party (members only). The meeting was uneventful but yours truly was re-elected to committee followed by Coote, Archer and MacLean in that order. The cocktail party was bright and kai was amply and nicely provided by Poppy.

 Your letter received 4.30 pm Saturday was delightful and much appreciated. I live for the end of the week and if you ever miss a mail well I'm all for Sulphur Creek…Glad to hear the Jays sleep in till 8am. Wonderful break and splendid training my girl.

 I would love to join you at the anniversary party. I guess you will look just as wonderful as ever in your long frock. I'm going to be envious or jealous of someone I can see that. Have a good time my sweet. I started this downstairs and am adding a word or two in bed. Have got the whole family lined up before me. Mother, John and Jill. I think I will say good night to you all. Its time I went to sleep. Before going however I must tell you how I love and miss you all. Goodnight Darling. Bill

Great excitement this morning. Lanson the cat fighting a snake. There was no clear-cut decision so in case the cat got bitten I made the boys kill the snake. Lanson and I are now bosom cobbers. He is very lonely and I can appreciate how he feels. Friends in adversity so to speak. Anyway I can talk to him and he talks to me.

We are all very miserable and uncomfortable up here. Matupi is worse now than she has been since she blew on 6th June. You've no idea how filthy the show is. I have just given up any idea of doing anything but sweep the house. I am doubly thankful you and the kids are out of it. Carpenter's have moved their offices to Toboi and BPs have moved their office into Jack Edwards house—he being on leave. It's a little bit clearer down there.

23 August 1941. Just received your wire you cad. It's a blow after looking forward to a letter for a week. Don't let it occur again young lady or I'll begin to suspect you of losing interest. However you have probably got some good explanation so lets hear it. The plane is late again today hence the reason for this extra letter. It may not go this week but I will give it a go. Cheers my love and I don't care what else is missed but don't miss the mail to me, I'll begin to suspect the city life is going to your head.

26 August 1941. Well Darling here I am again. I did get a letter from you on Saturday afternoon so all was well was looking forward to a bleak weekend and so was considerably cheered to get a letter after all. It sounds as though the censor held it up for over a week. The same thing happened some time ago to Tom Brennan.

I was amused to hear about John and his swearing. I must be considered blameless and it would look therefore as though you are the example. Tut tut my girl. Glad you are settling down in the house. I think Dear you will have to look on it as your home for some time as this place is getting worse all the time. There appears to be no chance of you coming back here. Matupi is just one continual roar and emits dust without stopping. Our 'good friend' the Sou East wind then takes it right across Rabaul. Carpenters and BPs removed their offices down to their respective wharves but they are now getting it as badly as anywhere else. Darling you should see the house. Everything is locked up and I have fastened the upstairs window with calico. I have dismantled all the beds and put the mattresses away. They are all beginning to go. Curtains towels sheets are all rotting away. The floors are thick with dust and the milk and butter and food has all got to be covered from the kitchen to the table or it will turn black with dust. A very pretty picture but quite true. I believe the Administration are removing immediately to Lae. It's not confirmed yet but is pretty correct.

Colin McInnes and a cove called Captain Ben Hall came up last night while I was in the middle of dinner. They had coffee with me and stayed till 11 pm talking over a couple of bottles of beer. Colin's wife has written up and reported a somewhat similar reaction on meeting you as you reported on meeting her. The feeling is apparently mutual. Ian MacLean is back and told me a bit about you on the way down.

Rich and Clarrie are living out at Nonga and I go out there frequently for a swim. Specially after drill as I'm short of water and the swim takes the place of a bath. Did you know that I now roll my own? Cigarettes are very difficult to get. How long this rolling business will last I don't know.

Just been interrupted by phone calls from Sydney. The Rabaul Electricity directors are getting very worried about the removal of capital etc. So are we all.

5 September 1941. Colyer is here and we of course have been living in each other's pockets and talking business almost 24 hours a day. I am glad to have him here because changes are in the making. To give you a rough picture we are going to decentralize. I have sold the idea to Colyer. That is why I sent Evans to Madang. To make the place self supporting. The same with Kavieng. We are opening these and will give the branch to Beyer. We will do the same at Kieta and either

*Evans or Bensley will go down there. When these changes are
completed I am going to have a break. Will fly to Sydney then on to
Melbourne and when the time comes I will be very ready*

> *Tick, life is a bloody lonely affair these days isn't it? How are
the babes? Tell John I'm coming and good luck to Jill tomorrow.
Our family is growing up.*

*10 September 1941. As you know a definite decision to move
Administration to Lae has been made. It's a little difficult to know yet
how this is going to affect us all.*

Bill became very close to Tom Brennan and they spent a great deal
of time together during those last months. They looked forward to
weekends at Toma, away from the volcanic dust and where the breeze
gave them some relief from the heat. There they relaxed, slept, played
deck tennis and unwound with various visitors. Tom's wife Ruth had
gone south, so they provided some company for each other. Tom
held the lease on the house at Toma. Before Tick went south, she and
Bill spent many happy weekends at the house and had already had
discussions with Tom about taking over the lease. They no longer
wanted to live in Rabaul as the smell of ash and sulphur was
suffocating. The house at Toma had views on both sides. They loved
sitting outside in the evening, watching the flying foxes and listening
to the distant drums, watching the smoke from the village fires and
smelling the wood burning. One day they lit a fire and pretended
they were cold, just to remember what a fire was like.

*10 September 1941. Feel a lot better today but full of quinine.
However the fever is behind me now. Had a bit of a blow today when
Tom told me he was going over to Lae by the plane on Saturday for a
week. I immediately thought of our Toma trip but it is all O.K. Bruce
Sinclair is over here from Salamaua and I will take him up with me.
I am looking forward to 2 or 3 days out of this show. I will take Gelu*

up with us as I don't want to leave her here on her own. Tell John and
Jill I'm coming down to catch them just as soon as I can. Gelu and the
boys want to know how they are getting on. Last night I was bidden to
drop in on the Bests, the occasion being Teddy's birthday. So after
dinner down I went and had a whisky. I was home again by 10.30
PM. Could not stay longer cause I couldn't drink. I'm so full up of
quinine I cant think straight. Delly and Jim Cromie were there. R.A.
Robinson of BPs, Colin McInnes, Ben Hall and several other lads.
Have not had a chance to speak to Colin recently but he will come up
and have some dinner with me shortly and then we will get together.
I have seen a fair bit of a cove here Major Mollard. I think you missed
him. He has shown photos of his wife on many occasions. Apparently
she is a capable woman as she is carrying on his business whatever it
may be. John has sent his wife your address so you may meet.

 I am missing you more each day darling and its becoming
unbearable. I miss the kids terribly. I'm afraid they will forget what
I look like. John maybe not so much but Jill may. However the fortunes
of war. I should say the misfortunes.

 I have staying with me the Best family. I called in at their place
last Saturday night the occasion being Ted's birthday. Apparently at
that party they were asked to stay with me while they packed up their
house in preparation for departure. I have no recollection of asking
them none whatever but when I returned from Toma half their gear
was up there.

 The District Services (Melrose & Co) go over to Salamaua at
the end of this month. Molly goes South I believe. Also the Admn are
sending a lot of Carpenters and a lot of building material to Lae. The
idea is to build more or less bachelor quarters at Lae until the war is
over. Then they will start some permanent building scheme. For those
of the Admn staff who are not transferring to Lae I believe they have
another scheme adjacent to Rabaul. I suspect they will erect a few
temporary huts on the site of the new native hospital ground at the foot
of tunnel hill. For other than Admn they will probably cut up Nonga.

I am trying hard to work our show to Kokopo and may have some success later. I have been fully occupied with the Copra Pool, which is about due to come into operation. The work entailed is terrific. The fever has all gone again but I am a bit full of quinine.

19 September 1941… The only thing of moment is the Best's boy Labeet or some such name tried to poison Gelu. Personally I think it was a native love philtre but he was caught red handed with the bottles and so I ran him straight in without any apologies to the Bests. Gelu poor thing knew nothing about this.

    Don't count on me getting down too much before Xmas. I am setting my mind on Xmas anyway as there is a hell of a lot to do yet. If I get down at Xmas it will mean over 5 months since I saw you and I will have to start in courting you all over again. However that wont be any hardship I can assure you and a few nights dancing with you alone appeals very much to me.

22 September 1941. Yesterday I spent erecting the billiard table at the club and now we can have our odd game. The Lands dept. are moving out at the end of the month to Wau. This makes two complete departments. I am glad to see some action being taken and we are assisting to the extent of diverting Hardie.

    Poor old Gelu had to appear in court today to give evidence against the Bests' boy. She did not like it a bit—reckoned it was the first time she had been in court. The boy got 6 weeks from Merrylees [magistrate]. It should have been 6 months.

In 1911 the anti-sorcery regulation made it illegal to practise or pretend to practise sorcery. In 1927 the Magistrates were instructed only to punish 'black magic' and not to interfere with charms and magic that were used by Papuans to assist them in gardening, hunting or fishing.[1]

24 September 1941. As regards returning to N.G. I simply cannot tell you anything yet. To Rabaul I should say definitely no but whether I can make a home outside is still beyond my ken at present. Be patient sweetheart, hard as it may be. We are in a transition period up here and its terribly hard to plan ahead in detail. I would suggest dear that you stay where you are if its comfortable and convenient as it appears to be.

26 September 1941. Tom Brennan tells me he has radioed Bob Cooper to come back. Tom wants to get away. Still as busy as ever here and seems there is no let up. Darling you must try and be patient about me coming down. It's much too far ahead for me to book up. Also I cannot foresee yet where we will eventually go in New Guinea. It's all dependent on so many things.

CHAPTER 11

MOUNTING TENSION
OCTOBER–DECEMBER 1941

Not this week nor this month dare I lie down

In languor under lime trees or smooth smile.

Love must not kiss my face pale that is brown.

WILFRED OWEN, 'Training'

OM BRENNAN WAS APPOINTED LIEUTENANT-COLONEL ADMS, 8th Military District. The headquarters were in Port Moresby and Bill, although pleased for his friend was sad to lose his companionship. In October he wrote of the farewell party arranged for Tom:

Well I am dodging drill this weekend. Tom Brennan's time is getting near so we have decided to throw a bachelors' party at Toma. Heron, Coldham, Nobby Clark, Brennan and self. You will note that all like a small game of draw [poker]. We go up Saturday afternoon and return Monday morning. On the Sunday Leggatt, Carr and the new C.O. are coming out for lunch. Do you remember Waterhouse Morris Smith & Co. at Toma?

This must have been quite an interesting lunch. The new Command-ing Officer was Colonel Scanlon and Major-General B. M. Morris was the commanding officer of all troops in Papua New Guinea (the 8th Military District) with headquarters in Port Moresby. Also present were Lieutenant-Colonel Sir William Leggatt and Lieu-tenant-Colonel Carr.

In September 1941 the Australian War Cabinet had accepted an offer by the Americans to provide minefields, anti-submarine nets, anti-aircraft equipment and radar to make Rabaul a more suitable base for a British and American fleet. An inter-service planning team visited Rabaul in November.[1]

I am now going to write to Colyer and try and convince him of the advisability and necessity of moving to Kokopo. I have of course Toma in the back of my mind but there are a great number of difficulties. Toma would be nice to get you back to but it cannot be for some months yet.

17 October 1941. I'm getting a bit worried about the Japanese situation which can flare up quite easily now that the Germans are making some progress round Moscow. This situation will of course have a bearing on your return as you will realise.

19 October 1941. Matupi is still our main topic and is certainly misbehaving herself. She has adopted new tactics. Remains very quiet for about half an hour and only a little bit of steam. Then with a hell of an explosion which shakes the town and specially our house she blows her top off and gushes up to about 4000 feet. This then settles quietly all over town. Actually the last week has been worse than any since 6th June. I am very seriously considering packing all the furniture etc. and storing it out at Ralum. I'd hate to lose the furniture we have got and the electrolux.

Next day… Matupi is still nasty so I got at Bay Loo [Storage &
Removalists] this morning and next week the Carpenters will start
packing I will stay at the club and let them have a fair go.

McNicoll and Lady have left Rabaul and taken up residence in
Lae. G./G. Treasury Govt. Stores and Customs go across next month.
There will be a lot of empty houses in the place. A lot of them will be
pulled down of course.

Although plans to transfer the Administration to Lae were discussed
quite openly, the actual move seemed to happen quite quickly. There
were no speeches, no formal farewells. Suddenly Harold Page, the
Secretary to the Administrator, became the acting Administrator of
Rabaul and the Administration was gone. This was a most
unfortunate time to move as communication and efficiency were
affected.

23 October 1941. Had a club meeting yesterday and have decided to
call a general meeting to discuss the future… As far as I can see the
only thing is to close up and sell what we can. Some pub keeper may
buy the club for removal to Kokopo. Seems a sad end to the place
doesn't it? Met Air Commodore Vic Hurley recently. I think I may have
heard you speak of him.

Had a stroke of luck last weekend. Drew Reading in the club
sweep and having drawn him had a bet on him also. With sweep and
bets came home about 6 pounds to the good. Put Pip Appel and
Mollard on to the horse too so they were satisfied and really believe I
know something about horses. Pip is coming up to have some dinner
with me tonight. In a note from Colyer last week he told me
Cunningham had reported that you were looking lovely and the kids
Number 1. I am getting a bit anxious to see you all myself. Went to
drill last night. First time for quite a while. They are trying to
organize or reorganize the NGVR in view of so many going across to
Lae. Don't know exactly what will happen.

Matupi is roaring her head off. I am in a way quite pleased as it will shake a few people out of their complacency and will encourage everyone towards Kokopo. Unfortunately we as a firm cannot make a 100% move to Kokopo on our own. We cannot get customs and quarantine facilities on our own and these are necessary. It only wants B.Ps [Burns Philp] to make a decision and then we are set. That's what I am working for. It's on the cards that we might be successful.

Poor old Pip got lots off his chest tonight. He is a man with a definite grouch. Very hard to follow because he infers [implies] a lot and talks in innuendoes. I have to guess a lot. However I gather no one else knows much about the war but he could win it. Ted Best was in to see me yesterday and was thrilled with some snaps of his kid. Quite the right way to be of course.

I spose the kids are well asleep and dreaming now. You have no idea how you miss them until you are without them. And the same goes for you too my sweet. There is something in this absence business after all. Goodnight my luv. Sweet dreams. I go now to a very lonely couch.

There is a local schooner going to Manus in about a week and I think I will send Gelu out on it. Elsie may be able to talk some sense into her. She is a bit of a worry at the moment with this Sam bloke. I have had to rouse him again and I am pretty certain she has gone the old way. Sam would not be hanging round so much if Gelu were knocking him back too. She is on her own too much and nothing to do besides costing money to keep etc. It seems too good a bargain from Sam's point of view. She can come in again if and when you return.

24 October 1941. Resistance is a bit low today. At a late hour yesterday I was bidden to a farewell spot to Leggatt. He is now promoted Lt. Colonel and goes to Darwin on Saturday. One thing led to another and about 6 o'clock I dashed home and had a bath and took Leggatt and Tom out to Tovakundum for dinner. Had a nice little game afterwards, which netted me 6 pounds and ten shillings. You have no idea how I loathe the beginning of the week but enthusiasm grows as Saturday approaches. I think it would be too much for me if Saturday came round with no letter.

    I got quite a surprise the other day when I put it to Gelu that she should go back to the Edgells at Manus. She told me no she was going to marry. Good oh says I who and when. Sam says she at the end of this month. Saves me the fare out. However she got a bit out of hand the other day as I asked her what day the wedding was scheduled. She didn't know so I told her to marry or go to Manus or get the hell out of it but do it quickly. Probably the girl's in love or some such thing but she is driving me a bit crazy.

31 October 1941. Phyl and Oscar returned last Saturday. I had forgotten about them coming but fortunately I happened to be down at the plane to say goodbye to Leggatt and it was no trouble to tell them that I was there to meet them.

    Well Tick it looks as though Kokopo will be the centre and in a few months too. The Administration are moving out there, that is those that don't go to Lae. I think we will get Ralum alright and I am just waiting the final word. Here is the story as far as I can tell you. I want to go South on 6ᵗʰ December by plane. I expect to return to N.G. early January. On my return Jack Evans will go to Kokopo and look after an office which we will transfer to Ralum. I will have to stay in Rabaul until the Admn move out or until we secure customs facilities at Kokopo. I expect that to happen in February or March. I have taken a lease on Toma with an option to purchase from the time Tom goes sometime next month. When I go out to Kokopo I will take over Toma and then if political conditions warrant you and the kids can come back. What do you think of these plans? They are subject to us securing Ralum and I am pressing to get that part fixed before I leave. Don't discuss these plans with anyone until they discuss them with you. Both BPs and WTC [Carpenters] are chasing Ralum and they have more money than we have. However I am more alive (I hope) than they are and I hope to pull off the lease within a week or two. I now look forward to the 6th December. Darling wont it be great to be together. I hope to have you back here in February or March.

4 November 1941. I now have the lease of Toma. Think I reported that but I also have an option to purchase for 600 pounds. I think I will exercise the option alright. Bob Cooper arrived back today and dropped in to say how do. Was pleased to see him and hear all about you.

    Well Cup Day has been and gone. What a day. On Saturday last we drew the Melbourne Cup Sweep at the Rabaul Club and I drew Skipton. That netted 21 pounds and twelve shillings. Very handy and much appreciated. Also drew 2nd horse in the Derby worth 3 pounds, ten shillings. Again very handy. As things seemed to be coming my way I had 1 pound each way on Skipton in the Derby thereby netting a further 3 pounds and fifteen shillings from our local books [bookmakers]. I officiated at the New Guinea Club sweep on the Monday and drew a horse called Vermont but scratched, however to even up I had 3 pounds each way Skipton in the cup and dragged in 30 pounds from the books. My expenses were comparatively light being under 3 pounds for various shouts. I will now defer any further betting until next cup day except that we hare having a final game of poker at Tovakundum tomorrow night.

12 November 1941. Toma is as dry and burnt up as can be. The well at Goss's has run dry and we are carting water up from Kokopo. On Sunday the military heads descended on us for lunch including Brig. Morris who remembers you and sent his kindest. While at Toma on Sunday we had a very good view of Matupi recommencing her activities. Coldham left today. On my return from Toma on Monday I found that over the weekend he had calmly established himself at home and was quite comfortable thank you.

    They had an earthquake at Lae and Salamaua last Sunday I believe. That makes you laugh. The Admin heads were out at Kokopo yesterday looking over the place. I am pretty confident that those that don't go to Lae will be going to Kokopo. I intend to get out there as soon as possible in the New Year. I have just about tied up the lease of Ralum and will [be] much happier when I get the document completed. Toma is set. If the Japs have declared themselves the right way when I come back you can come with me. Toma will be a nice spot for us I think.

Incidentally Colyer is not too keen on me going South as he thinks certain decisions will have to be made in December. The same thing can also happen in Jan. Feb. etc. in which case I will never get away. I have therefore forced the issue and unless anything untoward happens I will leave here either 13th or 20th. No later.

Colyer is over in N.Z. Before going he wrote me and asked me to stay up here and finish a job before going South. I will do this. It may affect my departure from here but not if I can help it. Rest assured my anxiety to get down is as great or greater than yours my sweet.

25 November 1941. There is still a lot of speculation about moving to Kokopo on the part of some people. BPs don't want to go and I believe are not going to. The Admn are going as far as I can make out. Unless Customs and Quarantine facilities are provided at Kokopo and BPs put their mail boat in there then it looks as though we will have to run both Rabaul and Kokopo which does not suit me, as I may have to stay in Rabaul. As you know dear I could not bring you back to Rabaul but will bring you back to Toma if the political situation is OK. If I must spend most of my time in Rabaul I can still get out to Toma frequently. That would certainly, from my point of view, be better than having you in Melbourne but we have got to be pretty sure of things.

CHAPTER 12

JAPAN ENTERS THE WAR

'What kind of people do they (the Japanese) think we are?'

WINSTON CHURCHILL TO US CONGRESS, 24 December 1941

JAPAN HAD INVADED MANCHURIA IN 1931 AND WAS STEADILY pushing towards controlling china. With the defeat of France by the Germans and the increasing isolation of Great Britain, Japan began to make a move into French-controlled Indo-China. Japan had only one year's supply of oil left and was dependent on imports from Canada, Holland and the United States of America. When the Japanese took Saigon, it became clear that they were moving west to Burma and its oilfields and aimed to completely cut off China. President Roosevelt became concerned in 1941 and America froze all Japanese assets in the U.S. and placed an embargo on all exports of fuel oil to Japan. This pushed Japan towards the sympathetic Axis powers and in 1941 they joined forces. The sanctions and oil embargo were a major threat to Japan's war effort in China and to its whole economy.[1]

Japanese trading ships often called into Rabaul Harbour and the Japanese were free to wander around the town, taking photographs. They even wandered into the Australian army camps. It was a difficult situation as Japan was not at war at this stage and the Australian troops were not supposed to be in Rabaul in a military capacity.[2]

The troops were becoming unsettled and began to get more restive as they felt they should be fighting in the Middle East. Discontent grew to such an extent that Brigadier Scanlon notified the authorities in Port Moresby that he feared a possible mutiny among the troops. Two VIPs were sent to restore discipline. They told the men that in the near future they would see more blood, destruction and death than they had bargained for, and ordered them to behave themselves and get back to the job.[3]

On 7 December 1941 the Japanese attacked Pearl Harbor and the United States could no longer remain neutral: President Roosevelt declared war on Japan. Japan had made it quite clear that it was total war.

It was now too late for the project of building up Rabaul as an American base. The Australian Chiefs of Staff stated that they saw Rabaul as 'an advanced observation line' but it would not be possible to reinforce it because of the difficulties of transporting and maintaining a force from the mainland. The Chiefs of Staff knew that Rabaul had no hope of defending itself against a Japanese onslaught but wanted the troops to fight for the Island. There was to be no withdrawal. Bill's letters continued.[4]

I am giving my seat in the plane to Gwen Evans as I think she should be away from here. The same applies to all the women. Toma is again in the air and honestly I don't know what to do at the moment. Can only wait and see. There is one thing very certain Tick which all of us must do and that is economize. Cost of living is going to rise and at the same time the standard of living will get lower.

There was a small air force attached to Rabaul aerodrome and this was used for reconnaissance work. The Catalina seaplanes kept the troops awake most of the night grinding their engines as they built up enough energy to take off. The ground planes were Wirraways and fairly ineffective. These planes took off daily on patrol to look for the enemy. Eventually reconnaissance indicated there was a large build-up of Japanese fighting ships and freighters at a place called Truk. Intelligence suggested that they would be proceeding south. People began to wonder how they were going to defend this island, which had such an extensive coastline, with so few troops and so little equipment.[5]

On 8 December 1941 Sister Berenice, a young Australian nun from the Order of Our Lady of the Sacred Heart, was teaching in the first international school in Rabaul. Although qualified for general teaching, her main teaching qualifications were in music, particularly piano and violin. She had requested a posting in the Islands and arrived in Rabaul in 1939 to open the St Joseph's school for children of mixed race. A soft, gentle young woman, she was to show great strength and intelligence as she now embarked on an experience which was to test and reaffirm her faith over the next four years.

A policeman arrived at the school and informed Sister Berenice that Pearl Harbor had been bombed and that the school would have to be closed. She was to move to the Sacred Heart Mission at Vunapope. The involvement of the Japanese was a surprise as there were Japanese families in Rabaul and Japanese children in Sister Berenice's classroom. Afterwards Sister Berenice realised that several of the families had quietly left Rabaul before the invasion of Pearl Harbor.

The Sacred Heart Mission Headquarters, established in 1891 by Father Louis Couppe, was named Vunapope or 'Place of the Pope'. He established schools and orphanages and several plantations for copra production around New Britain. The mission headquarters at Vunapope, near Kokopo, was a large sprawling establishment set in beautiful rolling lawns and with a marvellous view of the harbour. There were three convents, a hospital, boarding schools, a cathedral, the Bishop's residence, priests' presbytery and a seminary for New Guinea students training for the priesthood.[6]

Sister Berenice had been at the mission for a short while when the decision was made to evacuate the European women. The Australian nuns were told that they would have to go too. Bishop Scharmach approached each Sister individually and asked her if she wanted to go. Each one said she wanted to stay and continue with her work. They received permission to stay from the Australian Government in Canberra, provided they did Red Cross work and wore Red Cross badges on their habits.

After a couple of weeks, as nothing seemed to be happening, Sister Berenice requested permission to go to one of the outstations to do some nursing training. She was sent to the mission at Tapo, about 10 miles (16 kms) from Vunapope, where she worked with a German Father and two Dutch Sisters. She was taught to dress wounds and give injections. They waited to see what actions the Japanese were planning.

Bill's next letter illustrates the uncertainty of everyone's lives on the Island and perhaps the full realisation that Rabaul was to be the target.

12/12/41. Well my dear the balloon has gone up in spite of what a lot of us thought—and it appears to have gone up to some purpose. I did not start writing to you earlier in the week as I usually do as I wanted to consider the position for a few days. That is consider things in so far as one is able under the present uncertainty. The conclusions reached so far are not pleasant ones and have probably been anticipated by you. I will not be going South unless specially instructed to by Mr. Colyer. He will not do this unless there is a very urgent reason. I am more use up here and can also do a job in other directions which I think you will appreciate. Life is not normal today and will I'm afraid become much more abnormal as time goes on. We cannot therefore expect things to continue in a normal manner. In a way it is unfortunate I did not get away when I originally intended but on the other hand dear I think you will appreciate exactly what is in my mind when I say I would rather be here at present than with you. I feel that my place is here but I thank God hourly that you and the kids are not here. Sweetheart I know you will realize the position. My duty is here. Business is at a standstill of course and stocks cannot be replenished. All of us are however fully occupied. Commencing at 6 am we are all being put through our paces in no uncertain manner till 8 o'clock. Thence to our work. I have along with others given up the wearing of white clothes and we are all kept on alert day and night. You must use your imagination in trying to picture what I can't tell you in detail. Suffice it to say that my weight will now come down in leaps and bounds. However we did have the farewell to Tom and it was a very successful party indeed. It finished very late with every one very happy.

I am sure of one thing—the cost of living is going to get higher and the standard of living is going to get lower. We must anticipate this by getting ourselves accustomed to a lower standard. You must darling draw only what is essential. Ten pounds a week is not too much for your present standard but you must reduce your standard to enable you to draw less. This is rather a pessimistic letter Tick but you can see into the future as far as I can. It looks pretty murky. I am terribly disappointed at not seeing you for some time longer dear and the kids will be more grown up than ever. However your job is to look after yourself and the kids Tick till I can get down and take over the job. Well my sweet bear up and put that chin of yours out. Things may not be as bad as they look. It will be a great moment when I do eventually see you all again. Give the Jays a kiss apiece. Be good and God Bless. Cheers old thing.

On 12 December 1941 a cablegram from the Prime Minister's Department headed 'Most Secret and Important' was sent to the

Australian Ambassador in Washington, The Right Honourable Richard Casey, from the Chief of Naval Staff, Vice-Admiral Sir Guy Royal, who had been appointed to that position in July 1941. Copies were sent to the Defence Department and the Navy. The cablegram stated that the Naval Board had reviewed the proposals for the development of Rabaul as a defended base. It was regarded as an air operational base and, strategically, was too exposed for the very slender forces available. There was an implied understanding that the U.S. forces would at least occasionally operate in this area. The cablegram makes it clear that this plan involving the U.S. forces would be delayed or would be impossible to fulfil. Without the co-operation of the United States, it was decided that the reinforcement and supply of Rabaul would be hazardous and, therefore, the garrison should be regarded as 'hostages to fortune': 'Occupation by Japan would of course, prevent its use for offensive operations by United States, bring Japan nearer Australia and give the Japanese a base for air operations against Moresby'.[7] The dangers of a Japanese occupation were well recognised.

The difficulty in defending the coastline with so little equipment and so few men was indeed an issue, but two issues stand out clearly. First, the Australian Government made the decision to sacrifice 1399 Australian troops, 6 nurses, 150 members of the NGVR and the people still living in Rabaul who had not evacuated for different reasons.

Secondly, there was no efficiently co-ordinated plan to help any of these people escape. The troops were not taught how to manage to live in the jungle. They were not taught survival tech-niques, not given stores of quinine and food, not shown how to recognise native foods nor taught some basic Pidgin English. Had this been so, at least then they would have had a fighting chance. Initially, the 2/22 Battalion had spent several months in training in Australia based on desert warfare as it was anticipated they would be posted to the Middle East. With some careful planning, escape routes and escape craft could have been organised to assist all those still living in New Britain.[8]

19 December 1941…Everything looks a bit black at the moment darling but it will come right later on. Xmas for all of us will be right out of plumb and maybe the kids will be a lot bigger before I see them. You are all well and truly in my thoughts and I have got to be content with that.

I took Tom up to Toma the other day to say goodbye to the place. He hated doing it. Toma by the way is not much good to me now but I am going to hang on for the future and see what happens. Tonight if we are not interrupted I am giving a small dinner party at the Rabaul Pub to Gwen and Jack, Ron and Mrs Fetum and Mr and Mrs Herron. A sort of farewell to the female members of the staff. Darling there is very little news I can give you. I can't talk about the war and as nothing else but that is happening today I am very restricted. The lower standard of living I talked about in last letter will soon be enforced on us up here. Cigarettes and beer are short, the freezer is getting empty the stores are emptying their shelves and even if we wanted to spend money we couldn't. Am now resigned to walking most places. That's why I'm going to give up the house. Darling my very best wishes to the three of you for Xmas and with the hope that the New Year can bring us something better. Sweetheart Cheerio. Keep a stiff upper lip. We are busy fitting ourselves for whatever may occur. On the job every morning at 6 am which means getting up at 5 am. The same tomorrow morning and right on through Xmas except we have two full day shows. I should be getting fit although my weight is now 13 stone 11 lbs. However the weight is more in the right places than before.

A Chinese friend of mine came to light yesterday with two ducks, 6 bottles of whisky, 500 cigarettes and a Christmas cake. I'll have a few lads up to share the spoils. This is quite a man's town now as you may well imagine. Apart from work it has only been a man's town for me for 6 months so I am not feeling it quite so badly as some others. However in work it's a bit of a nuisance although we are slackening off terribly. I miss Tom and as a result am not so frequent a visitor at the club. However that would have been the case whether Tom went or not. Hell darling how I would love the next few days with you and the kids. Please give my Xmas cheers to everyone. I hope the early New Year brings a big change for us for the better. I think in a few months we will have the Japs' measure but it may get considerably worse during those months

~

CHAPTER 13

WARN THE OTHERS! GET OUT!

Bugles sang, saddening the evening air,

And bugles answered, sorrowful to hear.

WILFRED OWEN, 'Bugles Sang'

THE *Rabaul Times* STATED THAT 'THE WHOLE POSITION, regarding the huge vegetable oil monopoly and its activities should at the present time be made the subject of the closest investigation. For years Pacific Planters have been turned into serfs in order to swell the huge profits of internationalised money hogs'.[1]

Strange things were happening in the copra market. The prices paid to planters could not be reconciled with the prices paid in London. Prices were deliberately being held down. Coconut oil for margarine was urgently needed as more and more producers were cut off from their markets, yet there were few trading vessels still working in New Guinea waters. Copra has many uses, one of which is as a source of nitric acid which when added to gunpowder reduces the smoke.

In *Voices From a Lost World,* Jan Roberts transcribes an interview she had with Alice and Max Middleton who were plantation owners from Kar Kar Island. Because they were unhappy with the prices offered by Burns Philp for their copra, they began trading through Colyer Watson who were the agents for Norddeutscher Lloyd in the Islands. The Middletons liked the Germans and their Kulili Estates became very successful during their dealings. The Germans summoned Max and Alice to a meeting.[2]

They asked us to go to Hong Kong to settle the business dealings. And when we got to Hong Kong we found out the real reason for us coming there. It was to take us to Canton to meet the Germans there in their Settlement, and warn us there was to be a war and the Japs would take Rabaul first and then Singapore, and yes, the Japs were coming into the war on the side of Germany. And they told us their programme then, that the Japanese would come down on this empty sea from Japan. It's quite empty, and we've travelled on it before, you know. They gave us the route and the dates. And then the programme was that the Japanese would return the territory, the ex-colony of the Germans, back to Germany. And Mr. Mai said to Max he said, Mr. Middleton, you're too delicate. You wouldn't survive'. Because the time was drawing close, you see, they wanted us to come and tell the others to get out too. They said, 'Warn the others! Get out! They're coming!'

We had been their clients and always reliable cash-wise. And they said Tony Edgell from Manus, Fred Archer at Yame Island and the Campbells from Bougainville, and us were the four picked out by the Germans that they would allow back on their plantations.

My husband was horrified because we'd been making a certain type of copra for them, dried in the sun, with a high content of glycerine and chemicals, which could be used to make high explosives.

And my husband said, 'Do you really mean to say that you conned me into producing the type of copra for you, to be used in high explosives to shoot back at us?' And they said, 'Yes.' And he said 'Me, an old soldier of Gallipoli and fighting in the First World War, and a coastwatcher in this one?' He said, 'You horrify me. You devastate me. To think that I've been doing that for you!' The Germans were buying

metals in China, preparing for war, and we asked 'What are the
English doing?' and they said, 'The same, only they don't have as much
money!'

So we raced down to Melbourne to my brother [Dudley
Tregent]} and Tommy White who was the Minister for Defence, Alfred
Deakin's son-in-law. So we saw him and told him what we knew, and
he went up to Rabaul and that started, really, the evacuation of
women. Sure enough, within the time [schedule they gave us] the
Japanese came! They might have been a week or two late, but that's all.
Our Intelligence was all cock-eyed the business people always know first
and better! The point was, it was bypassing Singapore, taking Rabaul,
they went the back way to Singapore—they didn't go the front way.
Well, they told us that as well!

The evacuation of the women and children was recommended. On
22 December 1941 the men took their wives and family members to
the wharf. Everything was changing very fast with little time to
discuss matters, let alone grieve. Decisions had to be made quickly.
Who knew how long the ships would be able to get through to
Rabaul? Families did not want to leave, not knowing when or if they
would see each other again. Some believed that leaving was
unnecessary and many women wanted to stay with their husbands,
but felt responsible for their children. The MV *Macdhui*, under
heavy cover of cloud, began to move away from the pier. The women
waved as tears streamed down their faces; the men clustered on the
wharf wanting to farewell their wives and children. A week before
Christmas, the troops received Christmas gifts from Australia. At the
same time a message was received from the Japanese: 'You have
received your Christmas gifts, enjoy them, it will be your last'.

There was no attempt made to evacuate the Chinese
community who were left to their fate. This was particularly callous
as the Chinese had been at war with Japan for twenty years and were
also our allies. Understandably there was much ill feeling as they
were certainly at great risk in the hands of the Japanese.

27 December 1941…As I am on duty all day tomorrow I must write now. Had Xmas and Boxing day on the job. Only half day Xmas so was able to have a Xmas dinner. I was presented with a duck so had Clarrie, Rich and Chaunce to share it with me. All went off well. Ran into a tree in a blackout the other night doing about 5 miles an hour. Bent the front of the car a bit. I am in bed by 9.30 every night now and up at 5 in the mornings for stand to. You will have heard over the radio that scout planes have been over here frequently but been chased off. It is not as bad as it sounds so don't get worried. Sweetheart there is little to tell you. The main question has not been touched on and cannot be. Hong Kong was a bit of a blow but the same fate can happen to Manila. Singapore will be alright and until that falls if it ever does then I think that our Islands might get away with sporadic bombings, maybe to even those. The town as you may imagine is dead and no social gatherings to gossip about. I hope to goodness this is all over soon as I want to see you.

30 December 1941…I loved that snap of you dear. Its in my little wallet along with the snaps of the kids and is never very far from me. You look good-oh my sweet. You are as thin as when we were married. I will look out your nursing things and books. I have packed them and sent them up to Toma so I may not be able to get them for a while. I am not able to go out of Rabaul just yet. This is a bleak place Tick. Not a woman to be seen and what is worse not a woman to do our typing. That is where it hurts most. The plane yesterday took away the last of them. Ann Townsend, Mrs Fisher and somebody else. Am pretty busy exercising to be a General. Our Brown Brothers with the slant eyes are over daily but have not dropped anything yet. They may be cooking up something. You would be amused to see all the sandbags about Beeps [Burns Philp] store and WRC [Carpenter] offices. Toowong and the lads have dug themselves a hole in the ground which goes straight down and turns corners. They will be buried alive. Trenches everywhere for shelter. I have had a couple dug just outside my office window. I am saving on electric light too.

31 December 1941. Its New Year's Eve my sweet and you're not with me. Undoubtedly it is the worst Xmas and New Year period I have ever spent. I don't like it. You won't like it any better either.

Daylight saving commences with you tomorrow. They [the army] tried to start it here but it does not apply to this territory. If they had got it through we would have been on duty at 4 am instead of 5am.

Well Darling I am having some duck tonight. I told you I had two given to me for Xmas. The second one is small and I will eat it alone. Thanks for your Xmas wire darling. It arrived practically on time signed Pick Spensley. My intelligence was equal to the occasion and I knew it was from you. Darling keep that money of yours intact. Shove it in a savings bank. Do not use it unless you must. Try and scrape through without dipping into it. God knows you may need it very badly later on. You never know but what my salary may cease altogether and with it your allowance.

1 January 1942…Today is New Year's Day. Just returned from drill. Its 10 am and I'm going to try and pick up a bit on work. Strangely enough there is quite a bit to do. Apparently most of the town was on the scoot last night. I had numerous rings to join in but I wouldn't leave the house. I can get tight anytime but last night I wanted to stay at home with you or all that I can have of you up here. So although you may not have known it you and I had New Year's Eve together.

The mosquitoes are very bad everywhere just at present. As bad as they were when we first went into House Rakaia. Do you remember them then? How we captured a bottle full on your legs.

On New Year's Day Colonel Scanlan announced to his troops that 'There shall be no withdrawal'. The NGVR members were not informed of any decisions and had no control over their destiny. They were older than the enlisted men and many of them had previous militia experience. They were men in responsible civilian positions and were intelligent, competent businessmen. They were volunteers, training with inadequate weaponry, which was obsolete in many cases. They were intent on protecting their homes and businesses, and they were aware that the only escape was into the hills surrounding Rabaul.[3]

3 January 1942. Just heard the Japs have occupied Manila. This was to be expected as the place was declared an open city and the defences destroyed. The Americans are apparently still resisting outside Manila and I am hoping their resistance will immobilise the large army the Japs have there. We get daily visits from them but so far they are restricted to reconnaissance. I am terribly glad you and the kids are away. The food question for kids is already very difficult. With us it does not matter but John and Jill wouldn't understand why they could not get this and that.

All day on parade tomorrow and next week we go into camp. I should get quite fit shortly darling. I now work and drill and there is no play. One does not mind that of course but I do miss you all. I live for your letters.

On 4 January the voice of the coastwatcher, Con Page, was heard, warning that about a dozen Japanese bombers had just passed over Tabar and were heading towards Rabaul. It gave the people in Rabaul a warning of about 20 minutes which was enough to prevent many casualties. The coastwatchers did a wonderful job of warning Naval Intelligence in Rabaul of approaching raids. At one stage the attacks were happening almost daily.[4]

9 January 1942. Have had a couple of alerts today but the rain has saved us. A very low ceiling. I understand our friend Spencer Roberts has been talking in Sydney. He got a month's leave to go and get married and flew down. He has only just returned from his leave. Dearest I would love some thick socks. Short ones are OK. Our boots are heavy and I can't buy any thick socks up here. Any you make would be treasured. How is Clare Cooper? Haven't seen Bob for some time. Hope Tom has been able to ring you up. He left before the trouble started here but he will be able to tell you something.

10 January 1942. Didn't even finish this letter because of an alert. They are becoming a bit of a bore. So far the Japs have concentrated on the dromes and Rabaul is untouched.

12 January 1941. As you see I did not get this away last mail. It was not extended. The weekend was a quiet one although we were on the job most of the day. Was tickled to death to get two letters from you. Keep it up my darling you have no idea how I look forward to them. I look forward to the sox. They sound good oh to me.

   Darling don't get worried about the raids. Rabaul town has not been touched and all is well.

   There is in my opinion no need for you to evacuate. You will get ample notice of any intended raid I should think and in any case I can't see that happening until all these places are gone. If we get knocked and then Moresby and Darwin then is the time for you to consider evacuation.

The comment made that there was no need for Tick to evacuate reflects what was happening on the Australian mainland at the time. The Japanese were advancing rapidly and the prospect of their invasion of Australia was a very real one. Many people were making arrangements to leave Melbourne and Sydney and move into the country in the hope that, by such evacuation, they would be out of harm's way. Most private schools established 'evacuation schools' to accommodate students whose parents were required to remain in the cities.

14 January 1942. Have not had any raids for a week. Plenty of alerts but no visitations. You will notice there has been no mention of Matupi for some weeks. I had all but forgotten the wretched thing.

We were therefore all very hurt when it went up again today. Thank God its Nor West or we would all be very uncomfortable.

    Gelu is going to have a baby. Sam I hear is a bit of a rotter. He owes money everywhere and from what I can gather he gambles a fair bit. However Gelu went into it in spite of all warnings so it can't be helped. She came and asked me for a tenner the other day for Malu but she really wanted it to give to Sam. Needless to say she was disappointed.

Meanwhile, in Melbourne, Tick was becoming anxious. She had left Rabaul six months previously and although she and Bill wrote almost daily, the mail was only delivered weekly and censorship meant that communication was guarded.

Melbourne 14/1/42…It's no good saying I didn't get a very nasty turn when I got your package yesterday—I did—and I still feel awfully ill with fear, apprehension—all the same I quite realise that it was a very wise precaution and I guess everybody is sending away important papers—you mightn't have time to grab them if you have to make for the tall timbers in a hurry. I hope you won't be backward in the doing if the need arises.

    I think Gordon Thomas' report is the fullest account we've had. It would be very heartening to hear that a few Japs had been shot down instead of getting away with it as they seem to be doing. The going in to camp. Is that for good or only for a time? Your letters don't tell me half the things I want to know. But that's not your fault I guess Darling—you would if you could. But you speak of work in the office—what work? Is there any business or is it just tidying up. Tell me every last little bit about everything about you. Nothing is too trivial to hear you know. I'm hungry for words. Things here go on much as usual. The only bit of news is that I'm being offered a job. Marjorie Chambers has been worrying about me apparently and this is what she raked up. The Principal of Toorak College—a very big swagger girls boarding school here at Frankston—Miss Allen wants me to go there as Resident Nurse and take the babies. We'd live there and I gather—have our own quarters and my duties would be to look after sore throats and colds and such. In case of evacuation I and mine would go too of course. For this I would be paid the magnificent sum of 150 pounds per year and 18 shillings a week for each child. It sounds a very soft job to me. But there are all sorts of little points that we will have to go into first about J & J but the main thing is that we would be living on 1 pound a week instead of 10 pounds and I would be doing something that wouldn't occupy me over much and I'd have loads of time to mind the babies too. Marjorie is very excited about the whole business and feels its just made for me but I'm not saying anything till I hear the details. All the same it would be nice to know that in the event of evacuation the Jays would go decently and comfortably. Not on the State and just anywhere as is the plan now.

The following entries dated 15 and 16 January were in the last letter Tick received from Bill.

15 January 1942. This letter has developed into a diary. I always seem to be interrupted. I have just had a full day at the typewriter and my fingers ache and my mind is a bit bruised from concentration. I will probably learn to type shortly.

I went to the pictures last night with Noel O'Dwyer, Rich and Field. They start at 6 PM now and out at nine. Usually it's a case of getting out and into the dugouts half way through. Noel's passion is apparently quite correct. He took the girl to the club several times recently and he rings her up three or four times a day. What it is to be young. Anyway I'd like to be able to ring you up as frequently. There is one thing I am able to do for Noel though and that is tell him all the good spots at the hospital to hide away in.

The plane I hear may be a bit early this week. I hope that doesn't mean that it left too early from your end and missed your letter.

That would never do. I haven't missed a week getting a letter from you yet and I'd hate to spoil the record. I guess you haven't missed from me either. Cheers till tomorrow my love.

16 January 1942. This is the last chapter to this letter dear as it is approaching mail closing time. We have really had a quiet week although Matupi is going great guns.

Saw Oscar for a moment this morning and he is very upset as he has not had a letter from Phil. In your last you said I think that Phil was only going to be a few hours in Melbourne.

Damn it darling since the above line I have been in the dugout for an hour. We had our fifth raid. (Malta has had over 1200.) I had better finish this my sweet as I've just had word of another raid. It's all a damn nuisance. My best to the kids and everyone darling and lots of love to you. I'm thinking of you all my sweet. Yours Bill.

On 20 January there was a big air raid—110 bombers and ten zeros. The coastwatchers down the coast rang in with warnings. As the warnings came from all directions, it became clear there were aircraft carriers in the area.

It was difficult for Tick and the other waiting wives to continue with their lives in Australia. As Tick wrote in the following letter, they often felt guilty.

20 JANUARY 1942   916 BURKE RD BALWYN.

My Darling,

I've made a sad mistake. Bathed the kids at 5.30 and when I'd finished found it was only 5 o'clock! Can't imagine how it happened I'm sure and I was stone cold sober too! So now, having an hour to spare, here I am to have a little chat. Came back from House Hunt last night after a very enjoyable weekend. After finishing my last letter to you, we all set about playing mah jong and drinking gin. May got

*more than a little tight by the end of it and missed the last bus. So we
finally shoved her into a taxi about 1.30 a.m. As she was the only one
who seemed even slightly undone by the liquor we feel she must have
been a few up on us when she arrived or else we others are harder
heads than we thought. Anyway notwithstanding May's efforts it was a
thoroughly jolly evening. Next morning I felt very bad when I realised
that while we were enjoying ourselves you were probably curled up in
your trench while the brown boys visited you. That account in
Saturday's paper was very brief, so we still don't know much about it.
As soon as I read that there were no casualties I felt a lot better...
The whole business is hellish isn't it? Jean heard yesterday that John has
been made an Instructor in a school in Palestine. Isn't that a thrill?
We're all feeling very pleased of course. For it must be a definite
promotion, I should think.*

*The Jays are tumbling all over the vestibule with Snoopy in the
middle of it all. They've brought out Toowong and all the dolls and put
them to sleep on the floor and strewed shoes and pots and things all
about and altogether had a very busy time. It's wet out. The north
wind has brought rain so that ought to do all my seedlings good. The
phlox are in bloom and I feel so proud of them. I only wish you could
see them darling. Did I tell you I'd planted beans and carrots? Beans
are one shilling and fourpence a pound and peas anything up to one
shilling. All vegetables are a dreadful price. A pumpkin brings
anything up to eight shillings. So I really feel that if we can grow
anything, it will be worthwhile. People say that these prices are the
highest ever known here. I believe them. Clare is going away for two
weeks and I'm going to miss her. Not that we see each other so very
often, but we do have lots of chats per telephone which is almost as
good.*

*The family have moved to the kitchen so I must go and see
what's to do. Something no good, I'll swear.*

*<u>Tuesday night</u>. Oh Darling how are you? It must have been
dreadful! News has just come over that there was a full scale raid today.*

I wept and prayed that you weren't hurt and now I wont rest till I get your next weeks letter telling me that you are still all in one piece.

At this stage Tick and the other wives and families were not fully aware of the magnitude of the attack on Rabaul. Mail was not received until a week after being posted. Next day Tick arrived home and found Bill's letter from the previous week. She answered immediately unaware of the human disaster that was about to occur on the island she considered her home.

When we got home, there was your letter and as usual it was devoured. Note all you say about the house and believe me, I'll stick here as long as I can for it really is so right for the babes. I'm sure it has as much to do as anything with the fact that they are both looking so well.

Trust your old lady darling. You've got enough to worry about where you are without worrying about us too. I'll worry for us and you too. I do, so much so, that by the time you see me I'll be snow white. As it is I'm grey as a badger now. When you come through and get back to us I wont have a care left in the world. This is getting silly, all these teraklings, so will close. All our love darling We are always thinking of you.

It was clear to many people in and outside Rabaul that an enemy attack on Australia would first involve the capture of Rabaul. Many people in Rabaul could not understand why RAAF fighters, naval vessels and essential equipment were not sent to Rabaul to secure it as a vital strategic base. They also believed the Administration would evacuate the remaining civilians, nurses and wounded when necessary. Fifty years later there is still an immense feeling of betrayal amongst the B-4s, the surviving army personnel and their families.

After I finished reading the letters passing between my parents it was well after midnight. I felt as though I had lived through the experience with my father. I felt wrung out but strangely elated. Such a mixture of feelings. I felt I had a much better sense of Bill as a real person. He had a tendency to be intolerant as evidenced by his dealings with the New Guineans and others he did not agree with, and his approach to Gelu and other New Guineans in his employ was paternalistic and today would be considered to be racist.

The letters also raised questions. Who were all these people mentioned in the letters? Although some names were familiar to me, many were not and I decided to carry out some research. I was surprised by the calibre of the people mentioned and it appears that some war meetings may have taken place at House Rakaia and that Bill showed hospitality to many of these people.

I also gained the impression that Bill was a stubborn man who was prepared to stand up for his beliefs. He and Tick visited the Chinese, were firm friends with Oscar Rondahl and were upset that Oscar was not permitted membership to the Rabaul Club. Bill's beliefs did not appear to have affected his place in Rabaul society. He was an office bearer at both clubs and invited regularly to Government House.

Of course, I was also conscious of the warmth and love expressed between Tick and Bill. He seemed to be a committed family man who was struggling to make a good home for his wife and children. He also seemed to have a strong sense of duty and the desire to do what he considered right.

CHAPTER 14

COLIN STIRLING'S ACCOUNT

The monstrous anger of our taciturn guns.

The majesty of the insults of their mouths.

WILFRED OWEN, 'Bugles Sang'

READING THE CORRESPONDENCE BETWEEN MY PARENTS, and the description of the build-up to the Japanese invasion, with all the underlying tension of their situation, gave me an impression from a civilian point of view. Colin Stirling's written account conveys the atmosphere among the Australian troops at the same time. Colin was the handsome, dashing and personable young officer who attended parties at House Rakaia.

At last there appeared to be action looming and excitement gradually grew. We then started to wonder how on earth we could defend this island which had a rather extensive coastline with so few troops. Many thoughts were given and unusual suggestions offered.

I can well remember our company commander who was then Captain Travers thinking of all sorts of odd things. His pet idea was to float out into the harbour a whole lot of 44-gallon fuel drums full of air force high-octane fuel and have them form a barricade across the harbour. The idea being that should an invasion be contemplated, we could fire machine gun tracer bullets into these drums thus exploding and igniting the fuel which could cover the whole sea in a huge fire. A great idea and maybe it would have worked but high command flatly refused to allow Captain Travers to even experiment with the idea.

It turned out that the fuel was high octane for some American planes that were supposed to arrive to reinforce our rather meagre air force comprising the very famous Wirraway, which was almost useless in combat.

The year came to an end and just before, on Christmas Day, the Japanese sent over an air attack on the island. This was quite a surprise and quite frightening. Fortunately they were not very accurate in their bombing and were bombing from a great height. Our brave anti-aircraft gunners did their best to try and deter the Japanese bombers. However without much success. I think the total was one shot down. Their planes seemed to know the gun range and kept just above them.

Air raids over Rabaul became fairly constant and this brought with it the obvious threat that things were starting to build up. Our two little anti-aircraft guns were still doing their best popping away at a range just slightly under the normal height of the planes.

It is interesting to note the anti-aircraft regiment was recruited in Sydney under command of David Selby. It comprised a group of teenage militia troops from in and around Sydney suburbs. They joined us at Rabaul still as militiamen not having formally been transferred to the AIF. This caused quite some problems as to benefits including that of returned servicemen etc. on returning to Australia. Further, there was some discussion as to having virtually pressed them into Rabaul without necessarily volunteering in the ordinary sense. However they did a mighty job and proved to be very grand troops in the long run.

When war was declared in 1939, security procedures and regulations in Papua New Guinea ordered all German and German mixed race residents to register as aliens and report at regular intervals to the nearest District Office and they were not allowed out at night without permission.

The 1933 Census recorded 446 German Nationals living in New Guinea. Of these, 353 were missionaries in a total white population of 4201. There was a belief among the German Nationals that the Territory would become German in a short time. Before war was declared with Germany, the Lutheran Mission in Finschhafen, on the Madang coast, decorated all stations with Swastika flags.

During many of the raids we became worried that the Japanese appeared to be very accurate in picking out targets to bomb particularly the two aerodromes. It was also discovered that flares appeared on the flight paths. The question then arose how did the flares get there. It was concluded that they were placed there by somebody on the island. This of course created consternation and investigations were commenced.

I remember that several of us were sure that a certain resident of the island who had a plantation on the north coast or at least near the north coast could very well be an enemy agent and that he could possibly be responsible for allocating some of the flares. Of course the more we talked about it the more certain we were that this was the case.

The upshot of it was of course that I was talked into leading a small group to go out to the area one dark night surround it and then break in and question the occupants of the plantation house hopefully to discover something. At the time we didn't seem to think about what we were going to find except perhaps imagining that there would be a whole pile of flares and maps and wirelesses and goodness knows what in the living room. I really don't recall.

I took with me three of the unit together with one of the local population to guide us and make sure we could move into the area

safely without being heard or seen before we actually entered the house.
We were armed to the teeth with revolvers and all sorts of things. We
borrowed the local publican's car and drove out to within half a mile
of the house. We got out of the car and proceeded to stealthily move to
the house.

All was quiet and in fact as we discovered in many other cases
like that it seemed to be so quiet that it was almost unnatural. Lights
were on in the house and it would appear that we made the house
perimeter without being discovered.

Under the cover of my companions I boldly went up the
staircase to the house and bashed on the door. It was one of those houses
that were up off the ground with air space incorporating stores and
garage on the ground level.

The occupant, his name now I don't recall, came to the door
and greeted me by some rather curt remarks about what the hell was
he being disturbed that hour of the night for. I might add that his
voice was rather terse and had a slight foreign accent. This of course
made me completely suspicious and even a little uncertain of the next
move. I informed him that I was from the battalion and that I had
orders to call at his house and discuss what he was doing in the area
and that I was empowered to go through his house in case there were
things in it that were not permitted by our army laws. This was a bit
of a bluff but I had hoped it would work.

He indicated some surprise but however said I could come in
and bring in my friends. I think it was two of us that entered leaving
the others outside to watch and take action if necessary. The occupant
did not know of our numbers and that we had done this.

We looked around the house, we talked with him for some
time and quite frankly, as my memory recalls, we didn't discover a
thing nor did we get any indication of what he was doing or whether
he was involved beyond the fact that we were still certain he was up to
no good of some sort.

We formally thanked him, apologised for our intrusion and left.
I recall that a formal complaint was lodged at battalion headquarters

of troops disturbing local citizens during the night without apparent authorisation. We were duly formally reprimanded to clear the air. Looking back I can say that I was quite frightened.

Flare rumours persisted and in fact appeared quite regularly during bombings but we never really got to the bottom of it beyond the fact that we knew they were being laid by people on the island and being laid quite accurately and often in different patterns which indicated that there was some form of communication.

During all this time we were smartening up our defences around Praed Point where we were in support of the coastal guns. We were making sure that slit trenches were in the right places that we could overlook various landing spots and that our communication line was intact.

Reports were coming through that the task force was moving south and that it was of considerable size and included aircraft carriers. Then the obvious started—that was the appearance of lighter Jap planes in the form of dive-bombers. These descended on various strategic spots and in particular on Praed Point coastal artillery. Our site.

I don't think I can remember anything much more frightening than seeing and hearing a dive bomber coming down almost straight into you till you felt it was almost going to crash then coming out of the dive and disappearing. As it came out of the dive that horrible thump sound of a shell going off. I suppose the reaction was that of relief when you heard the explosion. My particular trench was spot in line with their flight path and I felt that each time they came down the bomb they had on board was that one specially for me.

I well recall that command issued the very strict order that we were not to use our light weapons to fire on the dive-bombers. The reason being twofold. Firstly so as not to disclose our positions and secondly that our small arms fire would be of little use in stopping the aircraft. The message was passed down the line and all troops appeared to understand. But it was too much for one particular gun crew to see *these dive-bombers coming out of their dive and moving away directly over their heads. They just couldn't resist the opportunity of having a go. They only had one go. As soon as they opened up to fire on this particular dive-bomber they were in turn fired on by a tail gunner in the dive-bomber. They were very very lucky as their particular machine gun post was riddled with fire right around it and they escaped without a scratch.*

As it became clearer that Rabaul was the Japanese objective, Harold Page, the acting Administrator of Rabaul, and Reginald Halligan, who was Secretary for the Territories in Canberra, worked very hard to bring the plight of the people in Rabaul to the attention of the seemingly uninterested Prime Minister's Department in Australia.

Ian Downs wrote:

In Canberra, the Department of Territories was frustrated again and again in efforts to have a general evacuation approved...even if they were only transported to the New Guinea mainland...It's hard to believe that when Reg. Halligan rushed around to the Prime Minister's Department with Page's last signal from Rabaul he was told THE MATTER COULD NOT BE DEALT WITH FOR ANOTHER FIVE DAYS...not until the War Cabinet met on 19 January. He was lucky to even get Rabaul on to the Agenda. Halligan was a very junior head of department. At the Department of Defence, that entrenched monolith, Sir Frederick Shedden brushed him off as an irritating fly.[1]

A Norwegian vessel, the *Herstein*, was lying in port for days and could have been used to evacuate civilians, particularly the wounded and the nurses. It was eventually bombed as it lay in the harbour, taking several direct hits. (Thirty crew members were later captured by the Japanese.) The copra they were loading was highly flammable, being residue of dried coconut kernel. The civilians were very angry and becoming more and more frustrated by the lack of communication by the Administration, the Army and the Prime Minister's Department.[2]

Somewhere, among all this political turmoil, my parents, separated by circumstances, yearned for peace and for reunion. Tick had her own war on the domestic front, caring for two small children and surviving the loneliness of separation from Bill.

CHAPTER 15

THE INVASION

I dreamed kind Jesus fouled the big-gun gears;

And caused a permanent stoppage in all bolts;

And buckled with a smile Mausers and Colts;

And rusted every bayonet with His tears.

WILFRED OWEN, 'Soldier's Dream'

THE FIRST AERIAL BOMBING RAID BEGAN TWO WEEKS BEFORE THE INVASION. The brave men of the Australian air force flew the remaining eight frail Wirraways into battle against no less than 80 bombers and 40 Zero Japanese fighter planes. It was a suicidal mission as the Wirraways were never meant to have a responsible role in wartime operations other than for reconnaissance and spotting duties.[1] Completely outclassed in speed and manoeuvrability and firepower, the battle was over in ten minutes. Of the eight two-man crews, six men were killed and five wounded. Those watching the aerial battle saluted the bravery of the Australian airmen, who knew the battle was hopeless, but did not hesitate to fight.

Wing Commander Kemp Hewitt described his sortie with the Japanese airforce. He was flying a Wirraway with his gunner, Pilot Officer Tyrell, when he saw some float planes attacking the wharf. He flew in for the attack with his gunner firing away behind him. As he came out of his dive, a Japanese Zero appeared above him firing all guns. In attempting to evade the pursuing Zero, the Wirraway stalled and went into a spin. As the plane flicked over, a cannon shell exploded in the front cockpit. Shrapnel lodged in Hewitt's left knee. The hydraulic oil lines were severed, throwing oil in his face and intercom mask. The manoeuvre was violent and Tyrell was thrown out of the cockpit. He made a parachute landing with only a few bruises, convinced that Hewitt was badly wounded or dead. Hewitt pulled the plane out of the dive and saw the Zero still on his tail. He made for some thick cloud, knowing he was an easy target for the Zero, and was surprised when it didn't follow, but thought the Zero must have been out of ammunition. He managed to bring his severely damaged plane back to the aerodrome. When he walked into the mess, Tyrell looked as though he'd seen a ghost, believing that Hewitt had had no chance of surviving.[2]

By 21 January 1942 Wing Commander Lerew realised that the situation in Rabaul was hopeless. His air fleet now consisted of one Hudson bomber and two Wirraways. He was frustrated by the apparent misunderstanding of the seriousness of the situation in Rabaul by Area Combined Headquarters in Townsville. He had received one order—to attack the huge force coming down from Truk with all available aircraft.[3] By this time he had decided to use the Hudson bomber to evacuate the wounded. He sought permission to send his remaining Wirraways out of Rabaul. He received the order: 'Rabaul not yet fallen. Assist army in keeping aerodrome open. Maintain communications as long as possible'. A frustrated Lerew used the services of Latin scholar Padre John May and Flying Officer G. M. Lempriere to adjust the ancient Gladiators' salute to suit the situation. Lerew then sent a telegram to Headquarters: 'Nos morituri te salutamus'. It took Headquarters a little time to translate and

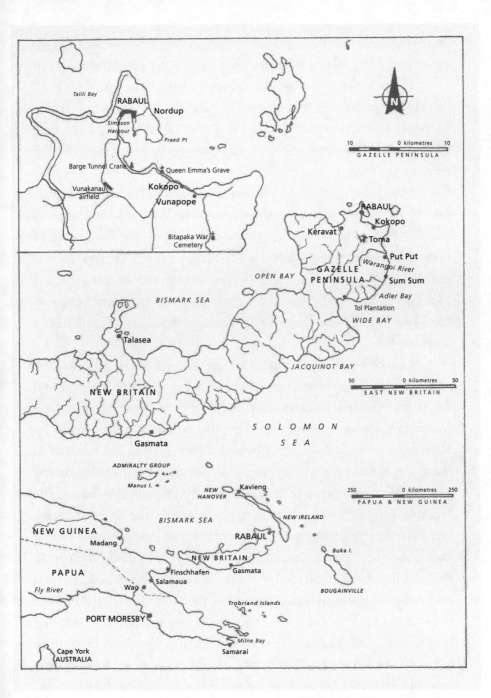

EAST NEW BRITAIN AND PAPUA NEW GUINEA

understand the significance of the message: 'We who are about to die salute you'. This telegram has become part of the 1942 Rabaul story.

Communication with the outside world ceased at 4.00 p.m. on 21 January. At 3.00 a.m. on 22 January 1942 the remaining Hudson bomber took off with the wounded. Also on board the final flight out of Rabaul were 300 or more letters, in many cases the last communication to loved ones.[4]

When the Japanese began bombing Rabaul, Bishop Scharmach offered the Sacred Heart Mission hospital at Vunapope to the army authorities for the wounded Australian soldiers. He also arranged with Dr Hosking, who was now the Senior Health Officer, for the transfer of patients and staff of the Namanula hospital to the Mission. Every day, for the last weeks, car loads of injured came to the Mission and were cared for by the nursing nuns in the Mission hospital.

On the night of 21 January a New Guinean arrived at the Tapo Mission from a neighbouring plantation. He told Sister Berenice and the other mission workers that they were to come and use the plantation owner's phone to ring the Mission headquarters at Vunapope immediately. The German brother there was unable to make the trek to the plantation as all Germans were under curfew and not allowed to leave their homes between 6 p.m. and 6 a.m. The German brother had left Germany to escape Hitler and the Nazis, but nevertheless he was still under curfew. Sister Berenice, a Dutch sister, and the New Guinean from the plantation, made the trip in the middle of the night. Sister Berenice rang mission headquarters and the phone was answered by one of the German fathers. He was too scared to say anything over the phone and told her that nothing was wrong. The phone call was suddenly interrupted by a male Australian voice saying, 'Sister, are you an Australian?' She said she was. He then told her that he was a soldier on duty at Kokopo and that there was something she should know. He told her they were expecting an invasion by the Japanese that night.

The two nuns hurried back to the Tapo Mission and relayed the message to the others. After much discussion they decided to stay where they were as there did not seem much they could do. The invasion did not begin that night, but they could hear the bombing and planes flying overhead.

The next morning Sister Berenice was called to one of the villages because there was an Australian soldier in a dugout and no one could rescue him. She took a couple of helpers with her, and a stretcher, and found a shell-shocked soldier frozen in the dugout. They got him out and one of the fathers took him to the Presbytery where they cared for him, together with several other shell-shocked soldiers.

The Sisters decided to make their way to the Sacred Heart Mission headquarters at Vunapope to report from there to the Australian Command that there were several soldiers at the Tapo Mission suffering from shell shock and needing assistance. Because of the bombing, it was too dangerous to walk along the open tracks so they cut across country. They became hopelessly lost and took the whole day to cover the ten-mile (16-km) distance to the Vunapope Mission.[5]

Meanwhile, the civilian nurses, patients and staff, supervised by Dr Hosking and Dr Bob Cooper, completed the move to the Mission in daylight on 22 January. They were able to calmly settle their patients into the large two-storey building, which was one of the Mission's native boarding schools hurriedly converted for their use.

Alice Bowman in 1996 reported that

The abrupt change from our last days in Rabaul to the tranquillity of Vunapope was so unbelievable as to make the present seem unreal. One of the nurses said to the others 'Don't let's talk about Japs and bombs, let's savour the peace of this evening'. The end of the day all over the tropics is the most pleasant time, when the humid air dissipates with the gentle evening breeze. At Vunapope, the air was flower-scented and free of smoke; we basked in the fragrant serenity, and even the mosquitoes seemed to be singing as they stung us kindly.

The experience of the army nurses was a little different and not nearly as pleasant. They received the order to evacuate the hospital immediately to the Sacred Heart Mission at Vunapope near Kokopo, which was about thirty miles (60 kilometres) around the harbour from Rabaul. They were not permitted to go to their own quarters to collect any personal belongings so only had what they were wearing at the time—grey uniform, shoes, socks and underpants. Evacuation took place immediately. There had been no order to evacuate the nurses on the last aircraft out, with the wounded, even though the nurses were certain to be caught by the Japanese. There had been a suggestion that they should leave, but Kaye Parker refused on behalf of the army nurses.

As soon as night fell, a convoy of four ambulances and three trucks slowly wended their way out of Rabaul. The journey was long and difficult. As the troops had evacuated Rabaul and gone to their posts in preparation for the attack, they had blown up the roads as they withdrew. Some of the natives took the nurses' convoy by the back roads and it was 2 a.m. before they arrived at the mission. After settling the patients, the nurses dug some slit trenches and air-raid shelters. By this time they had not slept for two days as the casualties from the bombings had kept them busy. They were not sure what was happening, but were looking forward to the moment when they could relieve each other for a few hours sleep. Heavy rain was falling and the sounds of bombing could be heard in the distance.[6]

The civilian nurses were concerned about Dr Bob Cooper, who was a diabetic, and they felt that he should have been evacuated. But they knew he would not leave as he was dedicated to the welfare of his patients. The Rabaul hospital nurses had also made the decision to stay with their patients, even though they had twice been offered the opportunity of evacuation.

Reports from the Catalinas had revealed that a Japanese task force was on its way to Rabaul and that invasion was imminent. All able men were required to meet in the Botanical Gardens on the late afternoon preceding the invasion, where instructions were given for their deployment. The members of the NGVR were deployed around Vulcan with the 2/22 Battalion.

Oscar Rondahl urged Bill to join him on his schooner, the *Kabakaul*, as he intended to help any survivors escape New Britain. Bill refused, because he was committed to be with the NGVR. Oscar left Rabaul on the eve of the invasion. He had twenty-three air force personnel (all married men) and eight civilians on board including Wing Commander Lerew, the commander of No. 24 Squadron. After reaching safety with his boat load, Oscar wanted to return to assist more people out of New Britain, but his offer was refused.[7] It was a mammoth and impossible task for an infantry battalion as enemy landings could have been effected almost anywhere over a coastal spread extending from the Kerevat River on the North Coast to the Warangoi River on the south coast of New Britain.[8]

22 JANUARY 1942: MIDNIGHT

Suddenly a parachute flare was dropped, illuminating the whole harbour. A fleet of transports entered the harbour and launched thousands of black-clad troops in 40-foot landing barges at six points around the harbour. Bill and the seventy members of the NGVR were positioned at Vulcan where one of the first landings took place. The suspense was unbearable as they waited, wondering what was in store for them, each man lost in his own private thoughts as he struggled to deal with the feelings hovering just under the surface.

At 2.25 a.m. they heard the sound of foreign voices across the black, still water, and then the sound of the barges grating on the shore, and they saw figures clad in black singlets and shorts emerge from the barges. The NGVR opened up with everything they had, causing the surprised Japanese to fall back and regroup. This initial barrage of fire used up all the ammunition and the volunteers retired to their waiting trucks. But they had fired the first shots at the invading Japanese. The Australian troops around the harbour put up a huge resistance until they, too, ran out of ammunition.[9] The main fighting was over in a couple of hours, by which time the Japanese had infiltrated and outflanked the defending forces. A general withdrawal was forced upon the defenders, but it was all to no avail as there was no defensive secondary plan provided. It was utter chaos.[10]

Bill Harry's report on the invasion stated that

By midmorning, Scanlan could see before him a seemingly impossible task to regroup his forces as he was without supply dumps developed in rear positions. There was no secondary plan to replace the beach defence when it came apart, as it must, under the weight of superior attacking forces. This situation precluded organised guerrilla operations being carried on from pre-planned inland bases.

The lack of a secondary defensive plan was difficult to understand and Colonel Scanlan was seemingly influenced by instructions from Army HQ in Australia that Lark Force could not be reinforced or withdrawn and that his role was to effect a delaying operation. This perhaps contributed to an instruction issued to the troops to the effect that the action would be fought out on the beaches—an unrealistic situation there being approximately eighty miles [120 kilometres] of coastline on the Gazelle Peninsula flanked by roads.

Although reconnaissance reports had indicated a large task force coming towards Rabaul, few were prepared for the enormity of the invasion force. In the early morning light, a screen of minesweepers advanced ahead of the transports. The entrance to the harbour was full of Japanese shipping, including at least one carrier and several cruisers. One eyewitness counted 32 Japanese ships in the harbour another said he counted 50. Aircraft carriers operated outside the harbour cushioning the take off and landings of the 100 fighter-bombers and Zeros. With no resistance, the Japanese planes fired and bombed at will, even putting on a display of aerobatics arrogantly highlighting their control of the sky above Rabaul. The remaining Australian troops were cut off from each other and the order came — 'Every man for himself'.

23 JANUARY 1942: DAWN AT
THE MISSION OF THE SACRED HEART

One of the Rabaul Hospital nurses described the scene that she saw from the waterfront at the Mission:

The sight that met our eyes was mind-boggling. Stretched as far as the eye could see were ships of every size and description: frigates, freighters, tankers, transports and barges. The fleet was moving slowly and silently around Praed Point at the tip of the Peninsula to join others already anchored at the foot of Rabaul and on the horizon two huge aircraft carriers stood like sentinels. The wrath of the waves breaking on the shore was all that could be heard. The watchers stood mesmerised in stunned disbelief by this terrible spectacle—the final evidence that the enemy had indeed landed and was now in control of this island of New Britain. The silence was broken by the Mission bell ringing for first mass.[11]

As dawn broke, the army nurses from another area in the Mission looked in bleary-eyed amazement at Rabaul Harbour. They saw the harbour filled with the huge convoy of Japanese ships. They noted the submarines, aircraft carriers and minesweepers and could not believe their eyes. They thought their lack of sleep was playing games with their imagination. Lorna Johnston remembers their astonishment: 'We didn't really think the Japanese had so many ships'.

Lorna and the people at the mission were stunned as, within a short time, they saw landing barges disgorge thousands of khaki-clad men. They were wearing what looked like black sand-shoes and were brandishing guns and bayonets. They ran up the beaches and across the beautiful lawns to the hospital, training their guns on the people at the mission. Chaplain John May surrendered on behalf of the hospital and, from then on, protected the nurses wherever possible. He walked out to meet the Japanese, reaching for a white handkerchief in his pocket, but quickly realised this was not a good move and put both his hands in the air. One of the nurses had a gun, but had been persuaded to dispose of it. She was cautioned in the first flush of the invasion that the Japanese soldiers were likely to be very trigger happy.[12]

With much shouting it was made clear that everyone was to come out of the hospital on to the lawns—patients, nuns, nurses and missionary workers. They were ordered to stand with their hands above their heads as the Japanese soldiers ran up and down poking their prisoners with rifles and bayonets. The prisoners stood for hours as the tropical sun grew hotter and hotter. Patients began to faint in the heat. The Japanese general seemed determined that radios or troops were hidden somewhere and his soldiers searched the hospital.

The nurse in charge, Sister Kay Parker, was a tall, lean woman of commanding presence and she was singled out by the Japanese general, because he thought that she had not bowed deeply enough. She then gave an answer which did not please the general and he attempted to slap her face. As she was much taller, he had some difficulty in doing this. He screamed orders to one of his soldiers, who disappeared and returned shortly with a box. The general then climbed on the box and slapped the nurse's face. The Japanese soldiers were often slapped by the officers for reasons unknown to the onlookers.. Some of the soldiers appeared to be only fourteen or fifteen years old and they looked really scared; but they were very disciplined.

Eventually the general decided that the women were harmless and allowed the nurses to help the patients back into the hospital. There were seven nurses from the civilian hospital, six army nurses and four Methodist Mission nurses. They were all allowed to go back to the convent to the nuns. The nuns were of many nationalities— German, French, Dutch, Polish and Australian. The Bishop, Leo Scharmach, was a Polish-German, and they hoped that his nation- ality would restrain the Japanese and that they would respect their Axis partners.

The nurses were so busy looking after their patients that at first they did not realise that the army doctors had taken the two ambulances, most of the medical supplies, and the orderlies, and had left the nurses in charge of the newly established hospital. They were dumbfounded at what they saw as the callous behaviour of the doctors, who had not informed them of their plans. They felt completely abandoned, although they had the full support of the Mission staff. They were able to do little, as they were left with ninety patients and very limited supplies.[13] In the tradition of the Royal Army Nursing Service, the nurses believed that their prime responsibility was to care for the sick and the wounded. They did not question the moving of their patients to the Catholic Mission at Kokopo. Two of the army doctors, Major Palmer and Captain Robinson, on the other hand, saw their duties out in the field with the troops, who were broken up in various locations after the defensive position had quickly fallen apart in utter confusion.

Captain Robinson was later captured and joined them at Vunapope. The army nurses refused to speak to him. Major Palmer moved down the south coast of New Britain where up to 350 troops were 'on the loose' with limited medical supplies. He endeavoured to give what medical care he could, but many troops died. At the same time he was attending to those who survived the Tol Plantation massacre. In due course, about 125 servicemen and civilians were picked up during a period of low cloud in a small craft which slipped through to Port Moresby. Major Palmer who later distinguished himself elsewhere in the Pacific in the course of the war, was among the group.[14]

23 JANUARY 1942: NIGHT

Lieutenant Colin Stirling and his unit were stationed at Praed Point and, once the guns there were demolished, they waited for the invasion they knew was coming. They were informed that the task force was just north of New Britain, and they were ordered to leave Praed Point and move around the north-eastern tip, down the pass, through Rabaul, to the upper aerodrome. There would be transport waiting for them below the pass. Because of the recent volcanic eruption, the road was covered in pumice and ash and many of the landmarks were obliterated; the unit was unable to find the entrance to the pass. The men were becoming more and more desperate as they searched for the opening, but kept their heads, and after an hour or so were able to find their way down to the main highway. They waited for the transport to arrive and eventually came to the conclusion that because they had been held up so long looking for the entrance to the pass, the transport had decided not to wait. So the unit moved on to Rabaul on foot, not knowing if the Japanese had landed. They did not know if they were moving through enemy, or their own, territory. They moved in a 'deployed set' up on the edges of the road, using forward scouts and covering each other as they advanced. As they approached Rabaul, they felt most uneasy as there was no sign of life. It was eerie: they did not see a soul, no people or even livestock, and became quite jittery, expecting to come across the Japanese at any moment.

They eventually caught up with the main body of their company and received hurried instructions to deploy themselves to cover the movement of forward troops who were down on the beaches to the west of the main harbour of Rabaul. Word came through that the Japanese had landed and that the unit was to maintain its position while the forward troops moved back through them. When it was clear, the unit was to move back towards the upper aerodrome.

There was sporadic gunfire from all directions and it was a most uncomfortable feeling not knowing where or from what direction the enemy was striking. There was now confusion, for the communication lines had been cut, and information was passed from one group to another as they met up along the tracks. Instructions were relayed that the units were to break up and form small, unrelated groups with a view to moving out into the bush and, with any luck, finding food dumps. They were then to make their way to the coast either north or south and attempt to get off the island.[15]

There began months of horror for the surviving troops. They had one 303 rifle and very few rounds of ammunition, and one pistol with about ten rounds. There were few if any food drops and their rations became one army biscuit and one twelfth of a tin of bully beef to each man daily. There was bush food, but they had not been trained in jungle survival, nor were they able to speak Pidgin and so were unable to barter effectively with the local people. They faced impenetrable jungle; the rain was constant and no man had dry clothing or dry feet. There were crocodiles in the river and the jungle was infested with malaria-carrying mosquitoes. The men were hungry and exhausted and many were developing malaria, dengue fever and dysentery.

The officers and men of the pre-war regular Australian Army had no idea how to conduct jungle warfare. The same lack of knowledge applied to all the Commonwealth armed forces—British, Indian and other dominions and colonies. Their manuals taught that the principles of war were unchanging and could be applied to all military situations.

Before the invasion some Rabaul civilians offered to teach the troops about the surrounding terrain. J. K. McCarthy, an experienced patrol officer, offered to give troops jungle experience if they were sent in batches to Talasea, but the offer was not taken up.[16] There were many lessons learned in the jungles of New Guinea from 1942 to 1945 but, sadly, too late for many young Australian men.

THE OCCUPATION BEGINS

'If ever a sledge hammer had been used to crack an egg, this was the time', said a disgusted Commander Mutsuo Fuchida, the leader of the attacking forces, when he realised how little opposition there was to the invasion.[17]

The hopeless imbalance between the strengths of the two foes becomes clear when it is noted that the Australian defences consisted of 1500 troops, two 6-inch naval guns and eight Wirraway fighter planes. The Japanese invading forces peaked at 200 000 (army, navy and air force), 390 fighter planes, ten cruisers, forty destroyers, ten submarines and one hundred troop carriers and freighters.

The Japanese now had control of Blanche Bay, on which Rabaul was situated. It was one of the best natural harbours in the south-west Pacific, with the inner harbour capable of handling 300 000 tons of shipping. The docking facilities of the port of Rabaul included seven wharves. The Japanese converted Rabaul into a major fortress and supply base for military action, which included the Kokoda Track, Milne Bay, the Coral Sea, Lae, Guadalcanal and Bougainville. There were many inlets and plenty of heavy foliage for cover in Blanche Bay where the Japanese set up their repair facilities. They also established submarine fuelling facilities and seaplane moorings.[18]

On the evening of the invasion the Japanese troops and naval units were able to move straight into beds left made up in homes and hotels. A Japanese general moved into House Rakaia, the house in which I was born and where Bill and Tick had spent many happy years until the last months in 1941.

In the abandoned homes, larders were stocked and cellars were full and the Japanese were happy to dispose of one thousand dozen bottles of beer. Businesses like Burns Philp, Carpenters, and Colyer Watson, had left food and equipment behind. The Japanese occupied every house and office. They erected ugly clusters of wooden huts even in the beautiful botanical gardens. Sanitation and hygiene lapsed and the township soon began to smell and became infested with flies.[19]

The Japanese Army and the Navy were continually at odds and the town was divided into two separate sections, naval and military. Rabaul became the main southern base for the Japanese forces, who were obviously settling in and expected to stay for a long time.

CHAPTER 16

THE SACRED HEART MISSION

JANUARY–JULY 1942

So secretly, like wrongs hushed-up, they went.

They were not ours:

We never heard to which front these were sent.

Nor if they yet mock what women meant

Who gave them flowers.

WILFRED OWEN, 'The Send-Off'

SISTER BERENICE AND HER COMPANION EVENTUALLY ARRIVED AT the Sacred Heart Mission headquarters after a day of walking around in circles trying to find their way. As they approached the main Mission House, a truck full of Japanese soldiers came round the corner. When they saw the two sisters they jumped up, shouting and pointing their bayonets at the two frightened women. There was a shout from within the truck and the soldiers all sat down as the truck drove on. Sister Berenice thinks that was one time when the Red Cross badge saved them.

When the two nuns presented themselves to the Bishop, he told them they would have to stay, as they were now Japanese prisoners. They were imprisoned in the house, a two-storey building, and were forbidden to speak to the Fathers or the other Sisters, or any of the New Guineans or the seminarists. They were guarded day and night. Sister Berenice described some of the guards:

Many of the Japanese guards were just little boys. They had no idea of where they were or what they were doing. All they had was their army outfit, a rope around the thing and a spade hanging here, and a bayonet. They always had bayonets and they'd come around to us and say, 'Blood of Australian soldier', and throw it up in our faces, but we'd just laugh at them and say, 'It's only tomato sauce', but we didn't know, it could have been true.

The guards patrolled constantly. There were daily searches and the prisoners were often forced to stand out on the grass in the sun all day while the Japanese searched for the radio they were sure was hidden there. There was no radio, wireless or telephone, but the Japanese did not believe the sisters, and continued their searches throughout the occupation.

The nuns made the army nurses and the civilian nurses very welcome, and prepared beds for them because they realised the nurses were totally exhausted. Sister Berenice described the feelings of the prisoners: 'For the first two weeks or more we were terrified, absolutely terrified. We didn't know what would happen to us'. Sleep was difficult as the Japanese soldiers walked in and out through the bedrooms all night. Night after night they took pleasure in prodding the women in the ribs with their guns. Fear of rape was high and the nurses had many sleepless nights. The Japanese interpreter suggested they lock their doors and that helped, although they still had to listen to yelling and knocking from outside. The next step was for the nurses to move in with the nuns.

Lorna Johnston recalled one incident with amusement. Exasperated by the constant intimidation, Sister Marcella took matters into her own hands. She was a tall quiet nun who was usually dressed in a white habit. One night she changed into a black habit, hung a large gold cross around her neck and hid in the shadows on the balcony, outside the nurses' room. As the Japanese soldiers approached the room she sprang out of the shadows with her arms outstretched and yelled 'Bugger off!' The Mother Superior, a Dutch nun, asked Sister Marcella what she had said to cause the soldiers to run away. She replied, 'I just used a common Australian saying Mother'.

Finally, Bishop Scharmach spoke to the Japanese commander and from then on the Japanese soldiers were not allowed in the women's quarters. After several months, twenty 'comfort women' arrived and the threats to the nuns and the nurses lessened, but the fear of rape always remained during their imprisonment.[1] 'Comfort women' was a Japanese military euphemism for what were, in effect, sexual slaves. Girls were dragged, kidnapped and tricked into serving in military brothels. They were treated brutally, some forced into service before their bodies were fully developed. The 'comfort' system consisted of the legalised military rape of subject women on a scale unknown in history. Comfort women were in the vanguard of the Japanese forces. In Rabaul the women were brought in quickly, some arriving with the ammunition and sometimes even before essential military equipment. Their services were considered a priority by the Japanese: they believed that pilots became accident prone if sexually deprived, and it was therefore a duty for them to use comfort services.

The Japanese avoided the local women because of the prevalence of skin disease and also the odour of the coconut oil used as a mosquito repellent. The women were in short supply initially and so were used continuously. One survivor told how with no lunch break she was given three rice balls to eat between duties. The pressure of the next client on her stomach made her regurgitate and she would have to re-swallow. More women were brought in and one eyewitness described about twenty brothels operating around Rabaul. The men were issued with 'thirty-minute tickets'. A bell was rung five minutes before expiry. One report mentioned using one woman for two thousand men, so only the officers were accommodated in this case.[2]

Experts believe that up to 200 000 women—Korean, Chinese, Taiwanese, Malaysian, Filipino, Timorese, Indonesian and Dutch—were victims of the sadistic sexual slavery used to keep the troops happy in World War 2. Many of the women did not live to see the end of the Japanese occupation; they committed suicide, succumbed to illness, or were cold-bloodedly murdered to hide the army's dark secrets. Others succumbed to illness and trauma in the long years after the war. While the war continued and Rabaul was heavily under siege from allied bombing, over two hundred of these comfort women were shipped out of Rabaul. The ship was torpedoed and sunk by an American submarine and there were no survivors.[3]

The arrival of the comfort women was greeted with relief by the women at the mission who did not realise that these women were prisoners too. The nurses and nuns were subjected to various types of sexual harassment. The soldiers tried to urinate on them and frequently dropped their pants and laughed at their own unsophisticated humour. Although the situation eased with the arrival of the comfort women, the Japanese did not like having their sexual advances refused. Slappings and beatings were common, as was torture, which left one nun permanently crippled. The victim was made to kneel with a bamboo pole placed behind her knees, and the Japanese soldiers stood on either end of the pole and rocked. This was a common punishment.

On the night of the invasion, the managers of Burns Philp, and Carpenters, were staying at the Mission. As they had made the decision to 'go bush', they had given the keys to the stores to the

Bishop and suggested that he go and take whatever he wanted for the Mission. The nuns and some of the soldiers had then dug holes and buried the supplies all over the Mission. There were two rooms used to store supplies and the nuns called these the malaria room and the tuberculosis room, as they were aware of the Japanese fear of these two illnesses. It worked for a while and for some months the Mission had a supply of food. The nurses were allowed to look after the soldiers down in the hospital until the day when the Japanese discovered where the sisters had hidden some of the food. They had put some of the supplies in the roof, and they had to use a ladder to climb up and bring the food down—quite a risky procedure. After some time they became a little careless and one of the sisters mistakenly left the ladder in place to be discovered by one of the Japanese soldiers. The sisters were forbidden to nurse the men any longer and the patients were taken to Rabaul. Sister Berenice was sad to see the soldiers go. She had nursed them, cooked for them, and watched them recover. She had become close to many of them and did not know what would happen to them. Dr Cooper had heard a rumour that the nurses were to be taken to Rabaul and he suggested that they share medical equipment among themselves as it was less likely to be discovered.

With no patients to care for, the nurses helped the nuns with their daily chores, and were cared for in return by those marvellous women. The sisters and nurses at the Mission were not allowed to have any contact whatsoever with the New Guineans or anyone outside the Mission. From the balcony of the mission house the sisters had a full view of the harbour. They could see the ships coming and going and watched the combat taking place overhead when the American planes began to appear. They could hear the sounds of battle in the distance and saw the badly damaged Japanese ships return and tie up at the wharf right in front of the Mission. They learnt later that this was the battle of the Coral Sea.

Five months later the Japanese told the Bishop that all the Australian nurses would have to go to Japan. The Bishop knew he could not stop them taking the nurses, but he refused to let the Mission sisters go. The Japanese were a little afraid of the Bishop, who had stood up to them from the very beginning, and allowed the mission sisters to stay.

The Japanese rounded up the nurses, put them in trucks and drove them to the harbour where they boarded the ship that took them to Japan. The nurses were told they were to be taken to the land of milk and honey. Lorna Johnston and the other nurses spent the next three and a half years in Japan as prisoners of war, living in horrific conditions. They were imprisoned first at Yokohama and later moved to Totsuka, a small village in the shadow of Fujiyama, where they lived sometimes in freezing temperatures. The ingenuity, stamina, creativity and the bravery of those women is described by Bowman, Reeson and others in their books. Nineteen women were held as prisoners of war. There were seven civilian nurses from Namanula hospital, six army nurses, four Methodist mission nurses and two civilians, all from Rabaul or outlying areas. Lorna was the youngest.

CHAPTER 17

SUM SUM

JANUARY–JULY 1942

'How did the human primate become the most

violent primate on the planet when our closest

genetic relative, the bonobo chimpanzee,

who shares 99% of our genes, is the most peaceful

primate on the planet?'

JAMES W. PRESCOTT, PH.D.

ON 23 JANUARY 1942 THE FAMILIES WHO HAD LEFT RABAUL saw a small piece in the Australian metropolitan newspapers headed 'Rabaul Silent Since 4 pm Yesterday'. Radio contact had been lost and it was clear that the Japanese had attacked Rabaul and Kavieng. Further information was scarce and vague. Much of the information for this chapter was taken from Lieutenant Colin Stirling's paper on his experiences and also from Bill's final letter to Tick. The letters to Bill from Tick were returned to her as undelivered mail.

Tick wrote anxiously to Bill.

27 January. Sweetheart. We are thinking of you daily and hourly. You must be going through hell and I'm praying for your safety. Today I posted a small parcel of sox and handkerchiefs and hope they reach you soon. Sent them airmail, so maybe they will and I guess they'll be very welcome when they do. Will continue to send odds and ends and keep hoping that ultimately you'll get them. We are all well but terribly anxious about you darling. The news is so scarce that we really know very little of what is happening. I've abandoned hope of any personal news for awhile.

The kids and I take up our abode at Toorak Ladies College on 10 February so now theres no need to worry about us. We are self supporting. Col gets to Melbourne next week and I look forward to seeing him. He's always so comforting. No news—We've got our chins up and are barracking for you darling. All my love. Tick

Following the Japanese invasion Bill joined up with a small group of eight men, which included Colin Stirling. Colin and Bill knew each other socially, as Colin's unit was stationed at Sulphur Creek and he often came to luncheon parties at House Rakia. They eventually reached a plantation called Sum Sum which was owned by the Parkinson family. Colyer Watson had business dealings there and the Chinese overseer, recognising Bill, made the main house available to the group, in spite of his fear for his wife and child. The question of food became of pressing importance as they could not continue to use the meagre rations of the overseer. Bill had organised some food stores at the plantation in the days before the invasion and this helped for a short time.

Sum Sum Plantation was situated on the south-eastern side of the Gazelle Peninsula. To the north was Put Put Plantation and to the south was Tol Plantation, about six hours walk away. Next to this was Waitavalo Plantation. The Sum Sum River flowed out of the

Baining Mountains into beautiful waterfalls and hot springs. The bush around Sum Sum abounded with wild life, such as pigs, and all types of birds—cassowaries, pigeons, hornbills and parrots. There were fish in the bay and the river, and lobsters on the reef.

The homestead was on a hill, and at the back of it was a beautiful 4-acre (1.5-ha) garden planted with fruit trees, ornamental shrubs, and palms. In normal circumstances, Sum Sum was a paradise. The land had been acquired by Queen Emma and given to her niece Dolly Parkinson as a wedding gift in 1919. Queen Emma's brother-in-law, the botanist Richard Parkinson, brought in plants from around the world and planted them all over the east coast of New Britain. The Sum Sum garden was one of the areas he planted.[1]

Friendly natives helped the men look for fresh food and once they managed to catch a wild pig. The group set about pooling any knowledge they had on how to dress a pig. The most difficult task was removing the hair. They found that by pouring very hot water over the skin and scraping the surface while it was soaking, the process was relatively easy, but as the temperature of the water reduced quickly, it became increasingly difficult to complete the process.

There were daily appearances of small groups of Australian troops passing through to the south attempting to find a way off the island. The men set up guards every night, well away from, and also in, the house. No one knew where the Japanese were. The search for food and information took over their days. They discovered a 4-gallon (18-litre) drum of peanuts in one of the storerooms, and they enthusiastically began to devour them. Two hours later they all developed severe stomach pains and diarrhoea and were incapacitated for 24 hours. They discovered that the peanuts were not cooked and should not be eaten unbaked. Once baked, they caused no ill effects.

When the group had come down from the mountains towards the sea and Sum Sum, they had slept near the tracks in heavy jungle where they encountered swarms of mosquitoes. As a result they all developed malaria, which affected them in different ways. Colin had regular attacks every seven days. Bill's attacks occurred at slightly longer intervals, but he had cerebral malaria which produced some bizarre behaviour. Although suffering a high fever, he was still mobile and wanted his meals. He insisted on having his soup with a knife and even when the others gently replaced the knife with a spoon, he kept turning back to his knife. They eventually gave up and fed him with a spoon.

The attacks of malaria among the group were staggered, so the healthy ones would take care of the chores, the guarding, and the search for food. The stricken lay in their beds sweating profusely for 24 hours till the fever broke. It would then take a further 24 hours for them to recover.

As a result of different parties passing through the plantation, and through questioning the locals, a picture began to emerge. The Japanese were well entrenched in Rabaul and had moved to Kokopo. They were sending patrols out searching for escaping troops. There were rumours that some troops had managed to get off the island of New Britain. The group discussed this information and decided to stick to the original plan to stay where they were and try to explore north and south, gathering information. At the same time, they would continue with their plan to escape from the island. They continued their search up and down the coast looking for a suitable boat, but to no avail. After much bartering they eventually persuaded some natives to dig out a canoe. They began to collect some stores together.

The massacre at Tol was the forerunner of other massacres and atrocities. Tol and Waitavalo Plantations were on the north coast of Wide Bay about 90 kilometres due south of Rabaul and six hours walk south from Sum Sum. On 3 February 1942 at 7 a.m. five barges of Japanese troops arrived there and found about seventy Australian troops living in the houses on the plantations. They had no lookouts posted and were quickly rounded up. Other Australian troops emerged from the bush and surrendered peacefully. The following morning the captured men were assembled, their hands secured behind their backs and their thumbs tied together with fishing wire. They were roped together in lines, and marched into the bush in threes where they were bayoneted and shot. After the first three, the remainder were well aware of their fate, having heard the screams of their mates, and having seen the Japanese soldiers return, wiping their bayonets.

Private William Cook, a member of the 2/10 Field Ambulance, survived the ordeal after feigning death. Bleeding from eleven bayonet wounds and a horrific facial wound, he stumbled on a group led by Colonel Scanlon. They dressed his wounds and he eventually escaped on the *Laurabada*. His was a miraculous survival.

Private Robinson, formerly a clerk in Rabaul and a member of the NGVR, also escaped. He was fortunate not to be tied to the others, although his hands were tightly bound at the wrist. As he was marched with the others through thick undergrowth, he ducked into the growth and hid behind a bush. One of the other soldiers hissed to him, 'Keep your head down. You can be seen'. For three days he wandered, unable to release the fishing wire around his wrists and at the mercy of mosquitoes, leeches and insects. Unable to eat, he was eventually found in a very poor condition by two planters, Vic Pennefather and Harry Briggs. He too survived.

The estimated deaths were not less than 150. Six men survived to tell the tale, but the dead were left unburied, their private papers and mementoes burned by the Japanese.

On 11 February, after crossing the Baining Mountains, the Headquarters party arrived at Adler Bay on the south coast of New Britain. Leading the party were Colonel Scanlon and his second-in-command, Major John Mollard. There were 25 servicemen and civilians. Many of them were in a weakened state of health. Large numbers had gone down south looking for ways to escape from New

Britain. At the same time, a large number had found their way back to Rabaul and surrendered. While at Adler Bay, word reached the Headquarters party that there were half a dozen troops, including Bill Spensley and Colin Stirling, at Sum Sum.

On 12 February Captain Ivan Smith, the adjutant of 2/22 Battalion, and Private Bill Harry were despatched to Sum Sum Plantation to make contact. It was a three- to four-hour trip. They were given a great welcome when they arrived at the plantation. It was clear at this stage that the group was comfortable. Everything was calm and they decided to stay where they were, maintain their health as well as they could, and avoid panic. The plantation house was up off the beach and ideal for the time being. They had limited supplies, but there were pigs, cattle and bush foods available. The Sum Sum group felt that the Headquarters party had no plans and they saw no purpose in joining this party which was already large. At this stage, they had support from the local people: the group organised for a pig to be killed and dressed for Bill Harry and Ivan Smith to take back to the Headquarters party. They prepared a good lunch for the pair and sent them on their way with two locals supporting the pig on a pole. The two men made an impressive entrance at the Headquarters camp as darkness fell.[2]

Bill Harry made a tremendous contribution in the weeks following the invasion. He was one of a small Intelligence section detailed to prepare a comprehensive compass and chain survey of the eastern Gazelle Peninsula area, as no accurate or detailed maps were in existence. He had been carrying out this survey for most of 1941. Before the Japanese invasion, it was becoming increasingly clear to him that should an attack on Rabaul take place, the small garrison would not be able to hold on for long and it would need to withdraw into the Baining Mountains. While such an eventuality seemed obvious to Bill, the military command showed no signs of having such an appreciation and nothing was ever planned in that direction. Bill Harry accompanied a missionary friend on a patrol into the

Baining Mountains, where he spent two weeks before the invasion camping out in the bush, and the knowledge gained from this expedition proved invaluable. He was the only one of the 1400 troops to do this and his actions helped groups to communicate with each other and consequently saved lives. On one occasion he completed a 140-kilometre trek armed with a pistol but no supplies. He was to liaise with another group of men attempting to escape from New Britain. He completed this trek from Sitwi to Kalai and back in 30 hours, which was an amazing feat as the jungle, hunger, and hostile New Guineans, made the trip tough going and dangerous.

The story of the massacre at Tol and Waitavalo Plantations was becoming a certainty rather than a rumour, and made the men at Sum Sum even more determined to escape from the island, so they attempted to hurry their planned escape. They co-opted several local New Guineans to form a small crew as they were told that the boat was to be brought to the plantation at last.

Meanwhile a letter was circulated by the Japanese, addressed to 'Commander Scanalan' [sic]:

WRITING BY JAPANESE—TOL PLANTATION

To Commander Scanalan,
Now that the Island is took and in Jap hands and tightly surrounded
by our Air Force and Army, you have no means of escape. If your
religion does not allow you to commit suicide, it is up to you to
surrender yourself and beg mercy for your troops or you will be
responsible for the death of your men.

To Officers and Men and Australian Troops, surrender your-Self or you
will die of hunger or be killed by wild savages As there is no means of

escape. You will be treated as prisoners of war and when the war is over, you will be re-turned to your Motherland. To-day we caught many prisoners but killed only those that attacked us.

SIGNED JAPANESE COMMANDER IN CHIEF OF LANDING AT WIDE BAY.

Sadly, at Sum Sum it became clear that malaria had taken a toll on many in the group. One of the men died in spite of the efforts of his mates to keep him alive. The ones in the group who were most ill decided that they had little chance of survival in the bush; they did not want to hold up an escape bid, so they decided to surrender to the Japanese. This was discussed at length and, finally, five men left in two different groups, 24 hours apart. It was hoped that because they had surrendered, they would be treated as prisoners of war according to the Geneva Convention. Colonel Scanlan decided to surrender after coming across survivors of the Tol Massacre.

Major Palmer, the medical officer, had sent a report to Scanlan and this also influenced his decision.

100 percent of the men have malaria and have had at least one recurrence; 90 percent have had two or more recurrences, 10 percent have daily rigors only 33 percent are able to do any sort of work. At least 15 percent are suffering from debility following attacks of malaria and diarrhoea, and lack of food that it will not be possible to keep them alive for more than a few weeks.[3]

Ian Downs describes how Scanlan told Major Mollard of his decision and asked him to address the men.

That night, Mollard gathered the men together and surprised them by saying he was going to surrender with Scanlan. He gave these reasons.
• *An announcement that he was a prisoner of war would relieve the anxiety of his wife and relatives.*

- *Malaria had already attacked the party, and without more quinine this could be fatal.*
- *Clothes were beginning to fall to pieces—with no replacement.*
- *Natives were showing indifference to the soldiers' plight and might become actively hostile.*
- *Food supplies were so low there was danger of death from starvation.*
- *The Japanese would soon round them up and they would pay the penalty for not surrendering.*
- *It was impossible for white men to live a native life indefinitely in the climate, and even if they survived until the end of the war there was no guarantee that they would be repatriated.*
- *The war might drag on for years and end with Japan retaining captured territory.*
- *They had not seen a friendly reconnaissance plane to date and there was grave doubt whether authorities in Australia would make any effort to rescue them.*[4]

At Sum Sum there were now three men left—Lieutenant Colin Stirling, the only member of the forces. my father, Bill, and Bob Brain, who was manager of a sawmill in Rabaul. Bob Brain and Bill were both members of the New Guinea Volunteer Rifles. Of one hundred and fifty members of the NGVR, only seventy stayed behind to defend Rabaul.

These three men formed a strong friendship. Their ability to survive depended on sharing, and looking after each other. They were very different men but managed to pool their knowledge and survive for four months in the jungles of Rabaul. Bill was a born organiser and his knowledge of Pidgin and skill in bargaining with the natives was a great asset. He was a big quiet man with a lovely sense of humour and the ability to laugh at himself. Bob Brian was a rough, tough, wily little timber man who looked even rougher without his teeth, which he had lost somewhere during the escape from Rabaul. He was a bushman who used his knowledge very

TICK WITH JILL, RABAUL, 1940

THE JAYS, RABAUL, 1941

THE JAYS, MELBOURNE, ABOUT 1946

Montevideo Maru, ABOUT 1942

US SUBMARINE *Sturgeon*, ABOUT 1942

THE WEDDING OF JOHN COX AND JEAN CUNNINGHAM:
(FROM LEFT) UNKNOWN, JOHN COX, JEAN CUNNINGHAM, ISOBEL COX

TICK WITH JOHN AND JILL, MELBOURNE, 1945

TICK IN ABOUT 1958

TICK AND FAMILY AT HER SEVENTIETH BIRTHDAY, MELBOURNE, 4 DECEMBER 1980

THE HERCULES, 1992

Montevideo Maru MEMORIAL ON THE FORESHORE AT RABAUL, 1992

A JAPANESE TUNNEL IN 1992

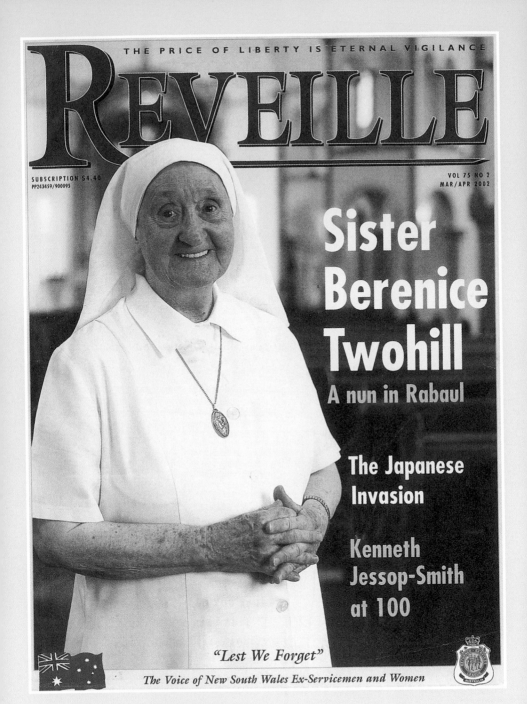

THE PRICE OF LIBERTY IS ETERNAL VIGILANCE

REVEILLE

SUBSCRIPTION $4.40
PP243459/900095

VOL 75 NO 2
MAR/APR 2002

Sister Berenice Twohill
A nun in Rabaul

The Japanese Invasion

Kenneth Jessop-Smith at 100

"Lest We Forget"

The Voice of New South Wales Ex-Servicemen and Women

SISTER BERENICE, PHOTOGRAPHED IN 1992

effectively in many difficult situations. Bob did a magnificent job as a runner attached to Battalion Headquarters on the night of the Japanese landing. Colin's expertise lay in his Army training and his knowledge of cars and engines. He was also excellent company and shared Bill's sense of humour. Bill had absolutely no mechanical skills so he and Bob were very grateful to have Colin with them.

The three men put pressure on the locals, prepared some rations for travelling and were due to leave within two days. They had obtained some rough maps and had decided to go south to the Trobriand Islands. They arranged for the canoe to be brought down so they could have a trial run and work out how to pack their stores.

While the New Guineans were organising the canoe at the water's edge, a Japanese patrol boat appeared on the horizon. Hiding in the bushes, the three men watched the boat cruise past them travelling south. It then turned and cruised back towards the north, as though it was looking for something. It disappeared out of sight, but so did the New Guineans and the canoe, and that was the last the men saw of them. They slowly settled back into a routine, relieved to have no more sightings of Japanese patrol boats, but bitterly disappointed about their failed escape bid.

Bill heard that there was a wild steer, called a 'Bullamacow' in the bush. They set off with their one rifle and some of the local New Guineans to capture it. The hunt proved successful and with the help of the locals they brought the huge beast back to the camp where they divided the meat. The next problem was how to preserve a huge quantity of meat in the heat of the New Guinea jungle and in extremely primitive conditions. The enterprising trio used a 44-gallon (200-litre) drum which they cleaned out and filled with sea water. They placed it over a fire and heated the water until evaporation rendered the contents into a slimy salty mess. For forty hours they added sea water until the bottom half of the drum was covered with this slimy mess. They cut the meat into lumps, made spikes, and speared the meat with the spikes while it sat in the brine.

The aim was to allow the brine to enter the meat and preserve it. They then wrapped the meat up tight and put it in the bottom of the drum covered by the salt mixture. Voilà! Corned beef.

While preparing the meat they were able to dine on the fresh meat and enjoyed themselves immensely. Although some of the meat lasted for three to four weeks, occasionally they would come across a particularly putrid piece, but in the circumstances this was a small price to pay in the face of such ingenuity.

Their food consisted mainly of taro, sweet potato and pawpaw. Tobacco, a variety grown in the highlands, was in great demand. Cigarette paper was difficult to obtain. Newspaper was most unsatisfactory and Colin discovered another form of paper which became a prized possession. It was a copy of the New Testament. The paper was very fine, and gilt edged, and stuck together when the tobacco was rolled. It became an effective bargaining currency. The other useful currency was the brine they manufactured for the meat, as the locals were short of salt. Most of the goods came from the 'hill boys' who would have nothing to do with the 'salt water boys'. So an effective bartering system was established.

Occasionally, the trio's diet was supplemented with fish, although fishing, particularly by spearing, was difficult. The three men decided to try a different method. They removed the pin from a grenade and dropped it in the pool. The secret was to scoop up the stunned fish as soon as possible, and eat or barter them quickly as they tended to deteriorate quicker than a normal catch. The fish were a valuable addition to their diet. Their methods of acquiring food were ingenious and creative, sometimes inspired by a craving, such as their desire for sugar. Chewing sugar cane was frustrating and the fibres unpleasant. They devised a plan to extract the juice from the cane. It involved using a large piece of timber. One end was placed under a beam of the house. That was the fulcrum which lay across a second piece of wood. The sugar cane was placed under the second piece. Two men stood on the end of the fulcrum while the third caught the juice in a bucket. It was tedious, sweaty work which took hours to extract a satisfactory amount of juice, but it provided another valuable item for bartering. An unfortunate complication was the weakening of the beams supporting the house caused by the weight of the men as they levered the beam to extract the sugar juice.

The three men constantly collected information and made notes of their observations and from talking to the locals. It was difficult to sort out fact from fiction as the locals were notorious for telling stories. The men had an understanding that one person would be in charge of the written information and would stay separate from the main camp. If the other two were captured, the one hidden with the notes would continue his attempt to escape from the island and give the information to the Allies. A pact was made not to voluntarily surrender.

From Sum Sum, the men had a clear view of the Straits and began to observe the activity of the Japanese warships. Overhead, they saw American planes appear and there were a number of air raids. At sundown one day they saw the planes flying towards Rabaul and it wasn't long before they heard them returning with Japanese fighter aircraft in pursuit. Suddenly, they heard a series of explosions nearby and the three raced for cover. The Americans had been unable to drop their bombs on Rabaul, and to enable them to gain more speed and mobility to escape their pursuers, they dropped their bombs in the jungle. Of course, they were unaware that there were a number of troops, civilians and ex-patrol officers hiding there.

Two civilians were hit, one quite badly. A shrapnel fragment went through the upper part of his leg and came out the other side, fortunately through the fleshy part, missing the bone. It was a nasty wound and the only antiseptic on hand was mercurochrome. They dipped a bit of rag in the mercurochrome and tied on a piece of string. They then threaded this through the holes in his leg, like cleaning a rifle, and continued this treatment two or three times a day for several days. To their amazement, the wounds healed up and he had no trouble from his wounds again.

On 30 March 1942 Bill began a letter to Mr Colyer.

The story of the invasion of Rabaul will be old history by the time this reaches you. I will not repeat it here, except to say that I was in action along with a few of the others. Greatly outnumbered, very poor defences, no supporting aircraft, and no ack ack defences. That's the story and the invasion in a few hours turned into a hasty retreat, and thence flight in headlong confusion. No one knew what had happened or was happening until late in the afternoon. We were told 'everybody for himself and go bush'. The whole show was [censored] and for my part, I am ashamed of it. However, with a party of twelve, I went bush; for a fortnight wandered round the mountains looking for food and absolutely buggered physically. Eventually all arrived at Sum Sum where we have been living on pigs and any native foods we can secure. Of the original party of 12, only six now remain. We at times have fed as many as fifty soldiers at one meal. They have been passing through mostly on their way to Rabaul to give themselves up. I do not propose to do that yet. I believe there is still a chance of getting away from the Island, intend with the two others here to give it a go. Have heard nothing of Evans or Bryen since before the action. I hope they are O.K. Moore has gone into Rabaul to give himself up. Have heard nothing of MacLean. Bensley I believe was lucky enough to get away to Australia by plane so will give you most of the office news. I have heard a rumour that the mainland is being evacuated so Thwaites and Cunningham may have got out. I hope so. This letter was started on 30/3/42. It is now somewhere round about 16/4/42. I have just come through an outsize crop of boils 'bad food', and negotiated a nice dose of fever, I was right off my head for two days, recovered now, and have in a couple of hours to try and recruit a boat crew for my canoe. Wong, Chinese Manager has done good work. The Plantation has fed a lot of soldiers and civilians over the past three months and a claim should be put to the Government for sustenance which should be collected by us and credited to Sum Sum account. The claim should be considerable as all of the pigs thirty odd, have been killed also three or four cows. Perhaps it would be better to claim on the basis of so much per head per day. Ah Wong has the particulars, I would like Wong to be recognised in some way also. His wages ten pounds monthly ceased on the outbreak of war or at [blank] *invasion. At the same time, he has come to light with a lot of his own private foodstuffs for our benefit. He cannot afford to keep soldiers etc.*

Mr Colyer received this letter in 1945.

The build-up of Japanese ships going south increased day and night and there was more air activity. A day later the trio observed Japanese ships returning slowly toward Rabaul. Some had their searchlights shining directly in the air, which is a signal of distress. Later they understood that the damaged ships were returning from the Battle of the Coral Sea. They hoped to see Allied ships following them to Rabaul but that was not to be. Nevertheless their morale lifted, as a result of seeing damage done to the enemy.

CHAPTER 18

PRISONERS

Give sorrow words; the grief that does not speak

Whispers the o'er fraught heart and bids it break.

WILLIAM SHAKESPEARE, *Macbeth*, IV, iii

THEIR HAPPIER FEELINGS DID NOT LAST LONG. THEY OBSERVED Japanese patrols moving down over the Warangoi River towards their plantation and then moving off again. Although not overly perturbed, they noticed that at the same time several New Guineans appeared not far from their camp and then disappeared into the jungle. One particular local, whom Bill recognised from one of the plantations he'd had dealings with, appeared on a small island off the coast on several occasions. Other locals told the three men that his appearance further up the coast was followed by Japanese patrol parties. A sense of uneasiness began to grow.

The three men decided to go to a plantation at Put Put just north of Sum Sum to barter with the local people for rations. They set up their base in a little hut in a clearing. It was Bob Brain's turn to look after the records, so he remained separate from the other two, hidden in the jungle. Colin and Bill had begun their bartering when they noticed that the suspiciously acting plantation hand had appeared on the island. Although decidedly uneasy by now, they continued their bartering till lunch time.

A movement at the edge of the clearing caught Colin's eye. Several New Guineans stood there staring at the hut. Colin was about to comment on this to Bill when he noticed behind them a group of Japanese soldiers. The New Guineans pointed at the hut and the Japanese soldiers dropped to the ground with two machine guns trained on the men in the hut. Bill and Colin were frozen to the spot. A terrible sinking feeling came over them and they sat immobile as their options flashed through their minds—run for it, or wait? But they were outflanked and escape was impossible; the Japanese called for them to come out of the hut. They emerged dressed in shorts and shirts, military boots, short socks and no hats. A Japanese officer who spoke English came towards the two men. The others had their rifles and machine-guns trained on them as the officer tried to interrogate them. 'Where are the other men?' Bill and Colin were evasive in their answers, saying they did not know, and that there could be hundreds. This confused the Japanese as they were not sure if there was a large force around the corner. The interrogation was accompanied with hitting around the head and body, but fortunately the officer only used his hand.

The two men were ordered to fall into line and march single file back towards Kokopo. They stopped at a plantation and the questioning began again. The Japanese received no satisfaction so decided to continue the journey to Kokopo as it was dusk. They trekked through the narrow jungle paths with troops behind and troops in front of them. Bill was a metre or so in front of Colin and, as they started winding through a swampy, narrow track, Bill whispered, 'Col, this will be the time we should make a break for it'. Colin replied, 'No, Bill. We wouldn't get anywhere'. A few seconds later Bill repeated his suggestion, adding that they didn't have anything to lose, that they would be dying anyway so why not make a break? Colin again said, 'No, Bill. We wouldn't have a chance. It's swamp either side of us infested with crocodiles and the Japs have machine-guns. They have their outpost and it wouldn't take long before they caught up with us again and I'm sure the only answer would be immediate death'. Bill agreed and in fact admitted that it was only wishful thinking and he was glad Col said no.

Colin has discussed this incident with John and me several times.

I will never know whether it was the right decision or not. At the time, I'm sure I felt it was the right one, but with the subsequent events I wonder whether or not it should have been a different one. I now feel that perhaps that was the time I should have given Bill the chance. He will be with me always.

The party arrived at the Warangoi River. The men were put in a small boat propelled by native push power with Japanese on both sides of the river. A couple of New Guineans who could speak English managed to say under their breaths how sorry they were. They would have liked to help the men escape but were too scared. Bill and Colin told them not to get involved and thanked them very much, saying that they would be back some day.

By the time they reached Kokopo it was the next day. They were again questioned and given a very small snack to eat. When they were outside, they noticed another camp in the distance and noticed that there were women in the camp. As they looked closer, they saw it was the army nurses and a couple of Catholic nuns. Bill realised that they were in the grounds of the Sacred Heart Mission. They waved and received waves in return before they were bundled into a truck and taken to Rabaul.

They arrived in Rabaul on 2 June 1942 and were taken to their old army camp, which was now a prison camp. Colin noted some familiar faces, but was unable to speak to anyone as he and Bill were kept segregated in little huts away from the main complex. Although they were in solitary confinement, a communication system was operating well within the prison camp and Colin and Bill were comforted by the knowledge that the troops knew they were there. Twice a day the two prisoners were allowed outside the hut for exercise and were watched by their fellow prisoners from the main camp. They were given meagre rations of rice and other unfamiliar food. Colin observed, 'I must say, on that diet, our systems didn't work as well as they should have'.

Each of them was interrogated daily. They were taken separately by car to a warehouse in Chinatown which was surrounded by Japanese troops. On the first floor there was a big room with a table in the centre. Colin felt the blood drain away and fear gripped his insides as he looked around the room. The scene would imprint on his memory. Japanese officers sat behind the table on which there were revolvers and a baton. There was a soldier on either side of him and he was pushed on to a chair about a metre in front of the table. In each corner of the room was a Japanese soldier with a sub-machine-gun trained on the prisoner. The interrogation took place with the usual slapping around the head. After they had finished Colin would then be taken back to the camp. The interrogations continued for five or six days. Although Bill was subjected to similar cross-examination, it was not quite as intense as Colin's interrogations. The Japanese realised that Bill was a civilian, and probably didn't know as much as Colin.

After the second day Bob Brain arrived. Alone in the bush he became despondent and felt he couldn't survive alone. He disposed of the ammunition and destroyed the notes and gave himself up. He felt depressed and guilty, aware of the pact the three of them had made never to surrender voluntarily.

Colin was scared as the interrogation was becoming more threatening and the Japanese were clearly not happy with his replies.

KILL THEM ALL ORDER
1/8/1944

Document No. 2701

(Certified as Exhibit "O" in D.c. No. 2687)

From the Journal of the Taiwan POW Camp H.Q. in Taihoku

Entry 1st August, 1944

(entries about money, promotions of Formosans at Branch camps, including promotion of Yo Yu-toku 1st Cl Keibiin — 5 entries).

The following answer about the extreme measures for POWs was sent to the Chief of Staff of the 11th Unit (Formosa POW Security No. 10).

"Under the present situation if there were a mere explosion or fire a shelter for the time being could be had in nearby buildings such as the school, a warehouse, or the like. However, at such time as the situation became urgent and it be extremely important, the POWs will be concentrated and confined in their present location and under heavy guard the preparation for the final disposition will be made.

The time and method of this disposition are as follows:

(1) The Time.

Although the basic aim is to act under superior orders, individual disposition may be made in the following circumstances:

(a) When an uprising of large numbers cannot be suppressed without the use of firearms.

(b) When escapes from the camp may turn into a hostile fighting force.

(2) The Methods.

(a) Whether they are destroyed individually or in groups, or however it is done, with mass bombing, poisonous smoke, poisons, drowning, decapitation, or what, dispose of them as the situation dictates.

(b) In any case it is the aim not to allow the escape of a single one, to annihilate them all, and not to leave any traces.

(3) To: The Commanding General
The Commanding General of Military Police
Reported matters conferred on with the 11th Unit,
the Keelung Fortified Are H.Q., and each
prefecture concerning the extreme security in
Taiwan POW Camps."

ENGLISH TEXT

'KILL THEM ALL', AUGUST 1944

The questioning continued endlessly and centred around whether or not there were other troops in the area. They wanted to know every detail of Colin's movements from the time of the invasion. Colin created a most plausible story which he managed to repeat every day without slipping up on his facts, and omitting every contact he had with troops. This seemed to infuriate the Japanese; Colin believed they hoped he would break down and change his story. At one stage the interrogation centred around radios. They accused Colin of leaking information from New Britain to the mainland, as the forces there seemed to know what was happening in New Britain. Colin's heart fell when the Japanese said that they had made a raid on their camp and found a radio nearby. They then produced the set as evidence. Colin continued to deny any knowledge of the transmitter. (He discovered later that it was the Australian coastwatchers who were transmitting information.) After five or six days, for some unknown reason, the questioning stopped and, with enormous relief, Colin found himself transferred to the main huts with the troops. His solitary confinement had ended at last.

Bob Lord, an infantry officer, had an even more frightening experience. He was captured by the Japanese and taken to the upper aerodrome where he was held prisoner; then he was tied up with a rope around his neck until the time came for interrogation. He was taken into a room where he was sat in front of a table on which was a sword and a map. Soldiers with machine-guns stood in each corner of the room. The Japanese seemed convinced that there were American troops in Rabaul. The interrogation began with 'We have killed your Captain. He has been beheaded'. Bob did not believe them at first, but as he observed the interrogating officer he slowly became convinced that he meant what he had said. The officer stood under one and a half metres tall and was very tense. He seemed ready to explode at any minute and Bob felt he could easily behead one of his own soldiers, he was so edgy. He put the map in front of Bob who was amazed at the detail. Every road, building, contour and section was marked. 'You were there the day before yesterday', the officer yelled. 'Why were you there the day we arrived?' The Japanese seemed to be very well informed. For reasons known only to the Japanese, after several hours of questioning, Bob was released. When I asked Bob why he thought the Japanese beheaded Captain Travers and not him, Bob replied, 'I believe senior officers felt they had to fulfil their samurai spirit. By beheading Captain Travers he probably thought he had done so'.

A few days later there was a lot of movement in the camp. The troops were separated from the officers. Rumours reported that there was a ship in the harbour and that the troops were to be taken on one ship and the officers on board the other. It was 8 a.m. on 22 June 1942. The prisoners began to assemble. Army Chaplain John May read part of Psalm 107 to a small group who were about to depart.

They that go down to the sea in ships,
that do business in great waters,
these see the works of the Lord,
and His wonders in the deep.
For He commandeth and raiseth the stormy wind,
which lifteth up the waves thereof.
They mount up to the heaven,
they go down again to the depths:
their soul is melted because of trouble.
They reel to and fro, and stagger like a drunken man,
and are at their wit's end.
Then they cry unto the Lord in their trouble,
And He bringeth them out of their distresses.
He maketh the storm a calm,
so that the waves thereof are still.
Then are they glad because they be quiet;
so He bringeth them unto their desired haven.

The prisoners included the troops and most of the white male civilian population of Rabaul, among them the deputy Administrator and Government Secretary, Harold Page, and eight heads of government departments, businessmen including Bill and other members of the NGVR, twelve Methodist missionaries, three Roman Catholic missionaries, twenty-three Salvation Army bandsmen, two Seventh Day Adventists and some of the Norwegian sailors from the M.V. *Hernstein*.

Colin and the other officers watched as the prisoners filed out. Colin was unable to speak to Bill or Bob Brain, but watched anxiously as they left the prison compound. Those left behind remembered the feigned cheerfulness of the departing men and the sound of their marching feet. Over one thousand people marched out of the camp that morning and were never seen again. A whole town disappeared!

On 6 July Colin and the other officers were put on board a small freighter, the *Naruto Maru*. As they boarded the ship they saw that the nurses were already there, and they gave each other a great welcome. The *Naruto Maru* took them to Japan where they spent the next three years as prisoners of war.

Colin had the honour of being the last of his unit captured and then only by force. He, Bill, and Bob Brain had survived in the bush for a little over four months and thought that they could have survived much longer if they hadn't been betrayed and captured.

In early 1942 Tick received a cryptic note from Mr Colyer.

Tell Tick have had 1ˢᵗ hand news of Bill. He had established himself and some others on a plantation temporarily with about four months supply of food and had expressed the intention of making himself a secret base. I can't tell you the name of the plantation but if Tick puts two and two together and doubles the Sum she should have it. My informant told me he was well and in the pink of condition.

Overjoyed, Tick scribbled an excited note to Bill.

Bill Darling. This may reach you and if so it is just to tell you how happy I am to know you are well. Its been a long time without news but now that I have heard nothing matters.

Our babies are so big and lovely—rosy cheeks and full of guile. They go to kindergarten now in the mornings and love it. We are living at home now and only Pop is there. Col has been an angel to me and if you get this it is only through his good offices. I can never be grateful enough for all his goodness.

Darling, I feel a new being since hearing that you are well and fit and am just living for the day when you return. I know it will be no longer than you can help for I know your feelings too. Keep your chin as high as mine and remember that my faith is in you and all my thoughts and love are for you.

6 February 1942. Hello Darling, Since meeting MacKenzie of the Com Bank, I feel a lot better about you. He told me lots and lots and my heart just bled for you all, going through all you did. It must have been far worse than anybody could possibly imagine, but I certainly feel better to think that you are all tucked away where you are, altho goodness knows that must be grim enough. There's nothing else to do but hang on and wait for news. At least you know that I am thinking of you lots and just living for the day we get these little yellow devils under control and you will return.

The pencil marks at the top of the page are where Jo was trying hard to add a line when he thought I wasn't looking. He really is the most adorable little boy and you'll just love his sweet considerate ways. Can you imagine a little boy of three, opening the door for his Mummie or rushing to get her a chair without being told? He does all that and is as faithful as can be to you. Don't think he'll forget you. He never will. Anybody more loveably wilful and hard to manage than Miss Jill would be very hard to find too. She's a fair young devil and sometimes I really do despair of ever teaching her any of the things a young girl should know. Oh well, I guess she'll improve in time too.

Ralph rang me from Sydney telling me that Bensley had rung from Cairns to say that you and Jack Evans were alright when he left. But that's days ago. This dearth of news officially is terrific and we can only hope it means that you are all tucked away somewhere where nobody can find you. There's one thing darling, a steady diet of taro and pineapple will do wonders for your figure. What a stream lined couple we'll be! I'm looking forward to the day when we toot about together again.

Clare is very anxious about Bob especially because of his need of insulin. Lets hope she gets some news soon, but not before me. I'm badly in need of some words from you. Cant be soon enough for my liking.

Have seen Mrs Mollard and Mrs Carr quite a lot lately, in fact it was through the former that I came in contact with McKenzie. He'd got in touch with her and she phoned me to go right over and see him—so needless to say, I did. I must water the beans and spinach. We are all being urged to grow our own vegetables, so being a good citizen I'm doing my best. My belated christmas present for you is ready at last but I'm not game to send it till I can be sure it will get to you as it is a very special picture of them and me, taken specially for you. All my love my darling. Tick.

Bill's last letter to Tick was written at Sum Sum and hidden in the rafters by a Chinese friend until the war ended. Tick finally received it at the end of 1945. Moisture had made some of the words illegible so there are some blanks in the letter.

SUM SUM 30/3/42

Dear Tick,
I have written several letters to you over the past 2 months, but they have all seemed so futile that I have torn them up. However it seems

*that we have prospects of making a move, so I will leave this letter to
be posted to you after the trouble is over just in case anything should
happen to me.*

I will probably be seeing you long before you get this.

*You will have had the history of the invasion from many others
and my experiences were the same. I was in action for a short time and
enjoyed it, but we were overwhelmed and eventually our retreat
developed into a debacle. None of us knew what was intended and
eventually were told it was everyone for himself and to go bush. This I
did in company with 12 others and with only the clothes I stood in.
After a fortnights tough (very tough) going, with little or no food and
without taking my boots off we arrived here. From 14 stone I dropped
to under 11 stone. It was a hard time my dear, for one as unfit as I
was. Further details are useless. I have been here 6 weeks or just over—
dodging Japs which has not been difficult. Our original party has
dropped to 3. Colin Stirling, Bob Brain and myself. All the others have
gone into Rabaul and given themselves up. I do not think there are
very many still out. However, we 3 do not intend becoming prisoners
without first making an attempt to get away. During my 6 weeks we
have all been very sick and the sickness has been prolonged through
lack of food and little medicine. I have had fever four times and each
time my ration of quinine has been 10 grams. Nothing in between. I
have had Dengue fever for over 10 days. _____ has had dysentery
which lasted 12 days and was very tough. Better now, but very weak
indeed. All that's wrong with me now is a bad tropical ulcer on my left
leg which is troublesome.*

*We have been working on a pinnace which is about 10 miles down the
road trying to get it seaworthy after the Japs had sunk it. Thought we
would be successful, but the job is too much for us. We had an engine
to put into it, but it is no go.*

*We have now an opportunity of getting a big canoe from the
S.D.A. Mission about 10 miles up the road. We can we think get 12*

natives to fill it and we intend making a break for it. We will in all probability leave for the Mission tomorrow so I must get this ready for posting. There is a Chinese man on the place on whom I can rely and I will give him this to post when the month is over.

Our intended journey is from Sum Sum to the SDA Mission straight across St. George's channel to a point some 5 or 10 miles north of Cape St. George on the west coast of New Ireland. The distance is roughly 40 miles and can be covered in one night. Second night will be to continue down New Ireland then round the cape and up the east coast to a point around about Muhaina. Third night across to Auea. Fourth night over to Nissan. Fifth night Nissan to Small Buka. From there we will work down the Bougain Ville coast according to circumstances (whether Japanese) and eventually hope to arrive at Tulagi in the BSI We believe Tulagi is still in British hands. We will be travelling only at night in order to avoid Japanese planes and we will pick up food and water as we go along. I hope to be in Australia in three weeks as we should be able to get a plane from Tulagi.

The above are our proposed plans and I will be very disappointed if we miss out on the canoe. It is a big [_____] and will take 16–17 people. There will be 3 or us and 12 natives we hope. Anyway, here's hoping.

I have not heard any word from or of Jack Evans—I hope he is allright. Most of the AIF on [__] have gone into Rabaul where I believe they are fairly well treated. All kinds of rumours are about, but we can't believe any of them. Its not much use giving you too many details of them as this will not reach you until the war is over and you will know everything. I am still very worried about you and the kids, but I know Mr Colyer will continue some kind of an allowance. It will probably be cut down, but that can't be helped. I want to get south as soon as I can to help you, but giving myself up is not the way to get down quickly. I have been tempted to give myself up several times *as I believe it is reported by the Japanese and you would know as a prisoner I was safe. However, it will be better to try and get away and the odds are in favour of us getting through.*

Tom Brennan was lucky getting out of it and Toma is in a bit of a mess and it seems our house is too so we can say goodbye to all of our furniture and what nots.

Bob Cooper I suppose is at Vunapope with Champ tending to the sick and God Tick I felt very sorry for some of the [_____] lads out in the bush. No food, real hard going and we buried one at Sum Sum. The only thing they could do was to just give themselves up.

Col Stirling is a good lad and Bob Brain is too—a bit boring at times —but then I suppose I bore him too. How I hope both of you and the kids are okay. It is worrying me like hell not being able to do anything. Still, you will

growing up fast............Jill has fulfilled her early promise and is probably talking like a parrot. God how I'd love to see you all again instead of just dreaming of you.

It's now about the 9th of April and we had some bad luck with our canoe trip. Got the canoe alright and still have it and also our boats crew of Buka natives. However, it just happened about the time we were to start off that the Japanese bombed one or two canoes on the coast and the natives got the wind up and refused to go. We were stuck. Then in my rundown condition developed a beautiful crop of boils which have given me hell. I still have a couple but I can now move about so am off tonight to try and rake up another boats crew. The others have done their best and can do no more. It all depends on whether I can get a crew or not. I don't like the chances too well as all of the boys are very frightened and in that condition they don't want to get too far away from the bush. However, this life is not at all interesting, so I must do my best to get away.

We are getting enough to eat, but it is all native food and unbalanced. It is going to be difficult to keep well. Natives can go in and out of Rabaul unhindered and one boy told me yesterday that all the bush was growing in Rabaul and that the Japs sanitation was terrible. There are a lot of Japs there, plus our own chaps and the sickness is bad now, so what it will be like later is terrible to contemplate. I want to get away from New Britain.

Looking back over this letter I see it was started on 30th of March '42 and added to on 9th April '42 and now it is about the 15th of April. My boils are progressing but have had rather a bad dose of fever. Went completely off my head for a couple of days. Couldn't talk coherently. They all had the wind up. I am much improved now and I leave in a couple of hours to try and recruit a boat crew. I don't expect much success as all the boys are very frightened of Japs. However, here's hoping.

Well darling I hope you can read this screed. Give my love to the Jay's I expect you have got to the stage of telling them bedtime stories—tell them some decent ones about their old man. This war is a devil.

    Good luck old thing and keep a stiff upper lip.
    Lots of love.

P.S. John old boy you have a big job ahead looking after Mummie and Jillipi. Do it well Goodbye. Dad.
PPS Jillipi be a good friend to Mummie and John. They will look after you. Goodbye. Dad.

CHAPTER 19

THE SACRED
HEART MISSION
1942–1945

Too much too-muchness we call trauma

LEONARD SHENGOLD, MD, *Soul Murder*

*R*ABAUL WAS COMPLETELY MILITARISED OVER THE NEXT couple of years. Before the invasion there were about 160 kilometres of road in the Rabaul vicinity and this was extended to 800 kilometres. In 1943 there were 4913 cars, trucks, motor cycles and repair vehicles in Rabaul.

From 1943 the Japanese garrison became more isolated as the allied bombing cut off the supply lines. The allied air attacks on Rabaul, Lae and on Japanese shipping, were a constant threat that damaged the Japanese resources and morale. The Japanese knew that their sea and air support was disappearing and the decision was made to dig into the hills. The Japanese navy did not think the Allies would attack but the army expected an invasion. It was easy to construct the tunnels by digging into the fine angular fragments of volcanic ash, pumice and scoria. These elements bound well together and the tunnels were strong enough to stand for some time without collapsing. The Japanese built interlinking passages between the main tunnel sections so it was easy to move from one area to another.[1]

It is not generally known that the Japanese virtually created the equivalent of a large town underground. Rabaul's pumice hills were honeycombed with tunnels estimated to have extended over between 300 and 500 kilometres. It is difficult to comprehend the ingenuity and extent of Japanese life in those tunnels. There was sufficient sleeping accommodation for 100 000 people; tunnels were equipped as workshops, cinemas, dormitories and mess rooms. The Japanese even used the underground hot springs to build a communal bath system. The tunnels included military installations, ammunition storage and supplies. Machine-guns and naval canons were moved underground. There were also bombs, gun emplacements, aircraft spare parts, photo flash and flame bombs, artillery propellants, suspected germ warfare shells or gas shells, torpedoes, depth charges, spigot mortars, aircraft engines, incendaries and much more. Some tunnels contained railway lines used to drag Japanese landing barges under cover. One was capable of containing five Daihatsu landing barges.

The labourers worked day and night as the bombings increased. Reports indicated that as well as Japanese labour, the heavy work in the tunnels was done predominantly by Koreans, Chinese, Indians (from Singapore) and New Guineans. The War Cemetery at Bitapaka is testimony to the hundreds of Indians who died in Rabaul during the occupation.

By January 1944 many hospitals above ground had been destroyed by allied bombing and the Japanese were forced to move their hospitals and medical facilities underground. One of the hospitals had room for 800 people. It had an operating room, X-ray rooms and pathology rooms. In 1944 the Japanese army tunnelled out 13 underground hospitals capable of accommodating a total of 4400 patients; the Japanese navy built two underground hospitals for 1000 patients. Many of the hospitals had cave-ins and were shored up with timber and had emergency exits. The only lighting was from an occasional electric light or small oil lamp. The ventilation was poor.[2]

The Japanese began to find substitutes for vital drugs, and there was considerable improvisation. Coconut husks and shells were burned to a fine charcoal and, applied externally, were used for gastro-intestinal disorders. For vitamin deficiencies they used yeast from fermenting potatoes and tapioca. Cocoa tree seeds were pulverised and used as a base for ointments, and chopped papaya leaves were used in the treatment of amoebic dysentery. Sulphur from the volcanoes was made into ointments for the treatment of dermatitis and wounds. Glue was made from the fruit of the breadfruit tree and used for adhesive tape. Oil from shark livers was used for vitamins and for antiseptic dressings. Fat from the abdominal wall of frogs and toads was melted down and added to potato and tapioca starch plus acriflavine and used for a haemorrhoid antiseptic salve. Malaria was a huge problem and stores of quinine and atabrine began to disappear as supply lines were cut. During the occupation 4400 military personnel died of disease in Rabaul; dysentery and typhoid fever were major causes of death. Infectious tuberculosis patients were crowded together with non-infectious patients and sanitary conditions were poor. Combined with the heat and poor ventilation it was not a healthy environment in the tunnels.

The Japanese did not harm the sisters at the Mission of the Sacred Heart although this may have been because they feared Bishop Scharmach who refused to be intimidated, and arrogantly bluffed his way through many interactions with the Japanese. After reading many accounts of the Japanese behaviour in New Britain it is almost impossible to understand their reasons for many of the things they did. Their behaviour was unpredictable, ranging from horrific cruelty to utmost courtesy.

In late 1942 the Japanese declared that the indigenous Sisters were now 'free from the slavery of their European masters'. They were now allowed to go anywhere and Bishop Scharmach gave them permission to exchange their habits for ordinary clothes and return to their homes. The local Sisters continued to wear the habit, and stayed together as a group, much to the fury of the Japanese. There were forty-five indigenous Sisters and none was permitted to go to the convents or churches. The mission prisoners were not given any food and the indigenous sisters established gardens and became self-supporting. They met regularly for prayer and on Sundays walked eight miles (about 12 kms) each way to Vunapope to bring food to the starving missionaries imprisoned in the compound. If discovered, they would have been executed.

The Japanese tried to separate them from each other and from the sisters at the convent. But they resisted and grouped together. These New Guinean sisters kept the prisoners in the Mission alive by creeping in and hiding food for them. The sisters in the Mission never saw or spoke to them, but the New Guinean boys in the seminary who remained did see them. They told the prisoners, not by word of mouth but in native fashion by using facial expressions and eye language. They could hold a conversation that way. The New Guinean sisters regularly brought food or a bunch of bananas for the 300 prisoners in the Mission. Sister Berenice was quite sure that 'only for them and the Bishop, we would not have survived because the Japanese plan was that we be starved'.

Humour helped the prisoners get through the long anxious days. Wherever possible the funny side of a situation was appreciated. Even the soldier's imitation of the Mission workers amused them. The soldiers made the sign of the cross, tried to genuflect and walked with outstretched arms whenever they saw the crucifix.

Sister Immaculata had a dog named Spot who could distinguish the sound of the American and Australian planes from those of the Japanese. If they were allied planes, Spot would head for the trenches and this alerted the nuns to follow suit even though they had not yet heard the planes. Spot did not like the guards and, although a good watch dog, he knew when to sit back. The guards changed duty every couple of hours and as they did so, they tramped heavily up the stairs, sometimes banging on the door of the Sisters' room. One night Spot could be heard barking so furiously that Sister Immaculata and Sister Berenice crept out to see what was happening. Below, two guards were trying to bayonet Spot who was springing to and fro endeavouring to avoid their stabs. Sister Immaculata spoke quietly to Spot, who calmed down immediately. Bayonets sheathed, the guards gave up the game. Spot unfortunately had to be shot later as there was no room for him in the trenches.

Eventually, the Japanese realised how much the Sisters could see from the mission and so they moved them to huts within the Mission grounds. These huts had a roof and only one wall and the Brothers erected a couple of walls to ensure that the Sisters had some privacy. The Japanese put up a barbed-wire fence to make sure the Sisters did not escape. Behind the Sisters' hut was a hut where the Missionary Brothers and other Mission workers were housed. The Japanese erected a hospital within a few yards of the fence. The Sisters were able to observe all that went on within the hospital as there were no walls but only a roof. On one side of the Sisters' huts were the nurses' quarters. Sister Berenice noticed how beautifully dressed and groomed the Japanese nurses were. On the other side was a hut housing Japanese soldiers suffering from shell shock, and so on three sides the Mission prisoners were surrounded by Japanese. The nuns had managed to persuade the Japanese to allow them to take their piano with them to their new home. They felt sorry for the wounded Japanese soldiers who lay against the fence listening to their music.

The Bishop demanded that nobody enter the missionaries' compound without first ringing a bell, and the Japanese complied with this demand. Bishop Leo Sharmach was an extraordinary man. Born in Poland and conscripted into the German Army during World War 1, as an ambulance bearer, he had learnt a lot about medicine during that time. Many prisoners believed they would not have survived without him. He was fearless and took enormous risks to protect his missionary workers. He bullied the Japanese and was always aware that the lives of the missionaries were in his hands. He was a stocky, suave man with a goatee, polished spectacles and an appearance of self-confidence and an arrogance that appears to have intimidated many of the Japanese who dealt with him.

Sister M. Editha loved animals and transported all her fowls and goats to their new home. Mother Martha sent Sister Berenice and Sister Catherine to the University to 'keep them out of mischief'. The University was a little one-room native hut with a sloping roof, and there was just room for a very small table at which the two young Sisters sat to study. The study took place between air raids and bombings, so concentration was very difficult. Sister Editha, envying their solitude, managed to squeeze herself into the room using a corner of the table to do her painting of exquisite tabernacle veils. On each shoulder sat a fowl and, strangely, the birds never disgraced themselves in the room, but all Sister Editha's animals were killed during the bombing.

Some of the scenes witnessed by the Mission prisoners were of unforgivable cruelty. Sister Berenice described one of these events.

One day to our horror we saw them bring an Australian soldier in and tie him up to a coconut tree some distance away from our barbed wire fence and he was kept there for some days. They seemed to be trying to get information out of him. He knew nothing—he didn't know. That's what it seemed to be. But he never opened his mouth. They tried all sorts of things with him. Then the day came when they untied him, took him down the back of the mission. We didn't see them but the seminarist boys living behind us, way down the back, said that he was taken there and they cut out his heart while he was still alive and that man I believe was Captain Grey.

The man who performed this horrific act was Dr Chikami. He later committed suicide before he could be put on trial for this and other war crimes.

Even in the midst of this horror, the beauty of the human spirit was present. Among the missionary people was a German composer who wrote some exquisite music for the prisoners. There were about three hundred prisoners in the Mission and some had excellent voices. The sound of their music lifted everyone's spirits enormously, and at Christmas they staged a play in the open. During the time of preparation and memorising parts, the prisoners again were able to transcend their surroundings. They performed *The Mikado*, organised by one of the Sisters who knew all the parts and was able to write them out for others to follow. Her enthusiasm and organisational skills inspired the other prisoners and they managed to have a lot of fun with this production. They staged the performance in between the rounds by the guards.

In about 1959 Bishop Scharmach wrote a series of articles for the Melbourne *Herald* describing events during the Occupation. He reported that he found that adhering to strict protocol was effective and that, time and again, aggressiveness paid when dealing with the Japanese, if he could summon up enough arrogance to impress them. That must have required courage as the Japanese temper was unpredictable and it was impossible to be certain of the reaction to any given situation.

Bishop Scharmach described several humorous situations which occurred during that grim and merciless time. Several months after the landing, a Japanese air force officer called on him bearing a gift of six tins of fish. He was a very serious young officer and came to the point after formally presenting the fish to the Bishop. He accused the Mission cows of drinking his high-octane aviation petrol. The Bishop remarked that the Mission cows had never done such a thing before. Perhaps, he suggested, it was because the Japanese had recently equipped the ox carts with motor car tyres and wheels and that must have put the idea into the cows' heads. The humour was lost on the officer. The Bishop acknowledged the seriousness of the situation; if the cows continued to behave in this way the consequences would be disastrous. Japanese planes wanting to take off to intercept enemy planes might find they couldn't do so as the cows had been at the petrol again. The Bishop was prepared for the death penalty to be ordered for the cows as their actions amounted to sabotage. The intense young officer assured the Bishop that honour demanded that the people of the Mission build a barbed-wire fence to prevent the cows from repeating their crime. The Bishop thankfully agreed.

There were other reports of misbehaviour by the Mission cows. The rice for the troops was cooked in the open in petrol drums which had been cut in half. One day several cows wandered up to the drums and began to eat the rice. They were seen and, in the ensuing uproar, their horns became stuck and they careered off, the drums attached to their heads. They ran wild through the Mission with the Japanese cooks in hot pursuit.

Another year went by. The Bishop gave orders for the Brothers and Fathers to build trenches in the mountains at the back of the compounds. They worked day and night until they built deep trenches in which people could stand up, or lie down at night. There was a sense of foreboding when the Japanese brought ammunition and put it close to the newly built trenches and put a red cross sign beside it.

Planes had been flying over for some time. The prisoners knew how many planes there were and how much damage the Japanese were incurring. Then the shelling and the bombing started in earnest. One day they emerged from the trenches after a particularly frightening bombing attack to find Vunapope in ruins. The mutilated bodies of Japanese soldiers were everywhere; the bodies were left there and nothing was done by the Japanese to bury their own.

When the Japanese had begun using the hospital which they had built near the Mission trenches, there was no sanitation provided. The soldiers just relieved themselves anywhere they wanted, and the smell and the flies were shocking. After the bombing, and when the Mission was virtually destroyed, the sisters picked up the parts of the bodies of dead Japanese soldiers, placed them in a bucket and put them over the fence for the other soldiers to bury. The heat in the trenches was unbearable and it was necessary to come up quickly for air and then disappear back in again as another wave of bombing took place. One of the prisoners, an elderly Brother, often continued working in the garden while the others raced to the trenches. After one particularly heavy bombing, he was not to be found. After searching, the mission prisoners found an arm that looked like his. The arm was buried and the prisoners prayed for his soul, but as they were finishing the prayers the Brother appeared from his hiding place very much alive.

The Mission people had created a niche in the wall where the blessed sacrament was kept. Mass was said every morning but, amazingly, the wine and bread never ran out. Attending Mass sustained the prisoners during a most terrifying period in their lives. The Allies dropped tons of bombs on the Mission and surrounding area where the nuns were hiding in the trenches. The whole mountain shook, terrifying the nuns. Sister Berenice remembers this as one of the worst periods of their imprisonment as every bomb felt like a direct hit.

As the bombing increased, the Mission prisoners were told they were to be moved to Ramale Valley, about 10 miles (16 kilometres) from their present position. The Japanese were persuaded by the Bishop to allow the Brothers to go on ahead to build a couple of huts for the other prisoners. Sister Berenice, with a knapsack on her back, was in the first party to arrive at Ramale. They looked down into the ravine and could see nothing. It was bottomless and the sides almost perpendicular. They hesitated and the Japanese guards began to scream at them—'DESCEND!' The prisoners began to slip and slide their way down through the dense undergrowth and trees until they could no longer see the sky, as it was hidden from view by the trees. Ramale Valley was hidden from all eyes. The dampness and lack of light made the valley smell dank and unhealthy. This was to be their home for the next 18 months. Sister Berenice wrote

It was a big step into the unknown. It was however to become a paradise compared with what we had left. God's Presence became tangible in so many ways as His Hand guided us unfailingly to safety. Drawn closer and closer to one another by our common suffering, we grew in admiration of one another's courage and forbearance.

There was a little river at the bottom of the gorge but the Mission people were forbidden to go near it as the Japanese bathed in it and did not want it contaminated by the prisoners. The Mission men built a little pump and the water that this produced was used for drinking after it was boiled repeatedly.

They had nothing to eat except the plants and shrubs. The Bishop taught the missionaries to collect weeds and to recognise what was poisonous and what was edible. Some weeds and plants were safe to eat, once the centre was taken out. The plants were often covered in grubs and the Sisters competed over who could pull off the most grubs. They would put them in the hollow part of a bamboo stick and this would pass many hours.

When the missionaries were removed to Ramale, the indigenous Sisters moved themselves to the same area and planted new gardens. They watched the missionaries conducting the Mass and although they could not hear it, they felt closer to their spitiual mothers and fathers. Sister Berenice described an incident which conveys the bravery and loyalty of these marvellous Little Sisters.

When one of the nuns, Sister Theresia, was accused of disparaging remarks about the Japs, all the sisters were assembled and the alleged culprit was tortured all night with bayonets and other humiliations.

Sister Cecilia refused to leave her and tried to protect her with her own body. When the Japs threatened to kill Sister Theresia, all the Sisters promptly begged to be killed in her place. As a result the other Sisters were subjected to the bamboo torture. This involved them being ordered to form lines and kneel down. A long piece of bamboo was laid across their legs and two local police boys were forced to stand on each end to weigh it down. This appalling mass torture continued until 4 in the morning after which the nuns were released. Seeing that it achieved nothing, the Japs finally gave up torturing them.

Once again it was necessary to build trenches. The men started from two ends and worked night and day until they met in the middle. It was an amazing feat as heat, illness and malnutrition made their lives miserable. The excitement in the camp was intense as they drew closer and closer and heard each other's voices. Finally the last shovelful was cleared away. Although the trenches were damp and unhealthy, they felt much safer to sleep in than the little huts outside.

The Japanese built a platform above Ramale and could see everything the prisoners did. They often brought New Guineans there and flogged them so that the prisoners could see what would happen to them if they disobeyed. The Mission workers lived under the threat that if one ran away, ten others would die.

There were casualties from the bombings. People died in the trenches and some died at Ramale. The nuns and the brothers built a little cemetery and tended it. They called Ramale 'The Valley of the Sacred Heart'.

As time went on, the undergrowth began to die and the sun began to peep through. The Mission workers were allowed to go outside and make their own gardens, always under guard. Once outside, they stayed there until the guards brought them back at the end of the day. If planes came over and bombed, the Sisters threw themselves on the ground as there were no trenches in which to take cover. As the sun began to peep through, the vegetables began to grow and life became a little easier, but they were always watched by the guards on the platform above.

A great deal of learning went on at Ramale. Everyone was treated in the same way whether they were German, Dutch, French, Irish or Australian. They learnt each other's languages and the doctor gave lessons in general medicine and in midwifery. They organised set times for the lessons and held examinations. The Japanese found it difficult to understand how the prisoners, who were different nationalities and whose countries were at war, could be so friendly toward each other.

The prisoners began to notice fewer planes overhead and a change in the attitude of their guards. The Japanese soldiers told them, 'We bombed Sydney today and killed many, many people. We bombed the Vatican and it's gone'. But their arrogance had disappeared and the Mission people were allowed to tend their gardens without escorts. Their hopes began to rise.

Then one unforgettable day they heard a 'COO-EE' and about twenty Australian soldiers came over the hill. The prisoners 'COO-EED' back and knew that their imprisonment was over. Sister Berenice described the feelings of joy, relief and excitement as being so overwhelming that she could not speak: there were no words to describe the depth of the emotions they were all feeling.

Sister Berenice raced around trying to find something to make an Australian flag. Everyone was laughing and crying. 'How did you get in? What's happening in Australia? What's happening in the world?'

The prisoners were taken out in groups of ten, the sickest going first. Sister Berenice was in the first group. She had suffered from a low fever all the time of her imprisonment, unable to sweat out the malaria. Her spleen was swollen and she was lethargic. She had a very nasty ovarian cyst which was operated on as soon as some of the malnutrition was reversed. The doctors informed her that she must never go back to the islands or allow herself to be exposed to malaria again.[3]

CHAPTER 20

JOHN MURPHY
1943

Torture and deprivation under conditions of complete

dependency have elicited a terrible and terrifying

combination of helplessness and rage—unbearable

feelings that must be suppressed for the victim to survive.

LEONARD SHENGOLD, MD, *Soul Murder*

*E*ARLY IN 1942 ALL THE AUSTRALIAN MILITARY PRISONERS captured in Rabaul were supposedly shipped north to Japan. From July 1942 those captured in the Rabaul area and the south-west Pacific were kept in the Rabaul area. Most of them were American airmen.

In 1943 Captain John Murphy of the Australian Army's Special Unit and a coastwatcher before the war, was dropped at Wide Bay to set up a coastwatching station. He was captured and taken to Rabaul. Murphy was a dynamic, intelligent, assertive man with a quick wit and a thorough knowledge of the islands from his days as a patrol officer. He had also been the officer-in-charge of the Otibanda police post in the Kukukuku country and knew New

Guinea well. He had studied Pidgin and had written a book on the subject, which was published in 1943 during his time as a prisoner of war. It includes a translation of Mark Antony's speech at the death of Julius Caesar, which sounds quite delightful in Pidgin.

When first captured, he was taken to Gasmata where he was handcuffed, blindfolded and interrogated. he Japanese used him for bayonet practice, although Murphy did not believe they intended to kill him. He had puncture marks from six bayonet thrusts in his chest and pock marks from the butts of cigarettes decorated his back. Some people believe that John Murphy gave away the coastwatchers' codes to the Japanese. Eric Feldt was in no doubt that Murphy would only have done so if drugged. He praised him as a brave man who would have been shrewd enough to leave out important facts if he had just been subjected to torture.[1] Sadly, the Japanese extracted a complete account of the coastwatching parties in New Britain and this enabled them to capture and execute one member for the assistance he gave. The Japanese seem to have used him for propaganda and the evidence, if given by the Japanese, would certainly be suspect. Matt Foley, ex-president of the Rabaul RSL, believes that John Murphy's only mistake was in marking the coastwatchers' positions on the map that he was unable to dispose of before his capture.

When taken to Rabaul, Murphy shared a cell with Joe Nason, one of the captured American pilots. Joe was 6 feet 3 inches (1.8 metres) tall and weighed 220 pounds (100 kilograms) when he was captured; he weighed 85 pounds (39 kilograms) when released from captivity. Joe wrote a sad and powerful book on his POW experience in Rabaul and in it he documents the senseless brutality and unpredictability of the Japanese. Joe Nason describes his first sight of John Murphy.

Both men peered out the window at a strange new prisoner coming into the courtyard. Accompanying a Jap in a black-and-white Navy uniform was a medium height white man. He strutted almost, keeping pace beside rather than behind his guard, as if he were still master of his own domain.

At the guard shelter before the cell-block, the Jap sailor turned over the prisoner. Stockily built, the new man had reddish brown hair, alert blue eyes and a red beard decorating his chin.

'He's not a pilot, that's for sure', commented Nason.

The stranger wore khaki shorts and shirt, plus sneakers.

One of the cell-block guards put a hand on the new prisoner's shoulder. Still handcuffed, the white man knocked the hand off with a sharp shrug and shouted, 'Watashi wa goishu!'

Disconcerted by the bold manner of the Japanese speaking prisoner, the guard stood frozen to his spot as the khaki clad white man took a few steps toward the cell-block.

The intimidated guard, keeping a respectful distance, caught up with his prisoner and guided him to the third cell.

At the door of Cell 3, the white man thrust his wrists before the nose of his guard as if ordering the handcuffs removed.

The guard hastily removed the cuffs and unlocked the cell door, anxious to be rid of his obstreperous charge.

Impressed by the entrance of the new prisoner, Nason and Wells watched wide-eyed as he entered their cell.

'Hi there!' he greeted them cheerfully.

'Welcome aboard', Joe responded and added, 'What the hell did you say to that guard?'

'I told him I'm an Australian.' The new man extended his hand. 'Name's John Murphy...of Brisbane.' [2]

John Murphy's knowledge of Pidgin meant that he was used by the Japanese to assist their questioning of the New Guineans. That gave him knowledge of what was happening outside the prison and he was able to pass messages out. He was also able to help one New Guinean to escape.

The ill-treatment of prisoners of war by the Japanese was the natural outcome of the code of Bushido, which was instilled into the

Japanese soldier as part of his basic training. It was considered cowardly to show one's back to the enemy and to do so brought dishonour on the family name.[3] Japanese warriors, the Samurai, no matter what rank, considered the maintenance of a spotless name more important than their lives. They were brought up to consider that the greatest honour was to die for the Emperor and that it was completely unacceptable to surrender to the enemy. The only honourable conduct for a Japanese soldier is to fight to the death. He should never surrender; rather he should keep his last round of ammunition for himself or charge the enemy in a final suicidal assault. Even if taken prisoner after being wounded, unable to move or unconscious, he could never again hold up his head in Japan. He and his family would be disgraced for ever. The code of behaviour led to a feeling of utter contempt for those who surrendered to the Japanese forces. They had forfeited all right to consideration.

Lord Russell, in *The Knights of Bushido*, describes the Kempei Tai:

The Kempei Tai was the Japanese counterpart of the Gestapo. Unlike the Gestapo they were the Army's military police administered by the War Ministry. They had a Kempei Tai training school, where many of their methods of interrogation were learnt and practised and this was maintained and operated in Japan by the same Ministry. They had full power of arrest over both civilian and military personnel.[4]

Lord Russell goes on to describe the opening speech for the prosecution in the Double Tenth Trial which began on 18 March 1946, by Lieutenant-Colonel Colin Sleeman in which he stated: 'To give an accurate description of the misdeeds of these men it will be necessary for me to describe actions which plumb the very depths of human depravity and degradation. The keynote of this whole case can be epitomised by two words—unspeakable horror'.[5]

At the War Crimes Tribunal in Rabaul from 1945 to 1947 Murphy and some of the other American prisoners described some of the medical experiments they had witnessed. One day a young Japanese doctor appeared in their prison. He told them his name was Lieutenant Einosuke Hirano and he hoped to study at the Mayo Clinic after the war. He told them he was doing research now, carrying on the work of the famous German doctor, Robert Koch. He selected five prisoners who seemed to be most resistant to malaria; these prisoners were then injected with blood from people who suffered from malaria. One prisoner tried to resist and was held down and told that if he developed malaria he would be given quinine. All five developed malaria. Two died, as they were not given quinine and in their weakened state were unable to fight off the illness.[6]

In the course of their investigations, the War Crimes Tribunal obtained information from some junior officers stationed in Rabaul as part of the 81st Naval Garrison Unit. They said some men were ordered to dig two large holes. Ten POWs were brought by truck to the site and divided into two groups. An officer decapitated POWs in one group, and the others were given lethal injections. The following is the testimony of one of the junior officers described by Yuki Tanaka in *Hidden Horrors*:

The executions were carried out by bringing one prisoner at a time to the front of the hole, making him lie flat on his back, opening his shirt and giving him an injection in the arm.

As I remember, there were three or four medical officers present at the executions. One would apply the injection while another observed the prisoner's reaction with watch in hand.

I am not familiar with medical matters, but I think most of them took about 15 minutes to die. I remember that one survived as long as 25 minutes. When one POW was dead, he was dropped into the hole and the next man was given an injection. This process was repeated until the executions were completed. By the time the executions by injection were completed, the decapitations had already been finished.

It seems that these POWs were injected with various poisons in order to test their effectiveness. The Japanese officer in charge committed suicide before he could be interrogated and, strangely, the War Crimes Section apparently did not investigate further.[7]

Tanaka also describes General MacArthur's reaction to the discovery of the activities carried out by the Japanese in the notorious Unit 731, in Manchuria:

After Japan surrendered, MacArthur sent the first occupation forces to Yokohama one week before he arrived. The first contingent included a number of intelligence officers, among them Murray Sanders, who was assigned the task of finding out as much as possible about the activities of Unit 731. General Ishii Shiro headed the notorious Unit 731. Sanders used Lieutenant Colonel Naito Ryoichi, a hematology specialist who had been close to Ishii, as an informant. Sanders asked Naito whether Unit 731 had used any POWs for experiments. Naito insisted that had never occurred. Later Ishii and other senior staff of Unit 731 approached Sanders through Naito and proposed that they would share all of their knowledge of biological warfare in return for immunity from prosecution for war crimes. Sanders conveyed the proposed arrangement to MacArthur, who instantly agreed to it. Soon after that deal was made, Sanders was told by an unknown Japanese informant that Unit 731 had definitely used POWs in human experiments on bacteriological bombs. Sanders conveyed this information to MacArthur, who did not repudiate the deal with Ishii and his co-workers, but instead ordered that there should be no investigations into experiments carried out on POWs.

The Soviet Union was also aware of the activities of Unit 731 and was able to obtain information from Japanese POWs captured by the Red Army in Manchuria. Soviet authorities approached the U.S. War Crimes Section and proposed a joint investigation into Unit 731. The U.S. authorities rejected the request, claiming it was unnecessary, and also rejected Soviet requests to prosecute Ishii and members of his staff at the Tokyo War Crimes Tribunal. Soviet officials reported to the United States in January 1947 that many of the Japanese POWs they had interrogated admitted that Allied and Chinese POWs were used as guinea pigs in experiments on biological weapons. It must have become apparent at this time that the scale of these experiments was much greater than the U.S. investigators had previously supposed. The United States apparently made further demands for information on biological warfare. None of this information was ever divulged to the other Allied powers; instead the U.S. government maintained a monopoly over the knowledge it had obtained.[8]

There seems little doubt that the POWs at Mukden, Manchuria, were used by Unit 731 to test the virulence of pathogens for use in biological weapons. Although the Ambon experiment came to light at the Tokyo War Crimes Tribunal, the Rabaul experiments did not.

John Murphy, Joe Nason and the other military prisoners held in Rabaul endured appalling unsanitary conditions, hard work in the hot sun, malaria, dysentery, beriberi, and the unpredictable atrocities inflicted by the Japanese. Prisoners lost up to two-thirds of their body weight and all suffered from malnutrition. They were kept constantly on the point of starvation. Their daily quota of food was three small balls of rice. Records of Japanese atrocities were given in evidence at Japanese war crime trials and before the International Military Tribunal, Far East. Murder, massacre, death marches, mutilation, vivisection and even cannibalism, were all practised by the Japanese. It was apparently condoned by the High Command. The mass destruction by starvation and forced labour, which turned tens of thousands of healthy men into disease-ridden skeletons, was deliberate military policy.

Joe Nason describes an incident that happened during his imprisonment. Many prisoners had quietly starved to death, but one prisoner whose stomach could no longer tolerate the prison food slowly began to deteriorate. He initially called out constantly to his fellow prisoners to give him some food. As his condition declined further, he called to his mother for more milk: 'Give me some milk, Mama. I'm hungry', or 'Mama, Mama. Hold me. Don't let them hurt me anymore'. His pleadings as he died haunted the starving men for a long time.[9]

The unpredictability of the Japanese made life very difficult for the prisoners. One day Captain Yamada and two guards came to the prison cell. One was carrying a shovel. They told John Murphy, 'You must put on proper crothes. At two-thirty you wirr be executed by the sword'.

Murphy promptly told the Japanese, 'Ah, get stuffed'. The interpreter refused to translate this for Captain Yamada. Murphy shook hands with the other prisoners and walked out with the three Japanese. When they reached the appointed spot one of the guards tried to hand Murphy the shovel and said, 'You must dig grave'.

Murphy pushed the shovel back at the guard. 'Dig it yourself, you bloody Jap'.

At the prompting of Yamada, the junior officer said, 'You die because you spy'.

Murphy lashed out. 'I am not a spy! I was in military uniform when I was captured…part of an advance detachment of the Australian Army.' He angrily added, 'who will be here soon!'

The Jap officers were silenced, but Yamada grinned with satisfaction at the prisoner's loss of composure. Murphy spoke to Tsukahara, the interpreter, in a low voice.

'Please ask your officers if they are aware I am the author of a book on pidgin-English? It's entitled 'The Book of Pidgin English'. It had been published in 1942 and proven useful to both Australian and American troops in the New Guinea campaign. The book was the proudest achievement of his life; and at this moment the condemned man wished to share the thought of it.

Captain Yamada didn't wait for an interpretation. 'Ah yes', he bragged. 'We capture one.'

'It took me five long years to write', Murphy stated, thinking it strange the Japs took pride in the 'capture' of one of his books. In an attempt to prolong his life, the Aussie said, 'I wish I could see one before I die'.

The junior officer promptly said, 'Okay. I bring you one tomollow'.

Captain Yamada roughly elbowed his colleague in the ribs and screamed at the junior officer. Later, when Murphy was returned to the other prisoners, he translated Yamada's words as 'You idiot goat! You've given the game away!' It had been nothing but a charade.[10]

After the surrender and before the allied soldiers arrived to release the prisoners, the Japanese gave the six remaining airmen and John Murphy gifts of candies, biscuits, cigarettes, sherry and whisky. As starvation had led to the diseases that killed so many prisoners, they were giddy at the sight of so much food. Murphy asked the Japanese guard, 'Why did you guys wait so long to give us this stuff?'

The guard reluctantly explained that it was the food the Kempei Tai guards were saving for their last feast before the banzai attack. All the Kempei Tai guards were to join other Nippon soldiers in a final attack against Australian and American troops on New Britain. It was to take place on 15 September 1945, two weeks later. All the prisoners were to be killed. The prisoners felt ice go through their veins as they realised the fate that might overtake them just weeks away from freedom and after two years of starvation, disease and torture.

At the end of the war John Murphy was accused of collaborating with the enemy. The fact that he survived led many to believe that it indicated his guilt. He was tried and exonerated. The six American airmen who were released with him in 1945 were stunned to hear of the accusations. They stated clearly that they would not have survived without his help. He was a leader and described by one American as having a dynamism about him that commanded respect. He was a wonderful story-teller. He stole food and medicines from the Japanese stores. He taught himself to speak and read Japanese so that he could win concessions from the camp commander and to glean valuable information about Japanese activities, some of which he was able to get back to headquarters through the local people. The extent of his bravery and the enormity of the injustice imposed on him became clear during the second day of his trial. In her moving obituary of John Murphy, Dr Susan Kelly commented that

he kept prisoners' depression at bay through a blend of badgering, humour, saying the rosary, making playing cards, cigarette rolling machine and packets, inventing games, using the Japanese concept of honour or 'bushido' to the prisoners' advantage, story telling, stealing food and enforcing rules.

He remains the only Australian soldier to have been honourably acquitted after a general court martial. He sold his house to cover his legal fees but never received any compensation; nor did he receive the honours to which he was entitled. The true extent of his courage becomes clear when reading Joe Nason's account of their POW experience.

There is a memory of John Murphy I recall fondly. He came to our room during a Christmas Eve party at home. It must have been 1946, and I was six years old. My brother John and I were lying at the end of our beds listening to the party downstairs. We were very excited, as we knew that Father Christmas was coming that very night. Tick brought John to our room. He told us that he was Father Christmas's leading reindeer and, because we were special, he would let us feel the bumps on his forehead where the antlers would come out later that night. I felt his forehead and I just knew I was feeling the antlers. He told us not to tell anyone, as this was our secret, and I kept this secret for many years.

John and I were enthralled by his story of Little Red Riding Hood:

She was a goody goody. In fact, she was so good that she was given all sorts of medals, which she wore on her chest. One day she packed a basket of food and set off through the woods, to visit her sick grandmother. She came across the wolf, which chased her. She outwitted him and hid behind a bush and the wolf just couldn't find her. He was about to give up. At that moment, Little Red Riding Hood was shaking so much that her medals began clinking together. The wolf heard the noise, found Red Riding Hood and gobbled her up. Sometimes it's better not to win all the medals.

CHAPTER 21

WAITING FOR NEWS

You meant everything in my destiny.

Then came the war, the disaster.

For a long, long time,

No trace, no news of you.

After all these years,

Again your voice has disturbed me.

All night I read your testament.

It was like reviving from a faint.

BORIS PASTERNAK, 'Daybreak'

MANY OF THE WOMEN EVACUATED FROM RABAUL AND surrounding islands had lived there for so long that they had lost touch with their Australian roots and had nowhere to go. Tick was lucky, as she was able to return to her parents' home; her father

Ross lived by himself in the house with two black Scotch Terriers, Vegemite and Whisky. Tick stayed with him until she was able to rent a place of her own.

The years of waiting now began. They lasted from early 1942 until September or October 1945. Scattered fragments of information came through over the years. Survivors began to appear, telling stories of horrific treks through the jungle but were unable to say what had happened to others left behind; no one seemed to know. Tick continued to write regularly.

Toorak College, 10 March 1942. It's hard to write about anything much these days. Life at the moment for me seems to consist mainly of rubbing girlish chests with Vicks and painting sore throats. There has been quite an epidemic here this last week and they've kept me pretty busy. Left the Jays at home last week with Mrs. Mac so that they would not be laid low.

We heard yesterday that the Japs have occupied Salamau now. It puts you further away than ever. I had so hoped that somehow you would be relieved. I still do, but those little beasts make it harder than ever. I do think about you so much and wonder how and where you are. I expect your whiskers are nice and long and curly now, but never mind Sweet, I'll love you just the same whiskers and all when you get home and I do so hope that at least some of the parcels are getting through to you. I've been sending socks and singlets and tomorrow will try and get some cigarettes to send. They are more precious than diamonds now, but I have a friendly tobacconist who may be able to oblige. I go home tomorrow and it will be good to see J and J again. Oh Darling, they really are sweet. Instead of saying 'It's mine' they say 'it's mise' and Jill always tags 'I did' on to the end of every sentence: 'I've been on the swing, I did'. You would love to hear Jo singing 'Run Rabbit Run' and 'Nursie, Nursie'. Amazingly too both he and Jill have an excellent ear for music and rhythm and sing in tune even at this early age. Isobel rang me tonight to tell me that Ron met with an accident last night. I think I mentioned before that he has been guarding the Japanese Consul (and hating it). Last night while patrolling the grounds, he tripped over a tap and his revolver went off and shot him in the leg. What a waste of a bullet!! Apparently he only got a flesh wound. The bullet just bruised his kneecap. Silly sort of thing to do wasn't it?

Just listening to the news. The Japs have just landed at Finschhafen. They certainly are digging their toes in aren't they? Oh dear where ever are we going to stop them. Surely we must be going to do something big soon, for they can't go much further.

13 March. The Japs seem to be getting tickled up a bit round your quarter at last and it is good news to hear believe me. I wonder how much longer all this will go on and how long before we meet again. I've got the fed ups today, rather. I guess it's not the time to be writing to you, but I just felt it would be nice to have a little chat. Your picture is right beside me and you are looking at me very hard. We have lots of long conversations you and I. The big trouble is I do all the talking— but then I've always been the chatty one in our family, haven't I? However, it will be your innings when you come home. There will be so much to tell and to hear, won't there? Albert Purnell told me the other day that Colyer is saving this Branch for you when you return. Colyer decided that I was entitled to a military allotment and put Purnell into getting it fixed up for me. So I was escorted up to Southern Command on Wednesday and its all fixed. Has Colyer told you that he is paying your insurance policies and looking after all your affairs for you? He said he'd written and would continue to do so; so maybe they'll get through too. News is as scanty as ever—however Gwen Mollard and I get together as often as possible and pool resources as it were. Wonder if you saw the R.A.A.F and American bombers when they did a bit of strafing. The news is just being broadcast and the man has just said there has been more activity. Good news. The Russians seem to be giving the Germans particular hell all along the line. Lets hope they soon beat the blighters completely and then we could all set about tidying up this side of the world.

Did I tell you that Oscar Rondahl is in the Air Force Ground Staff? He's doing a course at Laverton I believe. I haven't seen him but he got in touch with Clare and she told him I wasn't in town. I hate to stop writing. I feel I'm leaving you, but there really isn't anything else to tell you my darling. Things I'd like to say, are not for anybody but you to hear, so I'll not write them—but imagine all the nicest things and just think I'm thinking them of you.

Have got a new nib for my pen and it's going like a charm, and it's lovely to have it in working order again. Do you remember how we laughed that night we gave each other the pens? It was funny wasn't it?

The families made repeated attempts to obtain information from the Department of External Affairs, the Army Military Board, and the Attorney-General's Department. Military Intelligence was attempting to put together fragments of information they had received. One of the major sources of support for waiting family members was the New Guinea Women's Association. The women were able to spend time with others in a similar situation who understood the language of the islands. Here, they could share information and discuss any rumours that were circulating.

During this terrible period of waiting, the women had to cope with children who were reacting to their parents' distress. Both John and I had some problems settling in at school. Our language was sprinkled with words of Pidgin. I was very bossy, used to my native minders catering to my every wish. I remember telling the girls at school that I was from New Guinea. 'You can't be. You'd have brown skin and fuzzy hair', replied one of my more knowledgeable classmates. I was quite confused by this and indeed wondered why I did not have these attributes. Whereas I was bossy, John withdrew. He was diagnosed with a condition called melancholia. For a period of time he was inconsolable. He was tearful at school and refused to join in, isolating himself from the other boys. Tick was dealing with her own anxiety, which was exacerbated by her young son's grief. Not to be outdone, I created a situation which added to her burden. One day in 1944 I decided not to wait for my grandfather to pick me up from school. I was five years old and wanted to be independent. I caught the tram home, disembarked, walked behind the tram with my hat over my eyes and was hit by a truck. I spent the next two months in hospital in an extension bed waiting for the fracture in my femur to heal. Having just missed a lamp post as I was thrown on to the footpath, I was lucky to be alive. When Tick arrived at the hospital having been informed of the accident, she could hear my screams in the street outside Casualty. The nurses were applying Tinc Benz (Tincture of Benzoin Co) to my open wounds and I was not happy about this.

The war in Europe drew to an end and the world waited for the Japanese to surrender. For the Japanese this was not an option as they had sworn to die for the Emperor. Ominous news began to emerge. The Japanese planned a suicidal attack against all allied troops and would kill all prisoners of war in Japan and the Pacific. The decision was made by the Allies to use the atomic bomb as it was felt that nothing short of this would convince the Japanese to surrender. The 'Enola Gay' took off on 6 August 1945 carrying her deadly load.

In an article printed in the *Pacific Islands Monthly* in August 1945 the following comments were made:

As we go to press, Japan's unqualified acceptance of conditions laid down by the Allies is expected within hours. Word War 2—which has lasted 5 years and 11 months—is virtually over.

August 8: It is believed in many circles that the atomic bomb, used first on the Japanese city of Hiroshima on Aug. 6, will mean the end of the war. This terrifyingly devastating bomb, which relies on the release of atomic energy from a small quantity of uranium, has greater power than 20,000 tons of TNT. It was known that the Nazis were working feverishly on a bomb that depended for explosive force on atom-splitting. This was to be Hitler's greatest secret weapon, and probably what he spoke about in early 1945, when he said: 'God forgive me for the last ten minutes of the war'. Had the Nazis had a few months more in which to experiment there is no doubt that these bombs would have been launched against Britain. Britain was probably saved by a daring attack made on a Norwegian plant which produced heavy water, a modification of ordinary water, the best medium yet discovered for atom-splitting. Experiments and final manufacture of the atomic bomb were carried out in America by American and British scientists. This discovery of how to release atomic energy is hailed as the greatest discovery ever made. Its potentialities are endless—but in the hands of the unscrupulous could well mean the end of civilisation as we know it.

August 9: The second atomic bomb has been dropped on Japan—this time on the great industrial and shipbuilding centre of Nagasaki. Results are said to be the same as in the first atomic raid on Hiroshima.

August 10: Japan is seeking peace. She has informed Britain, the United States, Russia and China that she is ready to capitulate and will accept the terms of the Potsdam ultimatum on the condition that Hirohito, Emperor of Japan, continues as sovereign ruler.

The reply from the allies stated:

From the moment of surrender the authority of the Emperor and the Japanese Government to rule the State shall be subject to the Supreme Commander of the Allied Powers who will take such steps as he deems proper to effectuate the surrender terms.

In August 1945 Australia celebrated the Victory of the Pacific. Families experienced overwhelming feelings of hope, relief, joy, anticipation and fear as they waited for news. The rumours were put aside as Tick wrote excitedly to Bill.

25/8/45 Oh Darling, Darling, I'm so happy to think that by the time you get this you will be free again and that soon we'll be together again. Since Rabaul fell there has been no word from you or of you at all and it's been a long and anxious time. One of my greatest hopes has been that you would get at least some of the letter cards and swaps that I sent you for it must have been awful without any news at all. This will probably seem an awfully silly letter and wont tell you half of the things you want to know, but I'm going to try and cover as much as I can. Came over here from Burke Rd. in June 1942 and have stayed looking after Pop ever since. I can never be grateful enough to the Firm for all their care—financially and in every other way. They have all been marvellous—especially Mr Colyer. Well now I expect you would like to hear about the Jays. John was 7 the other day and Jill will be 6 in a minute. They started at Kindergarten when they were 3 and 4— and then went to Lauriston, a girls school near here. This year I started John at Malvern Grammar and he seems to be settling down quite well. They are both so big and tall. John is slim and still very like he was when you last saw him, but Jill has changed a lot. She is cultivating plaits for Daddy. She was unlucky enough to get knocked down by a car in February but has recovered quickly. She got a broken leg and is now perfect in mind and limb once again. Don't for goodness sake let that bit worry you for she is really and truly quite alright and will never have any after effects of any description. However, what with that and then they've both just recovered from measles. Poor old Jill hasn't had much school this year. The fact doesn't worry her at all. Of course. We leave on Friday for a week in the hills with Iris and Roger and we can hardly bear to tear our selves away from Town—even tho I know I can't hear anything of you for a few weeks yet. You are the main topic of conversation—are in all our thoughts all the time—My thoughts and private sayings darling, will be better said than written and all I do is keep praying 'Come happy day'—when we meet. All in Auckland seem to be well. Aunt Ets and I correspond at intervals. She too is longing for news of you and just at present I don't feel that I can write to her. Will wait till I have some real news for her and Kitty. She also seems to be well.

I hope you enjoy John and Jill's letters to you. Their excitement at being allowed to write was terrific and you have no need to be afraid of them not knowing you. They know you very well by your picture and we have seen that your memory has been kept green. I'm afraid you might think that I have spoilt them but if I have I couldn't help it. They're unmitigated devils but very lovable ones as I think you'll agree after you've all got thoroughly reacquainted again.

My dear there are many more things I want to tell you, but I'm hoping you'll know how it is—words won't come and yet I feel I can hardly tear myself away from this. One thing I do want you to know I'm just the same—loving you with all my heart. Your Tick.

After the surrender the first news began to come out of Rabaul in September. When Australian military personnel entered Rabaul, they found it in ruins. Not one building was standing and vines and creepers grew uncontrolled through the rubble. The town was devastated, no longer the tropical paradise of pre-war days. Parts of cars, trucks and planes lay rusting in the jungle and wrecked ships lay in the water beside wharves which had been wrecked by the bombing. Rabaul was the most blitzed centre in the Pacific. One hundred and fifty-four wrecks of over 1000 tonnes lay in Rabaul Harbour at the end of the war. Sixty-four are still there.[1]

The allied troops were amazed when they saw the tunnels: they discovered that they could drive their jeeps for several kilometres into them. Hundreds of tons of rice were discovered in underground stores and every imaginable piece of equipment. It became clear that the bombing alone would not have defeated the Japanese.[2]

Reports of the enemy's food supply were conflicting, but large-scale vegetable gardens were found in the Rabaul area. Although those in the township were well fed, this was not so in the outlying areas of the Gazelle Peninsula. The allied blockade prevented the food being distributed outside Rabaul.

There were thousands of prisoners—Chinese, Indonesians, Malaysians and Indians who had been brought to Rabaul—but no members of 2/22 Battalion or Rabaul civilians. How many thousands of Indians died in New Guinea will never be known. More than six thousand probably died on the mainland of New Guinea alone, apart from those on New Britain, who dug out the incredible fortress of Rabaul. After the surrender there were twenty-nine Indians left alive; twenty-eight were put on a Dakota to be flown home. The plane crashed shortly after take-off and there were no survivors. John Murphy was the only Australian army person in Rabaul. There were four pre-war Rabaul civilians who were kept in Rabaul to run the refrigeration and other utilities. One was the editor of the Rabaul Times, Gordon Thomas. The four men were reportedly moved to Ramale to be with the missionary prisoners from the Sacred Heart Mission some time before the surrender. In Rabaul there were eighteen British military prisoners, seven Americans, one New Zealander, one Dutchman and one Australian. Of sixty-three Americans imprisoned with John Murphy only seven survived.[3]

At the peak of the Japanese occupation there were nineteen generals and eleven admirals. It is interesting to note that the total number of generals in the Australian army was fourteen. About 300 000 Japanese, including 20 000 civilian workers, were landed in New Guinea and the Solomons from 1942 onwards. There were 127 000 survivors at the time of the surrender.[4]

In September news began to emerge of the sinking of the *Montevideo Maru* and its human cargo. The survivors of Lark Force began to arrive back in Australia after their period of time as POWs in Japan. During their imprisonment, they had been reduced to day-to-day survival and this survival was dependent on the caring and support of their mates. Their lives had been stripped back to basic needs and a tremendous bond had developed between them. When they arrived back in Australia the thing they noticed most was how people seemed so self-interested. This was such a complete contrast to the life they had led for the past three years. Colin Stirling found this very disappointing.

Colin got in touch with Tick and described his time with Bill at Sum Sum and his belief that Bill was indeed on the *Montevideo Maru*. But he did not see the men go on board the ship. Tick also received a letter from one of the officers who was with Bill before he left the camp. He said Bill was cheerful. He was also quite sure that the men did board the *Montevideo Maru*, although he did not see them, and that it was sunk by the American submarine.

Bill Harry is one person who has thoroughly investigated all aspects of the story. He has seen the logbook of the U.S.S. *Sturgeon*, the American submarine that torpedoed the unmarked Japanese ship and has studied the evidence for both sides of the controversy. He is quite convinced that the prisoners were on board and went down with the ship.

In May 1942 there was a major roll call by the Japanese. The four Rabaul civilians who survived the occupation, Thomas, Creswick, Ellis and McKechnie made a list of the prisoners they recognised when they were in the camp. These lists were thought to be the basis of the 'Katakana Script'. In late 1945 Major H. S. Williams went to Japan to try to trace the missing civilians and troops last seen in Rabaul in 1942. The Katakana Script was used by the Japanese to identify those on the *Montevideo Maru*.

Many B-4s did not believe the *Montevideo Maru* story. Bishop Scharmach, John Gilmore, John Murphy and many others had heard of, or seen first hand, the horrific deeds of which the Japanese were capable and were disgusted by the cruelty and tortures carried out by these people. There were stories circulating of cover-ups, treachery in high places, executions, death marches, cannibalism, and testing of biological warfare weapons on prisoners. These stories have been confirmed since confidential War Crime files became accessible through the Freedom of Information Act. Confusion and contra-diction surround the events. Some names appeared on the list of people lost on the ship and yet they were known to be alive after the ship was sunk. Others seem to have been killed twice. Many B-4s believe that men were executed on working parties out of Rabaul. They believe bodies were burnt or buried in tunnels later covered by earth. Around Matupi there are hot springs where bodies could be destroyed. Several New Guineans reported seeing executions at a place called the Malay Hole. This was a place where visits were forbidden by anyone but the Kempei Tai.

Reports say that the *Montevideo Maru* left Rabaul on 22 June and was sunk off the Philippines nine days later. The *Naruto Maru*, transporting the nurses and officers to Japan, took only nine days to reach its destination, yet the *Montevideo Maru* was still 1500 miles (2400 kilometres) from Japan when sunk. This seems to support the theory that the prisoners may have been off-loaded and executed on other islands.

At many plantations, the Japanese had tunnelled through the hills, trying to escape the incessant bombing by the Allies. Quantities of rusty Japanese equipment, helmets, guns and cooking utensils were scattered through the tunnels. So were human remains in various stages of decay.

A mass grave was discovered at Matupi and wrist watches and personal belongings of people supposedly on the ship were found, but the evidence was inconclusive. The grave was found to contain about forty bodies, many identified as American airmen.[5]

Just when the families began to accept one version of the loss, another rumour would occur. Tales circulated of civilians washed ashore. Bill MacGowan remembers a story told him by a Chinese man after the war. He witnessed the men being herded aboard the *Montevideo Maru.* It left port and returned a few hours later sitting much higher in the water. He believed the men were not on board when it left the same night for Japan.[6]

Alf Uechtritz returned to Rabaul as a young man, after the war. He was building a house, and employed two Tolai New Guineans to help. They told him that they were working on the wharves during the Japanese occupation. Although they did not know the name of the ship, they saw the 'mastas' being taken on board. The ship left that night and returned next morning with only Japanese soldiers on board. Alf believes that the prisoners were most likely executed at sea or on one of the nearby islands.

Professor Hank Nelson of the Australian National University states that although we cannot be completely certain, there is a high probability the Australian troops and civilians were on the *Montevideo Maru*: the Australians who carried out the post-war investigation were pretty thorough. They had reason to be suspicious of the Japanese story because the Japanese had lied about what had happened to the civilian prisoners in Kavieng. They certainly tried to shake the Japanese story, but too much of it seemed to be confirmed.

The story of the fate of the people of Kavieng is an example of the cruelty and hypocrisy of the Japanese. The men of Kavieng were imprisoned and many were executed. The native Bagail people were forced to attend the executions. Some prisoners died as a result of the privations suffered during imprisonment and a few were reportedly taken to Rabaul and placed on board the *Montevideo Maru*. It was later found that these people had in fact been executed and their names conveniently placed on the list. Between 17 and 25 March 1944 twenty-three Australians and nine German missionaries, the remaining occupants of the Kavieng internment camp, were strangled. Their bodies were weighted with cement and dumped in the bay.[5]

The *Akikaze* executions were particularly nasty as they involved missionaries, nuns, women and children from neutral countries. The executions were carried out efficiently and the sixty victims were disposed of within three hours. They were picked up from one of the smaller islands by the cruiser *Akikaze*. A plank was placed on the rear deck and a wooden structure built. The victims were hung by a rope and pulley and shot while the ship travelled at high speed. According to the report this achieved several results: the noise of the engines drowned the noise of the executions from the waiting victims; and the speed of the ship swept victims into the sea after the execution so that there was minimal blood on the deck and the bodies were disposed of efficiently.[6]

Pressure was put on the Government for an inquiry into the circumstances surrounding the capture of Rabaul and the abandonment of the civilians. In July 1946 *The Pacific Islands Monthly* reported the following:

AUSTRALIAN GOVERNMENT
WILL NOT INQUIRE INTO RABAUL.
Sacrifice of 300 Civilians by Officialdom to be Ignored, From Canberra, June 28.

The Australian Prime Minister (Mr Chiefley) [sic] told the House of Representatives today there would be no inquiry into the fall of Rabaul and other island bases in 1942.

Mr Chiefley made the blunt announcement after members of the Country and Liberal Parties had spent five hours putting the case of former New Guinea residents for an investigation, and, after the Labour members blocked a move to table secret documents on Rabaul.

The Prime Minister said 'I see nothing at all in raking over dead ashes. I think that opinion is held by men in higher positions than mine. I believe inquiries into old issues are justified only when some one has evidently been guilty of corruption or treason.

'If an inquiry was ordered into Rabaul or Ambon there would be demands for inquiries…and everywhere else…The names of men who served their country would be besmirched. I do not propose to be a party to supporting any inquiries into what may have been military mistakes.

'No matter what motion is moved by the Opposition, so far as I am concerned there will not be any of my party supporting them. There will be no inquiries of any kind at all'.

Mr H. L Anthony led the demand for inquiries into the fall of Rabaul, Ambon and Timor…

Mr Anthony produced in the House a thick sheaf of letters from organisations that wanted an inquiry into the fall of Ambon and Rabaul.

When the Minister of Postwar Reconstruction (Mr Dedman) laughed, Mr Anthony said 'This might be a very brave joke for the Minister, but the bereaved parents of these people who didn't come back are not amused'.

Mr Anthony went on 'At Rabaul, not only the army of about 1400 men, but also 300 civilians were sacrificed, I have good reason to believe there were cables exchanged between the Acting Administrator of New Guinea, Mr H.H.Page, and the Government, asking that these civilians be evacuated.

But the civilians were not evacuated even though there were ships in the harbour. Their lives were sacrificed by incompetence or negligence.'

Mr Anthony demanded that the Government produce copies of the cables sent by the late Mr Page.

All of Mr Anthony's proposals were quashed when the Labor members combined in a division to defeat the amendment by 33 votes to 20.

For pre-war residents, the reaction of the Government was difficult to understand. They felt angry, betrayed and powerless, as they grieved for lost family members and friends. The Australian Mandate to protect all races of New Guinea appeared to them now to be a farce.

There is enough evidence recorded to show that New Britain was a place of horror during the Japanese occupation. Hundreds of prisoners were executed or died of disease or starvation.

~

CHAPTER 22

AFTER THE WAR

And with rejection comes anger, and with anger

some kind of crime in revenge for the rejection,

and with the crime guilt—

and there is the story of mankind.

JOHN STEINBECK, *East of Eden*

TICK WAS DEPRESSED IN THOSE EARLY POST-WAR YEARS: SHE had nowhere to direct her anger and grief. She told me later that she wanted to take a machine-gun and shoot every Japanese she could find. We went to several memorial services at the Shrine of Remembrance. As soon as the Last Post was played on the bugle, Tick would dissolve into tears and we would leave abruptly. Her tears distressed us and we quickly stepped into the role of parent; we comforted her and worked hard to cheer her up. John and I developed a pattern of clowning to make Tick laugh and this continued until the day she died.

I realised very early that not having a father made me different from most other children I knew. Nonchalantly I would say, 'Not having a father doesn't worry me. I was too young to be affected'. I had mixed feelings about this statement. I rather liked the attention of being different from the other girls. I felt important. At the same time there was always a feeling of incompleteness, of missing out, of feeling not quite as worthy as others.

Although Legacy offered some assistance, bringing up children in Melbourne alone in the 1940s and 1950s was not easy. Because of our financial situation, Tick had to work. She decided to put John and me into private boarding schools for a short time, until she could establish an income and find a home nearer our schools. Both schools offered Tick financial assistance because of her circumstances.

With her children cared for, Tick leased a boarding house at 144 Royal Parade, Parkville. It was an old Victorian house with two imposing stone lions guarding the front steps. At the back of the house was a rabbit warren of rooms where people boarded. Tick was no businesswoman: after twelve months the gas company discovered that the meter was not registering correctly. It was either their negligence or, perhaps, the work of the previous owner attempting to reduce his overheads. Whatever the reason, Tick had not been paying the full amount and had to make up the shortfall. At about this time, one of the tenants went berserk with a gun and there were soon police swarming all over the place. Fortunately, no one was hurt, but Tick decided her time as a landlady had come to an end, and surrendered her lease.

Tick thrived on adventures, and often swept us all up in her enthusiasm. I remember arriving home for the school holidays and, on our first night home, Tick announced that we were leaving for New Zealand next day. It was time for us to meet Bill's family.

We set sail on a ship called the *Austurius* and John and I regarded the trip as a great adventure. It was 1947 and Australia and New Zealand were in the middle of a polio epidemic. Because of this, much of our travel was restricted. In fact we saw very little of the South Island. We managed to get special permission and sailed from Wellington to Port Lyttelton near Christchurch and met Mrs

Edwards, Bill's former landlady, who had been very special to him.

Bill had a sister called Kitty who was a nurse; she lived in Palmerston North with her friend Amy. I remember Kitty as a plain woman with straight hair cut in a bob and pinned back with a hair clip. Amy was a similar version of Kitty, thin and colourless. She and Amy were not at all interesting to an eight-year-old girl. I realised later that Kitty and Amy were in a relationship and I regret that I did not have an opportunity to talk to Kitty as an adult.

Most of our time was spent in Auckland with Aunt Ethel, Bill's maternal aunt, who had provided a home for Bill while he was attending Dilworth School in Auckland. Bill became very close to Aunt Ethel's daughter Ruth. In fact he was much closer to his cousin Ruth than he was to his sister Kitty. Ruth was a large, funny, extroverted woman who never married. Tick and Ruth got along famously and formed a lasting friendship. So many secrets! I wonder if Tick knew about Bill's father, running off with Mary. If so, she did not tell us. The trip used up any legacy left to us by Bill but, to Tick, relationships were more important than money.

Tick's next venture was to lease a clothing business in Balaclava Road, Caulfield. The previous owner sold her stock that was last season's and Tick had difficulty selling it. Fortunately, the cavalry arrived in the form of her sister Jean, who was home on leave, and decided that the best thing to do was for her to take the stock to New Guinea and sell it there. Tick was saved from a further financial disaster.

Every so often Jean would appear on the doorstep, home on leave or back from some exotic place. I dreaded her visits, as she seemed to assume the role of a disciplinary parent, criticising and chastising us as though she was trying to get in as much discipline as she could before she left again. She had a very sharp tongue and could be exceedingly cutting in her comments. I remember the day my admiration for my brother took root. Auntie Jean was standing over him telling him how to feed the ducks. This had been his job for a long time and he was proud of this responsibility. He stood firm, aged six, blonde hair, dressed in his overalls and holding an enamel dish under his arm, full of food for the ducks. Suddenly this strong childish voice with a lisp said, 'If you know how to feed the bloody ducks, you do it'. What courage! Nobody argued with Auntie Jean. My admiration was boundless.

At the end of the war Jean was appointed a lifetime major in the British Army. In October 1945 after the capitulation, Jean was sent to India. The Queen Alexandra Imperial Military Nursing Corps was responsible for the administration of the Indian Military Nursing Service and during the war had shouldered much of the responsibility of the nursing of the Indian Army and the nurse training of Indian auxiliaries. She was appointed Matron of the Military Hospital in Agra and then Rawalpindi. The principal Matron, Central Command Matron Fullalove, wrote of Jean:

Her work as Matron of the Military Hospital, Rawalpindi during the terrible riots when the partition of India and Pakistan took place, was specially outstanding. She was called upon to nurse civilian casualties, men, women and children under the most arduous conditions in addition to her own work which entailed extra long hours.

During this period in India Jean met Major St John Avery, also serving in the British Army. A romance blossomed and they became engaged to be married. Sadly St John contracted cholera and died in hospital in Lucknow. Jean never spoke of him and, I suspect, buried her pain and 'just got on with it'.

With the QAIMNC Jean was appointed Matron of the Beach Candy Hospital and Nursing Home, Bombay, in 1951. She bore the responsibility for equipping the hospital, including the wards and the operating theatre. In 1953 she finally returned to Australia.

The relationship between Tick and Jean was always volatile and I was often caught in the middle. Jean was angry and controlling when she returned to Australia and tried to take over the role of father, bossing Tick and disciplining us. Even as a young girl I was aware that Jean was jealous of my mother. Their personalities were so different. Tick was a happy person with many friends and a most forgiving nature. She was an attractive feminine woman with pretty features and a generous mouth. Jean was a big woman with sharp features and a sharp wit and clever tongue that lashed out at those she considered inferior. As an army nurse, she would not have tolerated any nonsense. I enjoyed the story of the hospital cleaning lady who was receiving a dressing down from Jean, as she hadn't mopped the floor to Jean's standard. The wardsmaid picked up her bucket of water and tipped it over Jean's head.

It was not until my adult years that I became aware of the physical punishments Jean had received from her mother and then handed out to Tick when they were children. As a child I could not understand why Tick allowed Jean to discipline us so harshly. Although she never hit us, the bad times I remember in my childhood were usually when Jean came to visit. I was constantly trying to make Tick stand up to her sister. Tick had more compassion. She had witnessed the terrible fights between her mother and Jean and felt guilty that their mother was only cruel to Jean and not to the other children. She was also aware of some of the horrors Jean had witnessed during her wartime experience and the terrible loss of her fiancée to cholera. I was not so tolerant, although I began to realise that there was another side to Jean.

Professionally she was admired; in all the hospitals she worked in, Jean fought for the rights of the patients and the nursing staff. Bill Harry once described her to me: 'She was a powerful personality. She knew where she was going. She had much to give New Guinea and her profession and she did not hold back. She was a legend'.

Tick found a position as a nursing receptionist to a doctor in general practice, Dr Brian Hughes, and stayed there for several years. He was a charming man with a deep booming voice and a laugh that matched. He smoked continuously so that in later years his laugh would end up in a fruity cough. He remained a firm friend of the family until he died.

In 1955 a position came up for a public relations officer with the Australian American Association. Tick applied and was successful. During her time there she helped the Association grow into a thriving, social, money-raising concern. It became responsible for granting funding for Australian Field Scholars to study in America. American businessmen were involved in companies like General Motors Holden and International Harvester and their wives were often dynamic charity workers encouraged by Tick to help in the organisation of fund-raising events, one of which was the annual Coral Sea Ball. It took place during Coral Sea Week when American ships visited Australian cities to commemorate the Battle of the Coral Sea. It was a good will exercise and helped to foster relationships between Australia and America. During Tick's time with the Association, membership reached its peak and a Junior Australian American group emerged, organising its own functions. Tick managed to relate well with people from all age groups and from all walks of life.

Tick organised and attended many parties. She enjoyed her life and met and entertained many prominent people and dignitaries. As part of her role as a public relations officer she met and organised speakers at lunches and dinners, among them people such as Katharine Hepburn and Robert Helpmann. She acted as hostess to the American admirals and captains at the official table at the Coral Sea Ball and attended many official functions on board the American naval vessels.

John and I referred to her as Noel Coward's heroine, Mrs Wentworth Brewster:

When both her daughter and her son said please come home Mama.
She answered rather ambiguously, who do you think you are.

Nobody can afford to be so lah-de-bloody-dah
In a bar on the piccolo marina.

John had taken out his medical degree and became a Member of the Royal College of Physicians and a paediatrician. I had graduated as a registered nurse and a midwife. After fifteen years, Tick decided it was time to move on from the Association.

Lady Casey and Tick had become friends during their time together with the Australian American Association. Lady Casey was President of the Women's Group and she was clearly very fond of Tick. She heard of a position for a community education officer with the Immigration Department, and suggested Tick apply. She and Lord Casey wrote glowing reports of Tick's abilities and she was offered the position. Tick loved Australian history and had quite an extensive library. Her knowledge was to prove invaluable in the following years as she answered questions from interested migrants. The job entailed looking after people emigrating from the United Kingdom on assisted passages. The fare cost them ten pounds. The position meant she travelled backwards and forwards between Southhampton and the Australian ports on either Chandris or the Flotta Lauro lines. Both shipping companies were competing for the contract, and the Immigration Department based its decision on the community education officer's report. Consequently both companies treated Tick very well. She loved the job and completed forty round-world trips. It also enabled her to visit many other countries all over the world. Most of the trips were on the Chandris line and she was very happy with this. She loved the Greek culture: she took Greek lessons, joined in the dancing and smashed plates at the appropriate times. She was expected to assist the Captain as his co-hostess and this she did with aplomb. She made many friends among the officers and passengers and many of these people have become my friends as well. She lived through many different experiences during this time including passengers falling overboard and a frightening fire at sea.

Her visits home were an event and her stories always entertaining.

Tick finally decided to leave the sea as she felt she was missing out on watching her grandchildren grow. She worked occasionally at Caulfield and Sandown racecourses, running the jockeys' casualty and also worked for a short period in the exotic diseases department at Fairfield hospital. She nursed patients with leprosy until eventually, as there was only one patient, the unit closed down.

Part of her never really recovered from Bill's death. She had male friends and a busy social life but she did not remarry. She often said to me, 'My life was like paradise for six years. No one could ever replace your father'.

Tick always told us, 'Remember that possessions mean nothing, it's people that count'. Tick lost everything, husband, possessions, lifestyle, friends, and a beautiful home. She had these things for only six years. In spite of this, there was no bitterness and very little anger in our home. Although we had lived in such a stratified society in Rabaul, we did not learn racist concepts in our childhood.

I am grateful that I had Tick as my mother. She was full of hugs and had the most delicious sense of the ridiculous. We sang and clowned and laughed and she welcomed our friends to the house. There was very little I could not discuss with her. She was depressed in those early years and perhaps could not help us as much as we needed help. She had her own pain but she gave us the skills to find the help we needed when it was time to face it.

She certainly wasn't perfect. She was inclined to be smothering. She could be manipulative, because she had a lot of trouble expressing her anger in a straightforward way. To teenage children she was at times irritatingly vague. It was sometimes hard to believe that she was a capable, intelligent, well-read woman. She liked her whisky and in fact her drinking became a bit out of control during her menopause. I had quite a few tearful, depressed phone calls during that time when she was feeling lonely, abandoned and invisible. Since I have experienced the same feelings during my menopause, I wish to apologise to her for my insensitivity.

In 1988 she had the cataracts removed from her eyes. She insisted on a general anaesthetic as her greatest fear was blindness. As her anxiety level was so high, the ophthalmologist agreed. She came to stay at my house to recuperate. One afternoon John called in to see her and the three of us were having a cup of tea in my sunroom. John suddenly stood up and walked over to her. He said, 'Tick, your eyes are jaundiced. How long have they been like that?' I felt a chill go through me.

She was admitted to hospital, and after tests, was diagnosed with cancer of the pancreas. We were stunned. The three of us sat together in her hospital room for a long time. We cried, talked, and even laughed a little. I remember such closeness that day.

And then the denial began. We began to plan a trip to India, a place she had always wanted to see. We pored over maps, talked to others who had been there, and marked out the places we wanted to go. As she became sicker, we let India go and concentrated on a trip to Port Douglas, in Queensland. She was gradually becoming weaker, and again we changed our plans and the three of us decided to go to Portsea, an hour's trip from Melbourne. She began to haemorrhage and was admitted to hospital. We put sunscreen on her nose, a baseball cap on her head, and a bikini top over her night dress, and she giggled as the nurses took her in to her bath. The then Reverend Peter Hollingworth conducted a communion service in hospital for Tick, John and me. John and I pushed the medical paraphernalia out of the way and stood on either side of her bed. It was a simple, beautiful little service. Tick loved the King James version of the Bible. She had a strong faith which she pursued quietly, never pushing her beliefs on to us. Reverend Hollingworth spent time with her and was able to help her attain spiritual peace.

She spent the last four weeks of her life in hospital. Old friends appeared from near and far. Sometimes she was well enough to see them and sometimes not. Colin Stirling, Ted Best and many others from her Rabaul past spent time with her. She was surrounded by people who loved her. She knew all the nurses and about their lives, and many of them were at her funeral. I often arrived at the hospital and found one of the grandchildren, or friends, lying on the bed, having a cuddle. She was such a cuddly lady. The one person she did not want to see in her last weeks was her sister Jean. I found it ironic that she was at last able to be assertive with her sister as she was dying.

The last days were traumatic and John and I sat with her during the long nights, watching her laboured breathing. She developed pneumonia and died within 48 hours.

There are many lessons learnt while being with someone when they are dying. In Tick's case, diagnosis to death took seven months. During the process it seemed like an eternity as we watched this woman we loved so much fade away before our eyes. Afterwards it seemed so quick, a blink of an eye in her 79 years on this earth. I have always thought I would like my death to be sudden, but watching Tick changed my mind. I saw her, in her own way, say goodbye to those she loved, and she allowed them to say goodbye to her. She had completion with all of us.

We did not have this with our father.

~

CHAPTER 23

REFLECTIONS

In the midst of dying life continues; in all untruth

truth survives; in the midst of the dark the light lasts.

There is an order in the universe,

an unchangeable law governs everything and all beings.

MAHATMA GANDHI

ATROCITIES HAVE A WAY OF RETURNING TO HAUNT THE perpetrators. Equally as powerful as the desire to deny atrocities is the conviction that denial does not work. Remembering and telling the truth about terrible events are pre-requisites both for the restoration of the social order and for the healing of individual victims. When the truth is finally recognised, survivors can begin their recovery. Working with people who have suffered trauma means bearing witness to horrible events. When the traumatic events are caused by humans, then those who bear witness are caught in the conflict between victim and perpetrator. We are morally forced to take sides. If siding with the perpetrator, all one has to do is hear, see and speak no evil. Our silence condones. On the other hand, the victim asks the bystander to share the burden of pain. The victim demands action; Not by words, but by triggering our feelings that what we are hearing is just not acceptable.

We may never know for sure what happened to the people supposedly on the *Montevideo Maru*, but I would like to know that the tragedy around the fall of Rabaul has been adequately investigated. The mystery surrounding the disappearance of these people clings to the children, family and friends. The ghosts of those on the list of people lost on the ship haunt the living, pushing us to seek answers so they can rest in peace. Many of the Administration responsible for the Rabaul débâcle have died. Perhaps now we can bring this story out in the open.

The Freedom of Information Act has meant that material previously hidden has begun to emerge. Documents were discovered in the early 1990s that revealed Japan's intention to use biological weapons against allied forces in the Pacific as early as 1942, when in April six regions were listed as possible targets—one of which was Australia. There is no concrete evidence that they were in fact used. It is clear that Australia was of little importance to the Allies except as a base to launch their attacks or to provide troops to reinforce numbers.[1] The Australian war historian, Dr Edwards, the author of Australia's official history of the Vietnam War, found the record of meetings between General MacArthur and John Curtin in which MacArthur rejected with brutal clarity Curtin's hope for U.S. protection: 'From what Mac Arthur said, it would not have mattered if Australians had brown or black or purple skins…or if they spoke 38 different languages, all incomprehensible to American ears', he said. 'The Australian landmass offered a geographically convenient base for American forces, and that was all that mattered to American policy makers.'[2]

The war crimes committed against Australian soldiers were never fully investigated. During World War 2, of the estimated

132 134 prisoners under the Japanese 35 756 died—a rate of 27 per cent. In contrast, deaths among the 235 473 allied POWs interned by the Germans and Italians reached 9348—a rate of 4 per cent. The death rate under the Japanese was seven times that of POWs under the Germans and Italians. Without diminishing Japanese responsibility for its crimes, Tanaka, in *Hidden Horrors*, attempts to understand the atrocities of ordinary fighting men not in popular mythic terms, but in historical, political, sociological, and psychological terms.[3] Large-scale atrocities are certainly not peculiar to Japan.

For many readers, however, the greatest shock may be in discovering that many of the individuals who committed these atrocities were simply ordinary men in extraordinary circumstances—manipulated by their leaders and dehumanised by the very nature of war itself. Their acts become all the more horrible when we no longer can regard them as having been committed by people utterly unlike ourselves...

War creates situations in which the moral framework of peace time ceases to be of any practical use. In looking at the acts of individuals caught up in such extreme situations, it is imperative to remember that guilt and innocence, the status of the perpetrator and that of the victim, are often indissolubly intertwined.

Every soldier is a victim of the state that drafts him, sends him to war, and demands that he kill the enemy. However, at the same time, this soldier still bears responsibility for his actions as an aggressor or war criminal.[4]

The war trials were conducted in Rabaul from December 1945 until November 1947. During the Japanese war trials, 93 Japanese war criminals suffered death by execution. In 1947, 277 war criminals were imprisoned in Rabaul after receiving sentences ranging from life to one year. From February 1946 until October 1947, 105 686 Asians were repatriated from Rabaul. They were Japanese, Formosans and Koreans.

In October 1946 Reginald Halligan sent a letter to the Administration of Papua New Guinea. He suggested that certain people be interrogated to discover whether they could provide any information regarding missing civilians.

Two natives also appear to have been employed by the Japanese Kempei Tai native police on duties which may well have required their presence at executions. One is an Arawe Boy, named Sam, who formerly worked on Put Put Plantation. This native is believed to have been 'boss boy' of the Japanese native police. The other is Gawa, a former 'boss boy' on Put Put.

As Bill and Colin were captured at Put Put Plantation, it seems likely that they were the New Guineans who notified the Japanese of their presence. I also wondered if Sam was Gelu's husband, the same Sam that Bill considered a rogue and had kicked out of Gelu's bedroom twelve months before.

In 1946 the Administration of Rabaul was reinstated. In 1947 John and Jean Cox returned to Rabaul and found it a very different place. Many natives had co-operated with the Japanese and were antagonistic towards the Europeans. Services were poorly managed. The Coxes moved to Port Moresby, where John took a teaching position at the Trades School. He became Headmaster and later took the position as Head of the Apprenticeship Board for New Guinea and in this capacity introduced the apprenticeship scheme. When he retired some of his old students got together and created the John Cox Prize. Little Jean worked for Reuter's News Agency and was very knowledgeable on New Guinea. The 'Virgins' Retreat' is now the site of the War Museum opposite the New Guinea Club. During the Japanese occupation a huge excavation was made beneath the 'Retreat' and it was used as the Japanese war room or map room complete with all modern conveniences, electricity and air filtering systems. On display in the museum is some of the radio transmission equipment used by the coastwatchers. On the ceiling is a map showing the whole Pacific region.

House Rakaia became the home of a Japanese general. It no longer exists, although the stone steps leading up to the house are still there. The house at Toma has disappeared and it is even difficult to find the place on which it stood.

In 2003 Neil Wilson, from the *Herald-Sun*, and Hiroshi Oosedo interviewed one of the seventeen Japanese survivors of the sinking of the *Montevideo Maru*. The most incredible part of this event is that Yoshiaki Yamaji, a merchant seaman, now eighty-one, was never interviewed by Australian investigators. Sixty-one years later, Mr Yamaji has contradicted the post-war stance of the Australian Government, that all prisoners perished at sea. Mr Yamaji said that there were no prisoners over 40 on the ship, and that all the men were fit and healthy. They were kept in three-tier bunks and brought out on deck every morning to exercise and keep fit.

When looking through the ages of the Rabaul civilians reportedly on the *Montevideo Maru*, one must question where the older men and the ill prisoners were. Those interviewing Mr Yamaji believe that when the men were marched down to the embarkation point, they were separated into two groups. The older prisoners and the ill or incapacitated were probably put on a ship, taken out to sea, and executed. There has been a report of another ship in the harbour that day. This would account for reports of bodies being washed up and the ship returning and leaving again.

Mr Yamaji said that prisoners on board the *Montevideo Maru* were kept in the lower decks and most would have died instantly when the torpedoes hit; but some did not. The crew and Japanese soldiers crowded into two lifeboats and made no attempt to rescue any POWs.

I remember seeing between forty or fifty Australian POWs swimming in the sea polluted with heavy oil. We have thrown them life jackets,

buoys, wood and anything that could come up to the sea's surface. Some
Australians were singing the song Hotaru-no-hikari [Auld Lang Syne]
in chorus.

Only seventeen Japanese crew members from one lifeboat survived
hostile Philippine locals and made it back to Japan one month later.
Mr Yamaji was told by a senior official from his company (OSL
Line) that some of the Australian prisoners were rescued and taken
to Kobe to work at the Kobe port. Four Australian officers of the
17th Anti-tank Battery on Rabaul saw a photo in a Japanese
newspaper, *Osaka Mainachi*, of allied POWs unloading sacks on a
dock near Tokyo in November 1942. They recognised two of their
close mates. Another man recognised a picture of his son among
POWs in Korea in 1943. This information was handed to the
Australian War Crimes Commission in late 1945. Frank Forde, the
army minister, informed the men that it was assumed all Australians
had died on the *Montevideo Maru.*

Mr Yamaji believes the surviving POWs may have been put to
work and death in Japanese gold mines on Sado Island. Two days
before the bombing of Hiroshima, four hundred POWs (Dutch,
English and Australian) were put down a disused mine shaft and it
was then collapsed on to them, burying them alive.

Bill's fate would probably have been decided in the selection
process. As he was thirty-seven, his health and physical condition
would have influenced this decision. His cerebral malaria flared up
at intervals and may have affected his mental state. If he was
suffering a relapse at the time of the selection he would probably not
have been on board the *Montevideo Maru.* It is more than likely that
he was one of those executed.

At this stage the account by Mr Yamaji is, for me, the most
plausible. It makes sense of the conflicting stories, but there are some
who dismiss Mr Ysamaji's account. There is some relief in writing
this, even though I am calmly discussing different horrific ways in

which my father might have died. Torpedoed, executed, or smothered in a disused mine shaft; somehow clarity of fact is easier to cope with than a huge wall of mystery.

As for my mother, Tick, long before the telegram came from the Minister for External Territories, she knew Bill was dead. One evening in 1942 when she was sitting in front of the fire, she felt a stabbing, agonising pain. At that moment, she said, she knew he was dead. The finality of that telegram, however, obliterated any last ray of hope.

It is with deep regret that I have to inform you that the transmission of the nominal roll of the Japanese vessel Montevideo Maru which was lost with all personnel after leaving Rabaul in June, 1942 shows that [name] was aboard the vessel and I desire to convey to you the profound sympathy of the Commonwealth Government. Signed Minister for External Territories.

Tick did not receive this telegram until later, as Bill's name was not on the original list. He was one of the last men captured and this was shortly before the ship sailed. It was thought that his name was added later. Sadly, Tick's letters were returned to her.

CHAPTER 24

RETURN TO RABAUL
FIFTY YEARS ON

Love goes very far beyond the physical person of

the beloved. It finds its deepest meaning in

his spiritual being, his inner self. Whether or not

he is actually present, whether or not he is still

alive at all ceases to be of importance.

VIKTOR E. FRANKL

ONE WARM MELBOURNE SUMMER DAY IN JANUARY 1992 I
received a phone call from John at the Health Centre:

*The RSL have organised a Hercules plane to take some of the survivors
from Lark Force back to Rabaul for the anniversary of the Japanese
invasion. There will be commemoration ceremonies for those who died
in Rabaul and those on the* Montevideo Maru. *If you can afford the
trip, there is enough room on the plane for us!*

There was never any doubt. I organised my leave and raided my money box and there we were on the way to the Richmond air force base in New South Wales.

On the tarmac at Richmond sat a Hercules plane looking like a big, old battered brown moth. We filed on to the plane carrying our air force rations—a white cardboard box containing nondescript sandwiches, a small carton of fruit juice and a piece of fruit cake. This was clearly going to be a primitive trip, very different from the commercial airlines. Also on the plane were young army personnel who were going to New Guinea to walk the Kokoda Track as a tribute to those who had died there.

The noise of the engines was horrendous and we sat with plugs in our ears, in long lines of bucket seats facing each other across an aisle. Condensation caused drips of vapour to drop on our heads and one enterprising gentleman produced an umbrella, which provided him with a little protection. We stopped at Amberley air force base in Queensland to pick up other members of the party and continued on to Madang where we stayed overnight. We transferred to a commercial jet for the last leg of our journey. Excitement in the group began to grow as the beautiful Rabaul Harbour came into view.

We were greeted at the airport by a brass band, and frangipani leis were presented to the women. We were then escorted to the Travel Lodge where a welcome party of members of the Rabaul RSL and other dignitaries were waiting. Delicious drinks were served in coconut shells decorated with red hibiscus. We stood around the pool chatting and absorbing the fact that we were back in Rabaul.

There were thirty-four people in the party (accompanied by two members of the Veterans Affairs medical team). There were twenty former members of 2/22 Battalion, including Colin Stirling, two army nurses (POWs), Sister Berenice (ex Vunapope Mission Sister) and eight children of fathers lost on the *Montevideo Maru*. The three sons and five daughters of the 'B-4s' were known as 'the camp followers' and we played an important role during the week that followed. We asked many questions and encouraged the survivors to tell us their stories. Together, we pieced together the events of 1942 and in many ways we were their counsellors and they were ours. We talked, shared and laughed together.

It was sad to realise that in 1942 these wonderful old soldiers were only nineteen or twenty. They were in Rabaul for less than twelve months, but their memories were sharp and clear. It had been a most traumatic experience for all of them at a time when they would normally have been studying or otherwise preparing for their life careers. They knew that not only had they been abandoned by their government but that they had not even been given equipment to protect themselves, let alone to fight a huge invading force. They were given little training in how to conduct jungle warfare and had witnessed friends killed and wounded in a battle they had no hope of winning or even surviving. The fact that they did survive is a tribute to the courage and tenacity shown by each of them.

As we attended the functions organised for us by the New Guineans and the Rabaul arm of the RSL, the conversation between the 'camp followers' and the surviving veterans continued. The stories kept rolling out, as did the questions we asked. Lorna Johnston expressed sympathy for the nurses employed by the Rabaul hospital. They were asked by the Administration to 'stay on' when they knew the invasion was imminent. They were captured by the Japanese and spent three and a half years in Japan as POWs with the Army and missionary nurses. After the war they received no pension or compensation from the government although, without exception, each had been badly affected by the experience.

Sister Berenice told us that initially they did not fear the Japanese. The nuns had taught Japanese children in the school and the parents were part of the community. On reflection, she remembers the families quietly leaving Rabaul in the months before the invasion. She believed that there was a valuable purpose to the sacrifice: 'When the Japanese first arrived in Rabaul, some of the troops thought they were in Australia. I'll maintain to my dying day that Rabaul saved Australia'.

Bob Lord was angrier with the Australian Government than with the Japanese: 'They sent us up there with no equipment, no thought of rescue, just a token to be swallowed up by the Japanese'. Bill Larkin thought that the Australians had made a difference: 'We held the Japs up for three months. They lost valuable time looking for the Americans that weren't there'. Colin Stirling said that he had no animosity towards the High Command; he understood that they had no experience in jungle warfare.

The first memorial service was on the foreshore of the harbour and was to commemorate the people who lost their lives on the *Montevideo Maru*. In the background was the wharf where the prisoners were loaded on to the ship. We laid wreaths at the stone plaque that commemorated those lost on the ship, as the New Guinea sun beat down on our tear-stained faces. The silence surrounded us all as we lost ourselves in our own private salutations. It was a most moving experience.

It was the same at the memorial service held at Bitapaka war cemetery. The magnificent rain trees provided some shade and the gardens were alive with brilliant banks of red and yellow crotons. The frangipani trees were full of flowers and the lush soft pine-green lawn cradled the white memorial plaques which filled the huge grounds of this beautiful place. As happened for Tick and me in 1984, the feeling of absolute peace soothed our wounds and was only broken by the sound of birds. This experience was more healing than I can describe in words. Part of me has always felt angry that my father had given his life and no one apart from his family seemed to know or care. But these men did. They had not forgotten. Nor had the other people there whose fathers had died on the *Montevideo Maru*. Our losses had affected us all in different ways and in this place we shared our grief. Our thoughts were of the events in 1942.

I remember particularly one man, Lex Frazer, a big tall Queenslander who ran an import and export firm. In his spare time he worked for Rotary and set up new groups wherever he could: 'My mates who died were young men, cut off at the prime of their lives. It's my way of making up for surviving when they died. I feel I have to live for them as well as me'. This affected me very much. I think it was because their deaths had meant so much to this man that he continued to honour them in his own quiet way. Another old soldier, Willis Crocker, had travelled by bus and public transport to join the group. He was a very sick man, who could only walk painfully with the help of two sticks. He attended every function, despite the pain, as he was determined to honour his friends in spite of his family's pleadings not to go. Sadly, he died a few months after the trip. Also present was Chaplain John May who had surrendered to the Japanese on behalf of the hospital and staff. He amused us all by returning to the New Guinea Club to demand a crab sandwich owing to him from the day of the surrender. He had paid for the sandwich and had to leave it uneaten when the invasion began. Chaplain John May was the only commissioned officer remaining in Rabaul. While his faith was strong, he described conducting a service while reciting the Lord's Prayer as bullets showered around them. It seemed more prudent to duck than rely on his faith at that moment.

On a trip to the Vunapope mission we lunched and gazed out over the wonderful view of the distant harbour where the Japanese planned their tactics during the Coral Sea battle. The mission has played a major role in the history of Rabaul. It is in a wonderful position at Kokopo—away from the volcanoes and strategically placed overlooking the whole of Blanche Bay.

This visit was one of the highlights of the trip. Young, Year 10 New Guinea girls from the Mission school took the hands of each member of the group and took them to a quiet place on the lawns where they questioned them on their experiences in Rabaul and conversed in English. We were then led into a huge hall where the girls sat on the floor while we were all seated on the stage. We were invited to stand and briefly share our experience with the girls. There then began a performance I will never forget. There was no glass on the windows, and the warm breeze drifted into the hall. In front of us, cross-legged on the floor were about 150 beautiful young women in their soft green and yellow uniforms, smiling up at us. They began to sing a welcome song. Their young voices filled the hall and no one remained unmoved.

John and Colin had arranged for us to visit the plantation at Sum Sum where Bill had spent his last five months. Ironically, a Japanese man now managed the plantation. There had been a recent spate of pay-roll robberies and violence on the road to Sum Sum. We knew this but were prepared to take the risk, but as we were about to leave, we were approached by the organisers who asked us not to go as they thought it was too dangerous. They argued that it would ruin the whole trip for the veterans if something happened to us. We were defiant, but gradually weighed down by the pressure of good sense. John rang the owner of the plantation and told him what had happened. The Japanese man responded angrily. He said he had marked out a route he knew to be safe. As he slammed down the phone, John heard him say, 'Another brave Australian!'

POSTSCRIPT

Dear Dad,

Saying that word is so unfamiliar to me and yet most other people don't even think about it.

For so many years you were a mythical person, part of a South Pacific Paradise, a legend created by Mum, a perfect man.

There came a time when I yearned to know the real man. You were thirty-eight years old when you died, and you died just before your birthday. When I was thirty-eight years old I had recently separated from my husband and become a single parent.

I have read many stories of Rabaul, looking for a mention of your name. Afterwards, when I found no mention I felt isolated. It was as though you didn't exist. This has been one of the worst aspects of our loss. No one seemed to care that you had died or even existed, apart from my mother and brother.

There was no body. There was no service. There was no ceremony.

My mother waited three and a half years to find out that you were dead—but how you died and where your body rests has never been clear.

Not knowing has been a theme through my life. When mourning someone you love these things become important— visualising, visiting the grave, putting to rest. It helps to complete the grieving.

For many people like me, the grieving is never quite completed.

I remember as a child, sitting in the hall playing with my dolls. I see a gold light behind the stained-glass window of the front door. I watch and wait expectantly for a shadow to appear, the door bell to be rung and for you to appear. In my fantasy played out with my dolls, you lift me up and I look down into your laughing face.

Was this a fantasy or a memory?

So Dad, writing this account of your time in Rabaul has taken me into your world and for the first time I have a sense of the real man.

At a recent Rabaul get-together I saw the sad faces of the other families who lost a loved one in Rabaul and I recognised the same sense of unfinished grief and lack of completion.

My grief became frozen until thirty years later it was triggered unexpectedly, as pristine and acute as it was when those words were spoken: 'Your father is not coming home'. At first I did not want to give it up. Holding the grief is a way of holding on to that person.

You are a part of my heart. I will not lay you down and rest unless I know what happened to you. I am your witness, as well as your daughter. I may never know what happened to you but I will keep the door open in case. If I don't do this, who will? I love you and now I feel I know you at last. I am so grateful for the life you gave me. Your life was worthwhile even though you were so young when you died. I'm sad that I did not have a chance to know you and tell you these things. Thank you for giving your life to protect your family and your home.

JILL

APPENDIX 1:
PEOPLE REFERRED TO IN BILL'S LETTERS

Appel, Captain 'Pip' Commanding Officer of C. Company. 2/22 Btn. Helped organise escape of men to Cairns. Encouraged troops not to surrender and to keep going. Paid tribute to Lt-Col. J. K. McCarthy for helping to save their lives.

Archer, Lieutenant J. C.(Clarrie), OBE Custodian Expropriation Board NGVR. Administrator of N.T. from 1956.

Bensley, Bob Shipping Manager. Escaped from Rabaul on the day before the invasion.

Best, Lieutenant E. W. 2/22 Btn. Captured at Gasamata. POW Japan. A former Olympian and Lord Mayor of Melbourne.

Best, Stanley and Betty (Stanley was Ted Best's brother). Close friends of Tick and Bill. Daughter Jocelyn born on night of eruption at Sacred Heart Mission.

Brennan, Dr E. T. Director of Health, Rabaul. Later appointed Lt-Col ADMS, 8th Division, in Port Moresby.

Carr, Lieutenant-Colonel. CO 2/22 Btn. Escaped from New Britain. Appointed District Telephone Officer in charge of the Western District of Victoria.

Clark, Hon. R. L. ('Nobby'). Chief Civil Warden, Air Raid Precautions. Member of Legislative Council. President of the R.S.L. Lost on the *Montevideo Maru.*

Coldham. Harold. No details available.

Cooper, Clare. Wife of Bob. A nurse, who trained at the Royal Melbourne Hospital with Tick. She and Tick remained friends.

Cooper, Dr R. W. Close friend of Tick and Bill. Was the last civilian to leave Rabaul before the invasion. Supervised the transfer of patients from civilian hospital (Namanula) to the Sacred Heart Mission hospital. Helped nurses whenever possible until he was transferred to prison camp in Rabaul, where he cared for prisoners. Lost on the *Montevideo Maru*.

Coote, Phil. Number One Manager of Burns Philp. Friends of Tick and Bill. Phil's wife Rhoda was a most gracious and charismatic lady. Phil was lost on the *Montevideo Maru*.

Cromie., Jim and Del. Jim was a solicitor. Escaped and remained friends of Tick after the war.

Edgell, Tony and Elsie. Plantation owners at Manus Island. Tick met Elsie on the boat coming to Rabaul. She became Jill's godmother.

Evans, Jack. Staff of Colyer Watson. Married Gwenyth Cunningham and was Tick's sister-in-law.

Feetum, ——. Police Officer. Rescued by Lieutenant Frank Holland.

Field, Lieutenant Ross. Director of Public Works, Rabaul. Had resigned his commission as a commanding officer of the NGVR in April 1941. Lost on *Montevideo Maru*.

Hosking, Dr H. Acting Director of Public Health, Rabaul. Lost on *Montevideo Maru*.

Leggatt, Lieutenant-Colonel Sir William, DSO MC ED, 2/22 Btn, CO 2/40, MLA, barrister.

McInnes, Major C. L. VX4646497, 2/22 Btn. Escaped to New Ireland and from there to Port Moresby in May 1942.

McNicoll, Brigadier General Sir Walter R. KBE CB CMG DSO, Administrator of New Guinea, 1934–43. Became ill and was airlifted out of Lae before invasion.

Mantle, F. W. A former District Officer. Acting Magistrate. Lost on *Montevideo Maru.*

Mollard, Gwen. She and Tick supported each other while waiting for news of their husbands. She was an active member of the New Guinea Womens Association during the long wait.

Mollard, Major J. C. Second in Charge of 2/22 Btn/Lark Force. Surrendered to Japanese. POW in Japan. On return was very helpful to waiting families.

Scanlan. Colonel J. J. DSO, Commander of Lark Force. Command HQ NG. Surrendered to Japanese. POW Japan. Veteran of World War 1. Became Deputy Governor of Hobart Gaol.

Townsend, H. O. Treasurer, Rabaul. Lost on *Montevideo Maru.*

APPENDIX 2:
LETTER RE WAR CRIMES

TERRITORY OF PAPUA AND NEW GUINEA

Confidential   No. C.A.

21/1/45

                                                               Port Moresby

3rd July 1950

The Secretary,

Department of External Territories,

CANBERRA. A.C.T

WAR CRIMES—RABAUL

1 During the past several weeks Flight Lieut. Rundle of the R.A.A.F. and Colonel Horton of the Imperial War Graves Commission have been re-opening graves situated on the shore of Greet Harbour, about one mile south of Matupi Volcano, Rabaul. Up to 27th June, last, 27 bodies had been recovered from the graves. Some of the bodies were buried in common graves and the area seems to have been used by the Japanese as an execution ground. There is evidence to show that some of the men suffered execution at the hands of the Japanese as their limbs are bound with wire. Some of the bodies show signs of terrible mistreatment before death.

2 The 27 bodies so far recovered are 15 R.A.A.F., 8 U.S. airmen and 4 unidentified—probably U.S. Airmen. In many cases the bodies have been buried complete with personal equipment and identification discs.

3 Flight Lieut. Rundle states that a complete crew of a missing Catalina were recovered from the one common grave. The identity discs serve to show the identity of the men. Records show that the Japanese Commander at Rabaul formerly stated that these men had been transferred to Japan on a destroyer which was later sunk. The statement of the Japanese Commander is now proved untrue and steps have been taken by Flight Lieut. Rundle to have the Commander detained as a war criminal in Japan.

4 It is possible that further investigation may show that the bodies of many missing civilian personnel at present believed to have been on board the "Montevideo Maru" are buried in Rabaul. To date there is no definite evidence of this, but in order to prevent undue hardship to the relatives of the missing men, steps have been taken to keep the whole work secret. Unfortunately, when the party commenced to exhume the bodies an unknown person reported the matter to the Australian Broadcasting Commission, with the result that an announcement was made over the National stations. It would be appreciated if the General Manager of the Australian Broadcasting Commission could be approached with a view to seeking co-operation in preventing any statement being broadcast at the present time. It is not the wish of the Administration to censor legitimate news, but it is felt that, at this stage, any premature announcements may cause unnecessary anguish to the relatives of the missing civilians.

APPENDIX 3:
CIVILIANS BELIEVED LOST ON THE
MONTEVIDEO MARU

NAME	AGE	POSITION
ABBOTT, E. M.	33	Pastor, S.D.A. Mission, Rabaul
ADAMS, H. A.	49	planter, Nostre Mal Plantation, New Britain
ALLEN, G. W.	49	planter, Duke of York Island, New Britain
ALLEN, W. E.	38	Warrant Officer of Police, Rabaul
ALLSOP, K. C.		Staff of W. R. Carpenter & Co. Ltd
ALLY, Rev. D. C.	35	Methodist Mission Society of N.Z., Bougainville
ASH, N. E.	40	Warrant Officer of Police, Rabaul
ASHBY, S. A.	47	planter, Maramakas Plantation, New Ireland
ATHERTON, J. W.	49	Administration Dispensary, Rabaul
ATKINSON, W.	38	recruiter and timbergetter
BANKS, A. E. D.	66	Manager of Pacific Hotel, Rabaul
BARNES, C. W.	67	Rabaul Printery, Rabaul

* Names appearing on the Nominal Roll compiled by Thomas, Creswick & Ellis after a visit to the civilians in the Rabaul Internment Camp at the end of May 1942. These names did not appear on the official list.

BATH, V. G.	53	Native Labour Overseer, W. R Carpenter & Co
BEAZLEY, S. C.	33	carpenter, Methodist Mission, Rabaul
BECK, N. R.	52	Public Works Dept, Rabaul
* BECKETT, H. J.		engineer/mechanic, Adm. Motor Transport
BELL, D. J.	30	Rabaul
BERMAN, R. A. A.	24	Lubba Plantation, Via Pondo
BICKMANN, Niels	25	MS *Herstein*
* BIGNELL, C. E.		resident, ?member of A.I.F.
* BIRD, R. A.		Customs Department, Rabaul
* BIGNELL, C. E.		resident, ?member of A.I.F.
* BISCHOFF, C. R.		son of H. Bischoff, liberated
BOLT, Benn	27	MS *Herstein*
BOWMAN, Herbert	21	Rabaul
BOX, W. C.	47	planter, Matalinge Plantation, New Ireland
* BRAIN, R. M.		Manager, New Britain Timbers Ltd, Rabaul
BRANDAL, Peter	47	MS *Herstein*
BRENNAN, C. A.	26	
BRETT, G. L.	49	Misima, Papua
BRINSTON, H. W. G.	44	Treasury, Rabaul
BROWN, R. A. L.	64	Adm Motor Transport, Rabaul
BROWN, T. G.		Rabaul
BRUCKSHAW, A. F.	45	Public Health Dept, Rabaul
BUNNY, J.	70	plantation manager, Wangamut, Rabaul
BURKE, J. D.	47	Titles Office, Rabaul
BYE, C.	60	master mariner, W. R. Carpenter & Co.
CAMPBELL, C. J.	61	

CANNON, C. F.	42	Chief Engineer, SS *Duranbah*
CARLYSLE, Lincoln	35	staff, W. R.Carpenter & Co.
CARR, L. A. A.	48	Public Works Department, Kokopo
CARSON, L. W.	48	planter, Fead I., New Ireland
CLARK, Ivan	43	Rabaul
CLARK, J. A. J.	48	Rabaul
CLARK, R. L.	52	Manager, Bay Loo Co, Rabaul
CLUNN, Colin	62	Staff of Burns Philp & Co. Ltd, Rabaul
COBB, Forbes	53	Plantation Manager, New Ireland
COE, P. E	36	Rabaul
COLLETT, T. D.	29	S.D.A. Mission, Rabaul
CONSIDINE, L. A.	36	Rabaul
COOK, R. E.	40	accountant, W. R. Carpenter & Co.
COOMBER, Arthur	43	medical assistant, Rabaul
COOPER, Dr R. W.	40	Public Health Department
COOTE, Philip	54	Manager, Burns Philp & Co, Rabaul
CROCKER, M. C.	45	agricultural inspector and instructor
CRUISE, J. B.	44	Chief Dispenser, Public Health Dept
DAVIES, Roger	41	Rabaul
DAYMOND, J .E.		A.D.O., Gasmata
DOCKRILL, William	60	poultry farmer, Rabaul
DODD, ————	54	accountant, Expropriation Board, Rabaul
DOYLE, H. G.	35	Selapiu Plantation, TNG
DOYLE, N.	21	Manager, Rentons Aerated Waterworks
DRANE, C. T.	56	Vacuum Oil Co. Ltd, Rabaul
DUUS, W. L.	25	Brisbane, Queensland
EARL, R. B.	47	planter, Rabaul
EDVARDSEN, Gunnar	25	MS *Herstein*
EDWARDS, J. H.	52	Native Labour Overseer, Burns Philp
EDWARDS, M. S.	29	Kavieng

EGLINTON, A. M.	36	Government Stores, Rabaul
EINSIEDEL, E. R.	41	staff, Burns Philp & Co., Rabaul
EVANS, T. E.	38	technical assistant, Public Health Dept
EVANS, W. J.	34	staff, Colyer Watson Ltd, Rabaul
* FIELD, C. T. R.	47	Director of Public Works, Rabaul
FILAN, S. H.	30	Treasury Department
* FLORANCE, V. A.		solicitor, Rabaul
FOGERVICK, Kare		MS *Herstein*
FORSYTH, D.	44	Government Store, Rabaul
FULTON, H.	33	staff, Burns Philp & Co.
GARRETT, T. V.	54	Kokopo, TNG
GASGOINE, C. J.	49	auctioneer, Rabaul
GASGOINE, I. N.	15	son of the above
GOAD, J. C.	49	senior medical assistant, Rabaul
* GOODWIN, H. R.		accountant, W. R. Carpenter & Co.
GRAY, K. M.	21	Kokopo
GREEN, A. S.	58	Ralawat Plantation, Rabaul
GREEN, E. C. D.	37	supervisor, Experimental Farm, Keravat
GREENWOOD, F. O.	57	planter, Rabaul
GREENWOOD, W.		planter, Kokopo
GREGORY, H. A.	44	district officer, Rabaul
GRYTNES, Reidar	17	MS *Herstein*
GUSTAVUSSEN, Gotha		MS *Herstein*
HAMILTON, J. E.	55	staff, W. R. Carpenter & Co., Rabaul
HAMILTON, L.	55	planter, Garua Plantation, Talasea
HANSEN, Jack		MS *Herstein*
HANSEN, Kaare	26	MS *Herstein*
HANSEN, Olaf	30	MS *Herstein*
* HASLAM, F.		draughtsman, Titles Office, Rabaul
HAWNT, E. W.	60	senior telephone mechanic, Rabaul
HAY, Arthur	35	Kavieng

HENNESSY, Rev. J. G.	36	Marist Mission, Buka Passage
HERKET, T. H.	44	inspector, Expropriation Board, Rabaul
HERON, G.	28	Commonwealth Bank, Rabaul
HERRON, W. L.	48	Tovakundam Plantation, Rabaul
HOGAN, G. G.	56	Crown Law officer, Rabaul
HOLDEN, H.	46	timber worker
HOLLAND, H. D.	49	Manager, Amalgamated Wireless Australasia
HOOGERWERTF, Jan		Manager, Rabaul Printing Works
* HOPKINS, E.		Rabaul Carrying Co., Rabaul
HOSKING, Dr H. C.	47	Acting Director of Public Health, Rabaul
* HOUGHTON, C.		Natava Plantation, Rabaul
JENTLAND, Alf	35	MS *Herstein*
JERVIS, A.	48	Plantation Manager, Nissan I., Bougainville
KELLY, E. C.	46	Kavieng, TNG
KING, A. J.	22	Commonwealth audit clerk, Rabaul
KNADSEN, Gunnar	28	MS *Herstein*
KOINBERG, Axel		MS *Herstein*
KRISTIANSEN, Kristian	26	MS *Herstein*
LANDHAUG, Arthur	34	MS *Herstein*
* LEDGER, W. A.		staff, W. R Carpenter & Co.
LIE, Ivar	22	MS *Herstein*
LINGGOOD, Rev W. L. I.	40	Methodist Mission, Rabaul
LIVINGSTONE, W. J.	37	Kavieng
LOCKHART, J.	44	Health Inspector, Rabaul
* McADAM, E. G.		accountant, New Britain Timbers Ltd
McARTHUR, Rev. L. A	38	Chairman, Methodist Mission, Rabaul
McCHEANE	32	butcher, Rabaul

McCULLAGH, D. B.	31	Sydney, NSW
MACDOUGALL, Donald	41	Rabaul
McEVOY, J. T.	46	planter, Maron I., Manus District
* McEWAN, W. F.		staff, Burns Philp & Co., Rabaul
McKELLAR, C.	45	planter, Tabar I., New Ireland District
McLAREN, T. W.	38	baker
* McLEAN, C. H.	61	shipping, W. R. Carpenter & Co.
McLEAN, C. I.		dental surgeon, Rabaul
McPHERSON, R. S.	32	Kavieng
MANTLE, F. W.	56	magistrate, Rabaul
MATER, C. S. P.	29	clerk, Post Office, Rabaul
MILLINGTON, B.	61	Plantation Manager, Rabaul
* MITCHELL, E. H. F.		patrol officer, Gasmata
MOLLER, Bjarne	31	MS *Herstein*
MOORE, R. K. P.	56	Tatavvana Plantation, Kokopo
* MORRELL, J. F.		Plantation Manager, Namatanai
MOSTAD, Knut	33	MS *Herstein*
MUGGLETON, H. R.	37	timber cutter
MULLIGAN, E. W.	28	baker
MULVEY, N. R.		civil engineer, Public Works Dept
MURRAY, G. H.	60	Director of Agriculture, Rabaul
MYHRE, Reidar	38	MS *Herstein*
NAULTY, P. G.	43	Warrant Officer of Police
NIELSEN, Gustav		MS *Herstein*
NIKOLAISEN, J. A.	37	MS *Herstein*
NUNAN, F. C.	30	Mandres, TNG
OAKES, Rev. W. D.	36	Methodist Mission, New Ireland
OATEN, Frederick	30	Manus I., TNG
O'DWYER, N. A.	49	planter, New Massawa Plantation, Rabaul
OLSEN, Gerhard	62	MS *Herstein*
ORMOND, J. L.	64	staff, Burns Philp & Co., Rabaul

PAGE, H. H.	53	Govt Secretary, Asst Administrator
PARRY, A. R.	47	medical assistant, Kokopo
PEARCE, Rev. E. W .	41	Methodist Mission, Rabaul
PEARSON, Rev. H. N. B.	29	Methodist Mission, Vunairima
PERRETT, A.		mechanic. Public Works Dept, Rabaul
PETTERSEN, Egil	42	MS *Herstein*
* PHILPOTT, W. H.		staff, Burns Philp & Co., Rabaul
PICKERING, M. B.	50	Titles Office, Rabaul
PINCHING, E.		Plantation Manager, South Coast
PINES, C. M.	46	medical assistant, Kokopo
* PLUMMER, H. O.		Senior Health Inspector, Rabaul
PLUNKETT, T. M.	23	Rabaul
POOLE, J. W.	28	Kalas, TNG
RAFF, G. S.	24	Rabaul
RAND, D. W. L.		Maritsoan Plantn, Namatauai
* RANKIN, D. J.		Govt Stores, Rabaul
REED, A. R.		dairy farmer, Rabaul
RENTON, Albany	49	sheet metal worker
REYNOLDS, J. A.	52	senior clerk, Public Works Dept, Rabaul
* REYNOLDS, R. W.	28	son of above, Commonwealth Bank
RINGSHAUG, Arthur	25	MS *Herstein*
ROBERTS, D. L.	29	Kavieng
ROBINSON, H. E.	42	Rabaul
ROBSINSON, Wright	23	Rabaul
* ROSS, H. J.		Burns Philp & Co., Rabaul
RYAN, W. J. or F. W.		staff, Burns Philp & Co., Rabaul
SAUNDERS, F. V.	50	planter and trader, Kavieng
* SAUNDERS, L.	50	Customs Dept, Rabaul
SAVAGE, S. K.	50	Kavieng
SAWKINS, A. G.	52	New Ireland
SCHMIDT, Adolf	37	headmaster, Malaguna Native School
SCOTT, H. M.		New Britain

* SEDGERS, J. C.		Plantation Inspector, Carpenter & Co.
SEIGERS. J. C.	44	Rabaul
SETCHELL, W. G.	38	Plantation Manager, Kokopo
SHEBLER, D. A.	36	chemist, Rabaul
SHELTON, H. B.	44	Duke of York Islands
* SHOOBRIDGE, I.		legal asst, Crown Law Office, Rabaul
SIMPSON, T. N.		New Hanover
SKAUG, Magnus		MS *Herstein*
SMITH, D. M. D.	39	Rabaul
SMITH, J. O.	63	Administration Native Labour overseer
SMITH, J. W.	43	postmaster, Rabaul
SNOOK, Samuel	50	Rabaul
SOLOMON, E. E.	26	Brighton Beach, Victoria
SOLOMONS, R. L.	52	clerk, Govt Stores, Rabaul
* SPENSLEY, G. W.	36	Manager, Colyer Watson & Co.
SQUIRES, R. T.	49	medical assistant, Rabaul
STALEY, W. G. S.	54	Roadmaster, Public Works Dept, Rabaul
STEPHEN, R. J.	46	W. R. Carpenter & Co., Rabaul
STEVENS, R. H.	35	clerk, Treasury, Rabaul
STEWART, James	60	Roadmaster, Public Works Dept, Rabaul
STRATHEAM, A. J.	36	clerk, Supreme Court, Rabaul
SYMES, H. H. C.	48	New Britain
* TAIT, R. E. jnr		accounts clerk, Rabaul
TEIEN, Hars	26	MS *Herstein*
THOMAS, Cecil	26	Rabaul
THOMPSON, I. C.	32	medical assistant, Rabaul
THORRSEN, Finn	32	MS *Herstein*
THORSELL, K. M. F.	36	MS *Herstein*
TITCHENER, J. W.	53	asst, Govt Experimental Farm, Keravat

TOWNSEND, H. O.	49	treasurer, Rabaul
TREVITT, Rev. J. W.	29	Methodist missionary, Vunairima
TRITTON, A. J.	34	staff, Commonwealth Bank, Rabaul
TURNBULL, H. F.	24	Laidley, Queensland
TYNAN, James	16	MS *Herstein*
*VENNING, F. O.		storeman, Govt Stores, Rabaul
VOSS, G. H. D.	37	teacher, Native School, Rabaul
WALKER, Thomas	53	Rabaul
WALLACE, T. V.	42	journalist and trader, Tobai, Rabaul
WALSH, T. R.	41	telephone mechanic, Rabaul
WASHINGTON, H. J.	55	planter, Kamberra Plantation, Rabaul
WAYNE, R. N.	38	interpreter, Supreme Court, Rabaul
WHITEMAN, A. K.	49	senior clerk, Customs Dept Rabaul
WILKIN, W. M.	56	New Hanover, TNG
WILLMET, W. P.	46	plantation assistant, Rabaul
YOULDEN, R. M.	48	clerk, Treasury Department, Rabaul

NOTES

3: JEAN DISCOVERS NEW GUINEA

1 Edward P. Wolfers, *Race Relations and Colonial Rule in Papua New Guinea*, pp. 30–1.

2 Ibid., p. 78.

3 Ibid., p. 45.

4 Ibid., pp. 96–7.

5 Ibid., p. 47.

6 Ibid., p. 58.

7 Nelson, *Taim Bilong Masta*, p. 168.

4: RABAUL

1 Peter Stone, *Hostages to Freedom*, pp. 1, 2.

2 Ibid.

3 R. W. Johnson and N. W. Threlfall, *Volcano Town*, p. 8.

4 Ibid., p. 10.

5 Hank Nelson, *Taim Bilong Masta*, p. 79.

6 *Una Voce*, March 2001.

7 G. L. Pearce, *A Heritage in Trust: James Dilworth and his School*.

5: LIFE IN RABAUL

1   R. W. Johnson and N. A. Threlfall, *Volcano Town*, p. 10.

2   Taped interviews, Tick Spensley (anecdotal).

3   In the 1920s after the Australians took over the administration of Papua New Guinea following World War 1 the Expropriation Board stripped Germans of their assets and deported them back to Germany, where they were to receive compensation. Expropriated property was sold by tender or auction. In many cases it was bought by Australian ex-servicemen who stayed on and, in spite of inexperience, began to run plantations. Jan Roberts, *Voices from a Lost World*.

4   Interview with Dr Elizabeth Banks, Phyllis Cooper's niece.

5   R. W. Robson, *Queen Emma*, p. 128.

6: VOLCANIC ERUPTION

1   R. W. Johnson and N. A. Threlfall, *Volcano Town*, p. 18.

2   Ibid., p. 25.

3   Ibid., p. 60.

7: THE AFTERMATH

1   R. W. Johnson and N. A. Threlfall, *Volcano Town*, p. 89.

2   Ibid., p. 106.

3   Ibid., p. 127.

4   *Rabaul Times*, June 1937.

5   Ibid., July 1937.

8: THE LULL BEFORE THE STORM

1 R. W. Johnson and N. A. Threlfall, *Volcano Town*, p. 8.
2 Interviews and correspondence, Jean Cunningham/Cox (Little Jean).

9: WAR IN EUROPE

1 Peter Stone, *Hostages to Freedom*, p. 37.
2 Edward P. Wolfers, *Race Relations and Colonial Rule in Papua New Guinea*, p. 69.
3 Ibid., pp. 96–7.
4 Colin Stirling, My Years in the Army, unpublished manuscript.

10: MEN'S TOWN

1 Edward P. Wolfers, *Race Relations and Colonial Rule in Papua New Guinea*, p. 21.

11: MOUNTING TENSION

1 Peter Stone, *Hostages to Freedom*, p. 40.

12: JAPAN ENTERS THE WAR

1 Peter Stone, *Hostages to Freedom*, p. 32.
2 Colin Stirling, My Years in the Army, unpublished manuscript.
3 Ibid.
4 Stone, *Hostages to Freedom*, pp. 42–3.
5 Sister Berenice, unpublished manuscript, interview and letters.

6 Ibid.

7 Stone, *Hostages to Freedom*, p. 43.

8 Bill Harry, The Japanese invasion and thereafter, as recorded by VX24.800; letters and interview with Bill Harry.

13: WARN THE OTHERS!

1 *Rabaul Times.*

2 Jan Roberts, *Voices from a Lost World*, pp. 256–8.

3 Ian Downs, *The New Guinea Volunteer Rifles*, p. 46.

4 Peter Stone, *Hostages to Freedom*, p. 45.

14: COLIN STIRLING'S ACCOUNT

1 Ian Downs, *New Guinea Volunteer Rifles*, p. 129.

2 Ibid., p. 53.

15: THE INVASION

1 Bill Harry, The Japanese invasion and thereafter as recorded by VX24.800; letters and interview.

2 Kemp Hewitt, interview, commemoration trip to Rabaul, 1992.

3 Interview with Canon John May, commemoration trip to Rabaul, 1992.

4 Peter Stone, *Hostages to Freedom*, p. 52.

5 Sister Berenice, interview and unpublished manuscript.

6 Lorna Johnston/Whyte, interview and correspondence.

7 Oscar Rondahl, interview.

8 Bill Harry, interview and correspondence.

9 Ian Downs, *The New Guinea Volunteer Rifles*, p. 82.

10 Bill Harry, interview and correspondence, November 2001.

11 Alice M. Bowman, *Not Now Tomorrow*, p. 42.

12 Interview with Canon John May.

13 Lorna Whyte/Johnston, interview and correspondence.

14 Bill Harry, interview and correspondence.

15 Colin Stirling, unpublished manuscript.

16 J. K. McCarthy, *Patrol Into Yesterday*, p. 188.

17 Stone, *Hostages to Freedom*, p. 42.

18 Ibid., pp. 123–5.

19 Ibid.

16: THE SACRED HEART MISSION 1942

1 *Age*, 9 December 2000.

2 George Hicks, *The Comfort Women*, pp. 81-8.

3 Sister Berenice, interview and unpublished papers.

17: SUM SUM

1 A. Uechtritz, correspondence and conversations.

2 Bill Harry, interview and correspondence.

3 Ian Downs, *The New Guinea Volunteer Rifles*, p. 109.

4 Ibid., pp. 109–10.

19: THE SACRED HEART MISSION 1942–1945

1 Peter Stone, *Hostages to Freedom*, pp. 135–7.

2 I have drawn on Peter Stone's excellent description of life in Rabaul during the Occupation. His book contains interviews with many of the Japanese stationed there at the time.

3 Sister Berenice, interviews and unpublished manuscripts.

20: JOHN MURPHY

1 Eric Feldt, *The Coastwatchers*, p. 345.
2 Joseph G. Nason and Robert Lawrence Holt, *Horio You Next Die!* pp. 68–9.
3 Lord Russell of Liverpool, *The Knights of Bushido*, p. 55.
4 Ibid., pp. 274, 280–1.
5 Ibid., p. 280.
6 Yuki Tanaka, *Hidden Horrors*, pp. 151–2.
7 Ibid., pp. 156–7.
8 Ibid., pp. 159–60.
9 Nason and Holt, *Horio You Next Die!* p. 197.
10 Ibid., pp. 140–1.

21: WAITING FOR NEWS

1 Peter Stone, *Hostages to Freedom*, pp. 340–1.
2 Ibid., p. 326.
3 Ibid., p. 341.
4 Margaret Reeson, *A Very Long War*, p. 83.
5 Yuki Tanaka, *Hidden Horrors*, pp. 190–1.
6 Ibid., pp. 174–5.

23: REFLECTIONS

1 Yuki Tanaka, *Hidden Horrors*, p. 139.
2 *Age*, 12 October 2001.
3 Tanaka, *Hidden Horrors*, p. 70.
4 Ibid., p. xv.

BIBLIOGRAPHY

PUBLISHED WORKS

Aplin, D., *Rabaul 1942*, published by 2/22 Battalion AIF Lark Force
   Association, Melbourne, 1980.

Bowman, Alice M. *Not Now Tomorrow*. Daisy Press, 1996.

Bulbeck, Chilla. *Australian Women in Papua New Guinea*. Cambridge University
   Press, 1992.

Clarence, Margaret. *Yield Not to the Wind*. Management Development Publishers
   Pty Limited, Sydney, 1982.

Downs, Ian. *The New Guinea Volunteer Rifles NGVR 1939–43*. Pacific Press, 1999.

Dutton, Geoffrey. *Queen Emma of the South Seas*. Macmillan, 1976.

Feldt, Eric. *The Coastwatchers*. Oxford University Press, 1946.

Gash, Noel and Whittaker, June. *A Pictorial History of New Guinea*. Jacaranda
   Press, 1975.

Hall, Timothy. *New Guinea 1942–1944*. Methuen, 1981.

Herman, Judith Lewis. *Trauma and Recovery*. Basic Books, 1992.

Idriess, Ion L. *Gold-dust and Ashes*. Angus & Robertson Ltd, 1945.

Johnson, R. W. and Threlfall, N. A. *Volcano Town—The 1937–43 Rabaul
   Eruptions*. Robert Brown & Associates (Qld), 1985.

Kenny, Catherine. *Captives: Australian Army Nurses in Japanese Prison Camps*.
   University of Queensland Press, 1986.

Lewis, C. Day (ed.). *The Collected Poems of Wilfred Owen*. Chatto & Windus, 1963.

McCarthy, J. K. *Patrol into Yesterday: My New Guinea Years*. J. K. McCarthy. 1963.

Murphy, John J. *The Book of Pidgin English*. 1st edition 1943, revised 1989. Robert Brown & Associates.

Nason, Joseph G. and Holt, Robert Lawrence. *Horio You Next Die!* Pacific Rim Press Inc., 1987.

Nelson, Hank. *Taim Bilong Masta: The Australian Involvement with Papua New Guinea*. ABC, 1982. Produced by Tim Bowden.

——. *Prisoners of War: Australians under Nippon*. ABC, 1985.

Pearce, G. L. *A Heritage in Trust: James Dilworth and his School*. Dilworth Trust Board, 1986.

——. *Whereabouts Unknown*. Albatros Books, 1993.

Reeson, Margaret. *A Very Long War*. Melbourne University Press, 2000.

——. *Whereabouts Unknown*. Albatros Books, 1993.

Roberts, Jan. *Voices from a Lost World*. Millennium Books, 1996.

Robson, R. W. *Queen Emma*. Pacific Publications, 1965.

Russell, Lord of Liverpool. *The Knights of Bushido*. Cassell & Company Ltd, London, 1958.

Stone, Peter. *Hostages to Freedom: The Fall of Rabaul*. Ocean Enterprises, 1994.

Tanaka, Yuki. *Hidden Horrors*. Westview Press, 1998.

Tudor, Judy. *Many a Green Isle*. Pacific Publications, 1966.

Wall, Don. *Heroes at Sea*. Griffin Press, 1991.

Wigmore, Lionel. *The Japanese Thrust: Australia in the War of 1939–45*, Australian War Memorial, 1957.

Wolfers, Edward P. *Race Relations and Colonial Rule in Papua New Guinea*. Australia & New Zealand Book Co., 1975.

NEWSPAPERS

Pacific Islands Monthly. 1939–1946 *Japan Will Strike Southward. Statement by an Admiral. PIM*, February 1941, page 42

Rabaul Times 1939–1942

Una Voce. Newsletter, Retired Officers Association of Papua New Guinea, no. 1, March 2001

ARCHIVAL SOURCES

Australian Archives—Canberra

A518	BJ16/2/1 Part 2	Evacuation of Women and Children from the Territories
A461/7	U337/1/4	Court Martial of Captain John Joseph Murphy
A1066	IC45/55/3/19	Internees—Australians abroad. Civilians reported lost on board SS *Montvideo Maru*
MP742/1	336/1/1943	Events Connected with Army Administration (War Crimes Trials etc.)
Ds16/2/1	Part 4	*Akikaze* executions, statements 1943, November 1946
Db16/2/1	Part 1	Report on Japanese atrocities. Sir William Webb 1942–1947
A1010/1/30		'Left Rabaul': List of Civilians seen by Thomas Creswick
A2671/1	333/41	War Cabinet Agenda Files

Australian Archives—Victoria

MP742/1	255/15/1643	Translation from Japanese of nominal roll for Rabaul civilians
	255/15/1643	Translation of part of civilian nominal roll, sent 8 October 1945
	336/1/1951	Sentencing of Japanese War Criminals from Kavieng, 1948
	336/1/1955	Box 801 (4 of 15). Major H. S. Williams, Japan, September to October 1945, search for identity of missing garrison and civilians from Rabaul
	336/1/1601	Australian War Crimes, Tokyo, investigating Kavieng 32, 1946 to 1947

	336/1/1955	(4 of 15) Army H.Q. Correspondence files 1943–1951
	336/1/1955	Investigation of War Crimes, Rabaul area, 1947 to 1948
MP742/1	336/1/1755	(4 of 15) Major Williams. Letter to H.Q. Melbourne, The Sinking of the *Montevideo Maru.*
	336/1/1955	War Crimes—Tunnel POW Camp— affidavits by [???] Nason J., Holquin J.

Australian War Memorial

AWM54	779/1/26	War Patrol Report, USS *Sturgeon*, 14 June–2 July 1942
	779/1/1	Missing civilians seen in camp by Thomas and Cresswick May 1942
	1010/9/32	Execution of Captain Grey at Vunapope early in 1942
AWM54	554/14/2	8th Division in captivity. Senior Officers' Group (Formosa and Manchuria.) Memorandum to Lieutenant-General Northcott, from Major General C. A. Callaghan, written from Chungking 32/8/45. Brief notes on Mukden Camp, Armistice and Release, Mukden to Chungking.
	1010/9/78	War Crimes and Trials—Investigation of Atrocities). Nominal Roll of civilians, in Rabaul internment camp, at the end of May 1942 (compiled by memory by Gordon Thomas, J. E. Ellis, A. L. Cresswick after a short visit). Most of all it is believed were moved from Rabaul in the ship 'Montvideo Maru' during June 1942. Letter to The Administrator of Papua New Guinea, Port Moresby from J. R. Halligan 1/10/46

MANUSCRIPTS, LETTERS, AND INTERVIEWS

Sister Berenice Twohill	Just One of the Crowd: The internment story of Sister Berenice of Rabaul 'May the Sacred Heart of Jesus be everywhere loved!' Austinmer, December 1983
Private Correspondence	between Captain J. Murphy and Sister Berenice Personal interviews, videotape
Lorna Whyte/Johnston	Radio interview Account of her experiences written for her grandchildren Personal interviews, audiotape Personal interviews, videotape and audiotape
John Murphy	Personal correspondence; eulogy by Susan Kelly
Bill Harry	Notes on the events of 11th February 1942; personal interview
Cox family	
Chambers family	
Stirling family	

A) Letter from Major H.S. Williams to AMF Headquarters in Melbourne. 1053 Australian POWs and Civilian Internees lost on *Montevideo Maru* torpedoed off LUZON on 1st July, 1942.

B) Translation of report received from Osaka Shosen Kaisha concerning The Sinking of the *Montevideo Maru*. AA MP742/1 336/1/1755 20/10/45

Letter to the Secretary, Department of External Territories, Canberra.
War Crimes — Rabaul. No. C.A. 21/1/45 Port Moresby. 3rd July, 1950.

Copy of lists of civilians believed lost on *Montevideo Maru*. A composite of the following lists which have been cross checked by the author. Some people were later found to have been killed in other circumstances (e.g. civilians from Kavieng).

(a) Official List

(b) List compiled by Thomas Cresswick & Ellis following visit to Civilian POW Camp in Rabaul in June 1942.

INDEX